UPTOWN, DOWNTOWN

UPTOWN,

DOWNTOWN

A Trip Through Time
on New York's Subways

STAN FISCHLER

RESEARCH EDITOR: Dave Rubenstein

DRAWINGS BY Ray Judd

HAWTHORN BOOKS, INC.
Publishers/ NEW YORK

A Howard & Wyndnam Company

Photograph on title page courtesy New York City Transit Authority Photo File

To the memory of the Ben who broke me in on the Myrtle Avenue (BMT) el and the Ben and Shirley who have made the Broadway (IRT) local as exciting and as much fun as a roller coaster.

Contents

Acknowledgments

The author wishes to thank Rich Friedman, Don Harold, David Rubenstein, Dennis Wendling, Ed Silberfarb, Hugh Dunne, Joe Spaulding, Len Ingalls, Bob Leon, Becky Morris, Karen Robertson, Ira Lacher, Joe Resnick, Bob Waterman, Joe Pagnotta, Jim Finkenstadt, Tom Mariam, Don O'Hanley, Charlie Cuttone, William J. Madden, Helene Elliott, Howard and Suzanne Samelson, and the New York City Transit Authority as well as the many others who helped so much in the preparation of this book.

The author wishes to thank Leonard Ingalls of the Transit Authority for permission to use excerpts of *Transit Magazine* in this book.

A special debt of thanks is in order for the Electric Railroaders' Association. The ERA, the most dedicated and knowledgeable group of train buffs I've ever encountered, provided invaluable assistance. ERA Librarian Olaf Olson unearthed rare subway publications and provided access to the association's extensive library. The ERA's magazine, *Headlights,* was an inexhaustible source of information, and authors such as Roger Arcara, Sy Reich, Bernard Linder, Leo Ross, and David Klepper, to name but a few, likewise have written extensively on the New York system. Their works were of immeasurable assistance.

Nobody on the face of the earth knows more about subways—or loves them more—than fellow hockey fan Hugh A. Dunne, the ERA ace. His encouragement and assistance in preparation of this book helped make it all possible.

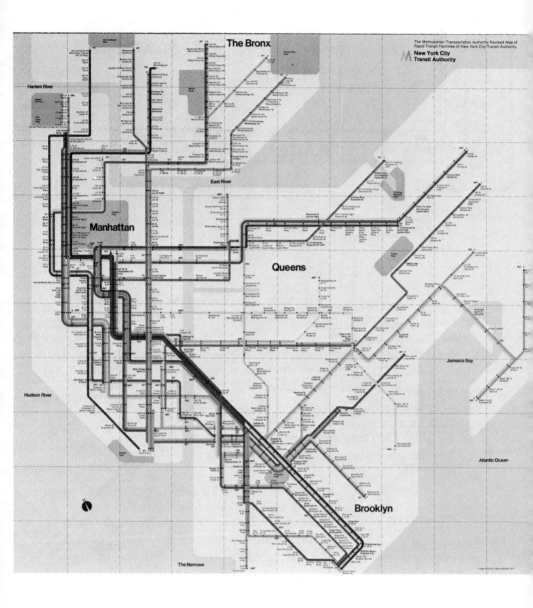

The Bronx

The Metropolitan Transportation Authority Revised Map of
Rapid Transit Facilities of New York City Transit Authority.

New York City
Transit Authority

Harlem River

East River

Manhattan

Queens

Hudson River

Jamaica Bay

Atlantic Ocean

Brooklyn

The Narrows

Introduction:
You Are the Greatest

The New York City subway does everything on a grand scale and, the law of averages being what it is, not everything is nice. From all available evidence it is the dirtiest underground in the world and surely as noisy as the noisiest. But even in its weakest moments the New York City subway takes more people where they want to go in a shorter amount of time—usually *on* time—than any means of urban transport anywhere.

On a global basis, the New York subway has formidable competition. London not only dug the first underground rapid transit system in the world but has continually enlarged its tubes and maintains an elaborate, well-run operation. Paris has, in parts, an ancient system but has also built a series of high-speed lines, including one that links the international airport to the city's center (which New York conspicuously never has done). No subway is more ornate than Moscow's or more modern than Berlin's.

But the winner, as far as I am concerned, remains the New York City subway and this book is written to tell the reason why.

UPTOWN,
DOWNTOWN

EARLY FORMS OF TRANSIT

Origins

Although the first practical railroad in the world was George Stephenson's steam engine built in England in 1825, America's original railway was a horse-drawn contraption that, curiously, was a direct lineal descendant of the American Revolution. It was built to haul granite from the quarries of West Quincy, Massachusetts, to historic Bunker Hill, where a monument honoring the patriotic colonials who fought on Bunker Hill would be erected. Even though a steam engine had just proven in Britain that it could haul large quantities of coal over wooden tracks, this first American railroad, which began operation on October 7, 1826, was nothing more than a horse-drawn tram whose roots could be traced back to the coal miners of England and Wales in the sixteenth and seventeenth centuries.

In that prerailway era, coals were routinely carried by horseback in double panniers. It was a slow and costly operation but eventually coal-mine owners developed a method to avoid the expense of maintaining large numbers of horses, which then was a staggering financial imposition.

The brainstorm that changed the complexion of Great Britain's coal industry consisted of a pair of parallel wooden rails on which coal carts rolled. The carts were pulled, of course, by horses. Utilizing rails on which to pull their carts, coal barons discovered that the capacity of the horse was increased twenty to thirty times and that sixty, instead of two, coal bushels could be hauled. (Strangely, there is a direct kinship between the original horse-drawn coal train and the modern New York City subway. The coalhaulers built their rails just four feet eight-and-a-half inches apart for cart wheels. This happens to be the standard gauge of all New York subways and els as well as most rail lines worldwide.)

By 1800 horse-powered railways had become commonplace in England, and in 1803 an erratic genius named Richard Trevithick built a "portable fire-engine," otherwise known as a steam carriage. For reasons known only to Trevithick he chose *not* to run his steam engine on rails. By no small coincidence Trevithick, having a fortune in grasp, died a financial failure. There would, in time, be many like him involved in the development of New York's subways.

Trevithick's major oversight was converted into a bonanza by George Stephenson, an unlettered engine-wright in a coal mine. He conceived the idea that the very coals themselves could be used to haul coal to the waterside, and in 1825 he built the first real steam railroad. What surprised Stephenson was that people wanted to ride his newfangled invention as much as they wanted to use it for coal carrying. That being the case, Stephenson began experimentation in passenger railroading, which meant that rapid transit development could not be far behind.

And it wasn't. In 1863 London opened its first "Underground." The world's first subway consisted of a steam railroad running through tubes far below London's streets. It was noisy and dirty, but it did reduce the unbearable surface traffic congestion and proved popular, despite its limitations.

Interestingly, the London Underground owed a debt of gratitude to America's very first railroad, the Granite Railway, and its creative

4

builder, Gridley Bryant. It was Bryant who produced, among other inventions, the original track switch, the first swivel-trucked eight-wheel freight car, the turntable, and the portable derrick.

Not only did Bryant influence British railway and Underground construction but his success with the Granite Railway inaugurated in America the grand era of railroad building and westward settlement. Bryant, like Trevithick, died a poor man, but in 1826 he seemed to have the world on a string—or on rails, as it were.

On January 4, 1826 Bryant petitioned the Massachusetts state legislature for funds and land upon which to build his granite-carrying railroad. The request was granted two months later, and ground for the line was broken on April 1 of the same year. In less than six months the Granite Railway was in business, and on October 9, 1826 the first railroad in America, costing all of $50,000, took its first run. The Boston *Daily Advertiser* described it as follows:

"A quantity of stone, weighing sixteen tons, taken from the ledge belonging to the Bunker Hill Association, and loaded on three wagons which together weigh five tons, making a load of twenty-one tons, was moved with ease by a single horse from the quarry to the landing above Neponset Bridge, a distance of more than three miles. . . . After the starting of the load, which required some exertion, the horse moved at ease in a fast walk. It may, therefore, be easily conceived how greatly transportation of heavy loads is facilitated by means of this road."

As for the line itself, *The First Railroad in America*, a commemorative book, prepared by a Boston advertising company in 1926 on the railroad's 100th anniversary, tells us what it was like:

"The road-bed, deep enough to be beyond the reach of frost was built of crushed granite, and the sleepers were made of stone, placed eight feet apart, on which were rested wooden rails twelve inches high. On top of the rail was an iron plate three inches wide and one quarter-inch thick which was fastened with spikes; but at all places where the railroad crossed public highways stone rails were used with an iron plate four inches wide and one quarter-inch thick bolted firmly on the stone. . . . As the wooden rails began to decay, they were replaced with stone rails. . . . On account of its construction, the upkeep of the road for many years was less than ten dollars a year."

Bryant created every inch of the railroad; not only was the idea for the design of the roadbed and the track his, but he also designed the Granite Railway's rolling stock, which was described as follows:

"It had high wheels, six and one-half feet in diameter, the load being suspended on a platform under the axles by chains. This platform was let down at any convenient place and loaded; the car was then run over the load, the chains attached to the platform, and the loaded platform raised a little above the track by machinery on the top of the car. The loads averaged six tons each."

Considering the era, Bryant had accomplished a monumental engineering feat, for nowhere in the United States was there a rail system, or any comparable transit system for that matter, able to deliver tons of granite over hilly, irregular terrain. Bryant himself described in his notes how he was able to surmount the physical obstacles with an ingenious device:

". . . The foot of the tablelands that ran around the main quarry had an elevation of 84 feet vertical," which had to be overcome. How? This was done by an inclined plane, 315 feet long, at an angle of about 15 degrees.

"It had an endless chain, to which the cars were attached in ascending or descending. At the head of this inclined plane I constructed a swing platform to receive the loaded cars as they came from the quarry. This platform was balanced by weights, and had gearing attached to it in such a manner that it would always return (after having dumped) to a horizontal position, being firmly supported on the periphery of the elevated cam."

There were other problems, but Bryant conquered them as well. "When the cars were out on the platform," he noted, "there was danger of their running entirely over, and I constructed a self-acting guard that would rise above the surface of the rail upon the platform as it rose from its connection with the inclined plane, or receded out of the way when the loaded car passed on the track; the weight of the car depressing the platform as it was lowered down.

"I also constructed a turn-table at the foot of the quarry. The railroad was continued in different grades around the quarry, the highest part of which was 93 feet above the general level; on the top of this was erected an obelisk or monument forty-five feet high."

When Gridley Bryant began operating his railroad in Massachusetts, the citizens of New York City were being transported about the southern tip of Manhattan Island by oxcart. At least one oxcart line was known to run from the Battery up Broadway, eventually being replaced in 1827 by lumbering, horse-drawn omnibuses. These, in turn, were succeeded by horsecars in the middle 1850s. Unlikely as it may seem today, horsecars remained in operation on New York City's streets until July 26, 1917, when the Bleecker Street–Broadway horsecar line made its last trip.

In time steam came to American railroads and, more important, electricity made its debut in Richmond, Virginia, in 1888 when the city's entire fleet of horse-drawn streetcars was equipped with electric motors. Once the Richmond electrified streetcars proved successful other metropoli turned away from steam to the new energy source. New York, Chicago, and Brooklyn abandoned their steam locomotives in favor of electricity on the elevated railroads.

Up until this time, however, nobody had installed electricity for underground transit purposes. In fact, politicians in Chicago and New York had successfully waged war against subways. Boston was the first to put an electric railway underground in the United States successfully. It happened because of Henry H. Whitney, boss of Boston's West End Street Railway and a man who was very impressed with—and yet concerned about—the Richmond trolley operation.

"Serious doubts plagued him at first," wrote rail historian Brian J. Cudahy in *Change at Park Street Under.*" "In the peaceful, almost rural precincts of the quiet Southern city electric trolleys performed their routines with leisurely ease. Would such prove practical in brisk, congested Boston?"

Whitney was persuaded to take the big gamble and installed a fleet of electric trolleys in Boston. The streetcars were an immediate hit; even the poet Oliver Wendell Holmes penned a few verses in their honor, describing the characteristic pulley arm of the trolley:

> Since then on many a car you'll see
> A broomstick plain as plain can be;
> On every stick there's a witch astride—
> The string you see to her leg is tied.

The trolleys proved so popular they became unpopular because of their ubiquitousness. The bumper-to-bumper lineup along Tremont Street brought demands for some way of removing the streetcars from the street and putting them somewhere—anywhere!—even if it meant building an elevated railway or a subway. The Massachusetts legislature approved the plans of a firm called the Boston Elevated Railway Company, which ultimately built the "elevated" railway underground!

Ground was broken for the monumental project on March 28, 1895, and two and one-half years and $5 million later the first leg of the subway was open for business. The *New York Times* observed: "That so conservative an American town should happen to be the pioneer in adopting this is viewed as remarkable."

If Boston could do it, why not New York? Boston's first four-wheel open-bench car rolled out of the Allston barns on September 1, 1897; it was only a matter of time before New York would built a subway system. But it did not come easily.

Elevated Railroads—
Phase I

In 1811 when City Hall was completed on Manhattan Island, New York planners estimated that the bulk of the city's population would reside in the area from the southern tip of the island (the Battery) to an area just south of City Hall. In fact, the builders of City Hall had used a cheaper, less cosmetic material on the northern facade of City Hall on the assumption that nobody would venture that far north and see the other side of the building.

Very quickly they were proved wrong. As immigrants poured into the United States from Europe, they were funneled through New York City and, naturally, many chose to live on Manhattan Island. The city grew so fast beyond City Hall that street congestion soon became a major problem for pedestrians and drivers of wagons, horse-drawn omnibuses, and horse-drawn carriages.

Each year the city extended its limits farther north and, as a result, horsecar lines did a thriving business, but they were inadequate to haul the growing throngs. By midcentury the Hudson River Railroad station at 30th Street had become a major terminus, yet it took almost an hour to reach it by horsecar because of congestion along the route. "It was a slow, bumpy ride just to reach the railroad," according to the Electric Railroaders Association account. "Plans had been offered to let the railroad trains run all the way down [Manhattan Island] as a sort of transit facility, but they would have hindered rather than helped the situation."

Almost everyone in town agreed that some improvement was necessary to ease the flow of traffic; especially in view of the reckless competition between stagecoaches and horsecars. Robert Daley, writing in *The World beneath the City*, described it as violent and cutthroat:

"No tracks hampered the operations of the stages, whose drivers ran over men, women and children in their haste to beat competitors to waiting passengers. Burly conductors shanghaied people into coaches and forced them to pay, so that heavy profits could be shown. Drivers were picked for heft not courtesy. Most swore at the passengers, and swindled them on tickets and on change. Axles broke, horses shied and policemen on boxes at intersections spent more time separating slugging rival drivers than directing snarled traffic."

Reflecting the public concern, the local press urged reform: "Modern martyrdom," asserted the New York *Herald* of October 2, 1862, "may be succinctly defined as riding in a New York omnibus." But the question remained: What kind of transit reform?

Since 1825 various plans had been developed to transfer surface transit to elevated structures. Proposed propulsion systems ran the gamut from steam to cable to compressed air.

By the start of the 1860s more than 700,000 people filled the city from the Battery to the "suburbs" around 42nd Street, and hundreds more were arriving by the week. The mostly undeveloped land north of 42nd Street was sprinkled with squatters' shanties and pasture. Farms still abounded north of Harlem, which was hardly populated, and deer could be seen grazing among the woodlands and meadow of what now is Central Park. This was unexploited land that soon would be developed if some convenient means could be devised to make it readily accessible.

The 10-cent stagecoach was not the answer, nor was the 6-cent horsecar. "The answer," said Hugh B. Willson, a Michigan railroad man, "is a subway line under Manhattan."

Willson promoted a Metropolitan Railway Company with $5 million of his own in working capital. A. P. Robinson, engineer for the project, conceived an elaborate right-of-way on his drawing board. It would be covered with glass sidewalks to allow light down into the tunnel while hollow lampposts on the street would transmit fresh air to the subway below.

"Our subway," boasted Robinson, "will signal the end of mud and dust, of delays due to snow and ice. The end of the hazardous walk into the middle of the street to board the car, the end of waiting for lazy or obstinate truckmen. Everything will be out of sight, out of hearing. Nothing will indicate the thoroughfare below."

But neither Willson nor Robinson bargained for the byzantine turns of New York politics. Opponents included such Gotham heavyweights as Origen Vandenburgh and Jacob Sharpe, not to mention the powerful rail baron, Cornelius Vanderbilt. When Commodore Vanderbilt learned of Willson's subway proposal he snapped, "I'll be underground a damned sight sooner than this thing!"

Most awesome of all the obstacles was William Marcy ("Boss") Tweed, kingpin of New York's Tammany Hall Democratic machine and the man who dominated, via the backrooms, the horsecar and stage companies. Clearly it was in Tweed's best interests to protect the horsecar and stage outfits from any competition, which is precisely what he did.

When the New York State Assembly approved the Willson subway proposal in the spring of 1865 by an unexpectedly large 89 votes, Tweed's puppet governor, Ruben E. Fenton, vetoed the bill. When Willson attempted to negotiate with the governor personally, he was shown the door. To be sure, there were those who truly believed that a subway would be a menace to Manhattan. A. W. Craven, chief engineer of the Croton Reservoir, feared that the underground railway would impinge on sewerage systems and contaminate the water supply. Others pointed out that the smoke pouring out of the subway's steam engines would damage the riders' throat and nasal passages. A second attempt by Willson to persuade the state legislature failed under Tweed's pressure.

Curiously, Tweed was indifferent to another transit proposal developed by inventor Charles Harvey. This was an elevated cable car to be built along the sidewalk line of Greenwich Street in downtown Manhattan. According to Harvey's plan, the cable pulling the train would be activated by stationary engines, anchored to bedrock every 1,500 feet.

Like Willson, Harvey went to Albany with his blueprints but, unlike Willson, he met no opposition. He called his company the West Side & Yonkers Patent (Elevated) Railway and went about the business of constructing an experimental track. On October 10, 1867 the first column of the line was erected on Greenwich Street. Preliminary field work had started on July 1 for construction of the first quarter mile of the line to Morris Street.

Relentlessly, Harvey pushed forward on his unique project and, on December 7, 1867, he demonstrated use of the line by riding a car truck instead of a car. This was a pivotal day for Harvey. If the ride failed in any way—many citizens were convinced that the el would collapse of its own weight—its inventor would lose the support of his financial backers. But the test ride worked, and directors of the West Side & Yonkers Patent Railway Company authorized expenditures to complete the remainder of the line to Cortlandt Street, which was approved by the state legislature.

In 1868 the elevated project moved full speed ahead. On July 1 Harvey again successfully tested the device before a large and skeptical audience. Just two days later members of the Board of Railroad Commissioners made a test trip in a passenger car from Battery Place to Cortlandt Street. Pulled by a Roebling-made cable, powered by a stationary steam engine, the train worked well enough to win official approval.

In terms of its cable grip device Harvey's el was similar to the San Francisco cable-car system of the day. Harvey's track gauge was four feet ten and one-half inches with the rails on longitudinal girders without crossties so familiar on traditional railroads.

With offices at 48 Cortlandt Street, the West Side & Yonkers Patent Railway was ready for its great leap forward—uptown. All that was needed was money. But finding it proved to be difficult. Harvey had to go begging for lenders and eventually found enough to enable construction to continue toward the 30th Street railroad terminal.

Harvey knew that if his elevated railroad was to make money, it had to link with the Hudson River Railroad Terminal. On September

26, 1869 it was just a mile away, but on that same day the Great Depression of the sixties took place, and Harvey was broke.

He looked everywhere for more backers and finally capitulated to a group of fast-buck operators who took over control of the el but temporarily retained its inventor as the titular boss. Construction moved forward to the target destination, and on February 14, 1870 regular operation for passenger service began from the Dey Street station in lower Manhattan to the line's new terminus at Ninth Avenue and 29th Street. The single-track structure followed the easterly curb line of Greenwich Street and the westerly curb line of Ninth Avenue. The line was powered by four new cable-operating plants. The railroad had three passenger cars in service.

To move the cars, the West Side & Yonkers Railway had its first cable-operating plant at Cortlandt and Greenwich streets. This plant powered the line from Battery Place to Franklin Street. A plant at Franklin Street operated another cable from there to Houston Street, while another engine at Bank Street propelled the cable between Houston and Little West 12th streets. From Little West 12th Street to the northern end at West 29th Street another cable ran to and from a plant at the northwest corner of West 22nd Street and Ninth Avenue. The original steam cable engine at 107 Greenwich Street, built for the first experiments, was closed down.

In its early months of operation the el proved both a blessing and a curse. The idea of carrying passengers above the street was a good one, and planners soon realized that in theory Harvey had the ultimate cure for New York's transit problems. But mechanically the el left a lot to be desired. The cable frequently snapped, forcing the emergency crew to haul out a team of horses and pull the stranded car and passengers to the end of the line. Following this, the entire line had to be closed down for a considerable period while necessary repairs were made.

Despite the chronic disruption of service, it was apparent that the el was here to stay, and that is precisely what began to annoy Boss Tweed. At first he had treated it as just another crazy idea, but suddenly he realized it threatened his many surface transit interests. Tweed swiftly contacted his aides in Albany who pushed a bill through the New York State Senate branding the el a public nuisance. The bill authorized the commissioner of public works—one William Marcy Tweed—to raze it within three months. Since Tweed had the governor's vote in his pocket, he needed only the approval of the State Assembly to wipe out Harvey's el. But the desperate inventor was not about to throw in the towel. In fact, Harvey had a trump card sitting in Albany named Erastus Corning, an old friend. Corning was a major figure in New York State politics, having served as state senator, congressman, and vice chancellor of the University of New York. What's more, Corning was deeply indebted to Harvey dating back to the time when Corning was building a canal at the outlet of Lake Superior and was stymied by a major rock ledge. Corning's sandbar dredges could not break the ledge, and the promoter appeared doomed to a financial debacle.

It was then that Harvey invented a device for crumbling the ledge, and Corning was able to complete the canal. Now Harvey needed a favor from his friend. Corning, then seventy-eight years old, was not afraid to take on Boss Tweed. He went before the assembly and filibustered in favor of the newfangled elevated railroad. Corning had respect and he had clout. When the assembly voted on the measure Tweed went down to defeat and the Ninth Avenue el lived.

On April 20, 1871 operation on the el resumed with one essential difference; instead of using cable cars the West Side & Yonkers Patent Railway had a small steam locomotive pulling the three former cable cars. The steam engine was boxed in to prevent it from frightening horses in the streets below. A 10-cent fare was charged and 237 passengers were carried on reopening day.

Despite optimism about the el, financial troubles continually intruded. In November 1870 the line had been auctioned off for $960 to bondholders, and now in 1871 it was auctioned off again for $5,000 to another group of bondholders who were organizing a new company, the New York Elevated Railroad Company.

The new company was chartered on October 27, 1871 with a capital stock of $10 million. By now Charles Harvey had been eased out of the el operation altogether, but the railroad prospered and many of his original ideas were soon realized. In the summer of 1872 the Little West 12th Street station opened with an innovation for the elevated. Instead of limiting the operation to a single track, which allowed just one train running back and forth, the directors built a passing track at the new station, thus enabling trains to roll in both directions, meeting at the double-track point. Shortly thereafter the Morris Street station was opened. On January 21, 1873 a station opened at Franklin Street, and running time over the entire route was twenty-eight minutes.

Having defeated Boss Tweed and a legion of skeptics, the elevated railroad proved—at least in the seventies—that it was the panacea for all Manhattan's street-level traffic problems. Year by year, the el grew like a horizontal beanstalk. In July 1873 it was extended to West 34th Street and Ninth Avenue. Later in the year an additional station was opened at West 21st Street. Some officials of the New York Elevated Railroad Company believed it should carry freight as well as passengers and voted to alter the superstructure.

In March 1875 the entire line was closed for major alterations. More than 200 men were hired to change the wheel widths on rolling stock to four feet eight and one-half inches. Rails were relaid on crossties and the general superstructure was beefed up from start to finish. While they were at it, engineers installed a new siding at Franklin Street. By the end of 1875 trains were rolling as far north as 42nd Street, and sidings were installed at Bethune Street and 34th Street.

Business boomed up and down the line. In January 1876 the el was averaging 5,600 fares daily and was a full five miles long. Its bosses, Simeon E. Church and Cyrus Field, pushed it ever northward to 53rd Street. Because of the demand, double tracking was begun in April 1877 and, during Christmas week that year, the directors celebrated their el with a dinner at posh Delmonico's Restaurant. "The el sold out to the sheriff in 1870," chortled Field, "but it seems to be doing all right now!" And so it was. In 1878 it was averaging 8,500 daily passengers, and work was progressing on a Sixth Avenue elevated line, under the direction of Dr. Rufus H. Gilbert, a former medical practitioner who had become avidly interested in transit.

Dr. Gilbert's line suffered through much of the same financial affliction that befell Harvey. After a series of internal problems and legal complications, the company changed its name from the Gilbert Elevated Railway Co. to the Metropolitan Elevated Railway and erected an impressive line along Sixth Avenue.

Although the girder work on Gilbert's Sixth Avenue el differed from the style utilized by Harvey's railroad, it was constructed to conventional standards. The line began in downtown Manhattan at Morris Street on Trinity Place and proceeded north along Trinity Place and Church Street with stations at Rector Street, Cortlandt

Street and Park Place. Then it moved up West Broadway with stops at Chambers Street, Franklin Street, Grand Street, Bleecker Street, and finally north on Sixth Avenue itself, stopping at 8th Street, 14th Street, 23rd Street, 33rd Street, 42nd Street, 50th Street, and 58th Street. At later dates stations at 18th Street, 28th Street, and 38th Street were opened.

To move rolling stock up to the elevated tracks an inclined plane was installed on Trinity Place behind Trinity Church, near Rector Street. Everything from the small steam locomotives to the passenger cars were hauled up the artificial train hill. The locomotives had a two-four-two wheel arrangement, weighed fifteen tons, and were painted pea-green. The passenger cars were painted a light green, with pea-green and gold trim, and had wheels of highly compressed paper with steel rims. The interiors had woodwork of oak and mahogany, Axminster carpeting, and kerosene chandeliers. The fare was 10 cents.

Like its predecessor on Ninth Avenue, the Sixth Avenue el did very well and eventually would link up with the Harvey road in 1879. The move northward in Manhattan continued through the end of the nineteenth century. Meanwhile, railroad planners were busily stretching their tracks through New York City's sister municipality across the river, Brooklyn. The growth of elevated railroads in Brooklyn was significantly different from that on Manhattan Island because of the then rural nature of Kings County and the fact that it boasted several attractive seaside resorts.

Elevated Railroads— Phase II

A year before Charles Harvey made his initial test run on the Ninth Avenue el, Brooklyn's first major steam railroad line reached Coney Island. Like so many of that city's railroads, the Brooklyn, Bath & Coney Island Railroad was constructed to link the populous northern section of the city (Brooklyn remained an independent city until it incorporated as one of the five boroughs in 1898) with the popular seaside resorts at Coney Island, Manhattan Beach, and Sea Gate, all on the southern tip.

In time the Brooklyn, Bath & Coney Island would be known as the West End line of the Transit Authority's BMT system. But in 1867 it was called the "Dummy Road," a euphemism for the steam dummies used for motive power. The line had two starting points to provide linkage with Brooklyn horsecars as well as the ferry boats to Manhattan.

The ferry boat connection was located at 39th Street west of Second Avenue in Brooklyn. The ferry floated north across New York harbor to its Manhattan destination at South Ferry. The horsecar link was situated at 27th Street and Fifth Avenue, Brooklyn, from where the horsecars fanned out to various districts such as Park Slope, Borough Park, Bay Ridge, and the downtown area in the north. After traversing the westerly portion of Brooklyn, the Brooklyn, Bath & Coney Island Railroad terminated at Tivoli's Hotel in Coney Island.

Swank came to Coney Island in 1875 when Cable's Hotel (later known as the Ocean View) opened, and with it came another key rail link, the Prospect Park & Coney Island Railroad, founded by Andrew R. Culver.

Culver's first line started at a northern terminus near Prospect Park, 20th Street and Ninth Avenue, and concluded its twenty-minute steam journey to Cable's Hotel in the West Brighton section of Coney Island. The Prospect Park & Coney Island Railroad charged 43 cents for a round-trip ticket and did a lively summer business.

There still were no elevated lines in Brooklyn when the Brooklyn, Flatbush & Coney Island Railroad opened in 1878 along much the same route now traversed by the Transit Authority's Brighton line. One of the most successful operations, the Brooklyn, Flatbush & Coney Island operated between Atlantic Avenue, where it connected with the Long Island Rail Road, and the Hotel Brighton in Coney Island.

As more and more New Yorkers discovered the glories of Coney Island's clean sands and sparkling waters, there was increased demand for still another railroad to the Atlantic. Finally, in 1879 the New York & Sea Beach Railroad shot its line through the farms and small towns of Brooklyn from 65th Street in Bay Ridge (connecting

16

with the steamboats to South Ferry) and the Sea Beach Palace Hotel in Coney Island.

The steamers cruised from Bay Ridge Landing to Whitehall Street, Leroy Street, and West 22nd Street in New York City. "Thus," wrote Electric Railroaders Association historian Bernard Linder, "Manhattanites discovered that a steamboat ride of an hour and 20 minutes, plus a half hour on the NYSB brought them to this lovely spot, where fresh-dug clams were available by the bushel. The flavor of Coney Island clams became quite as famous as the huge schooners of beer. Clams and beer were the universal food and drink of the early excursionists."

By 1880 Coney Island's beer, clams, and sea breezes assured an endless boom and, as a result, promoters erected the first authentic —albeit unconventional—elevated line in Kings County.

Only a mile long, Brooklyn's pioneering el was built within view of the ocean to connect the Hotel Brighton with a terminal just west of the Culver Depot in Coney Island. It was completed in 1881 and called the Coney Island Elevated Railway. Purists hesitated to call it an authentic el, since the line actually was more a long trestle than an elevated railway. Still, it was built above ground on wooden pilings and columns, utilizing iron bridges at road crossings. There were only two stations, at the start and finish of the route, and the Coney Island Elevated Railway ran only in the summer for the tourist trade. At first the wooden passenger cars were pulled by a steam engine but, years later, in 1898, after it was purchased by the huge Brooklyn Rapid Transit Company, the line was electrified with overhead wire.

Meanwhile the Brooklyn Bridge opened in May 24, 1883. Exactly four months later a cable-operated train service—with steam switching engines at the terminals—commenced across the span connecting Brooklyn and Manhattan.

Bridge planners, anticipating a brisk business on the railway, hired six locomotive engineers, six locomotive firemen, one master of transportation, forty-five conductors, one trainmaster, four train dispatchers, four yardmen, and five switchmen, among other bridge railway employees. Train business was more than brisk. In the first year of operation the bridge cable line carried 9,234,690 passengers.

Still more business was guaranteed because construction had begun on Brooklyn's first conventional elevated railway from the Fulton Street ferry, located on the East River, to Van Sicklen Avenue, near the city limits. The Brooklyn Elevated Railroad opened in 1885 and stimulated service on the bridge cable line. In 1885 the bridge trains, running twenty-four hours a day, handled nearly 20 million passengers. As a result its terminals were expanded and more cars were installed.

To New Yorkers the year 1888 is synonymous with the most awesome blizzard the city has known. To rail historians it is significant as the year of the great leap forward in Brooklyn's elevated railroad construction. From East River terminals no less than three major els fanned out across the city on Long Island. The Broadway (Brooklyn) el began at the ferry terminal at the East River and Broadway, the Myrtle Avenue Line started at Sands Street near the Navy Yard, and the Fulton Street line left from the Fulton ferry. In less than six years five major elevated lines snaked eastward and southward to Brooklyn's city limits.

Coney Island's many steam lines were doing so well that rail promoters felt the need to exploit the shore resort with assorted attractions. Perhaps the most lavish of all Coney Island's extravaganzas was the Brighton Beach Hotel, built by the Brooklyn Rapid Transit Company (BRT). An enormous, rococo wooden structure, the hotel was among the first to have electric lights.

The BRT designers made one colossal mistake to go with their colossal hotel. They originally erected it at the very edge of the Atlantic Ocean. Once completed, the hotel was assaulted by so high a tide that some guests were nearly drowned by the swirling waters. To prevent this happening in the future the BRT had to move the entire structure back from the edge of the beach, using Long Island Rail Road steam locomotives to accomplish the move.

Brooklyn's elevated lines continued proliferating through the turn of the century, and by 1900 every line in the borough but the Canarsie route was controlled by the Brooklyn Rapid Transit Company. By 1910 the borough of Brooklyn had a population of 1,634,000, and the 157-mile Brooklyn elevated network carried a total of 170,752,487 passengers in 928 cars.

The growth of elevated lines in Brooklyn was matched from the late seventies to the early 1900s only by the seemingly endless movement of the steel girders northward up Manhattan Island. The Ninth Avenue line was a veteran of nine years when construction started on the Third Avenue el which, by 1891, marched all the way from

South Ferry at the lower tip of Manhattan, across the Harlem River and up to 177th Street in the Bronx. In 1902 it got to Bronx Park and was electrified. Originally it was a two-track road, but the heavy residential and business development that followed it overburdened the two-track capacity. A third, or express, track was installed from Chatham Square, Manhattan, to East 149th Street in the Bronx in 1916 and extended to 177th Street a year later, being used for southbound traffic in the morning, northbound in the evening. The golden era of elevated railroading had reached its peak.

Beach's Bizarre Broadway Subway

Contrary to popular belief the Interborough Rapid Transit (IRT) subway line, which began operation in 1904, was *not* New York City's first public underground transportation system. The original Manhattan line actually ran under Broadway as early as 1870, following one of the most outlandish engineering operations the city has known.

The chief protagonist of what developed into an undercover underground operation was one Alfred Ely Beach, a gentleman of grand insight and dynamism. Beach had already invented the cable railway, the pneumatic tube, and a device that was to be pivotal in his subway production—the hydraulic tunneling bore. Journalists had revered Alfred Ely since he produced the world's first practical typewriter, which won him a gold medal at the Crystal Palace Exposition in 1853.

When he wasn't busy inventing something, Beach managed the affairs of the New York *Sun* (he and his brother were co-publishers), and founded several magazines while simultaneously working as a patent lawyer. Beach had been entertaining the idea of a subway since his early twenties. From his office overlooking City Hall in downtown Manhattan, Beach would regularly worry about the congestion that developed at the corner of Broadway and Chambers Street where neighing horses, screaming wagon drivers, and pedestrians vied for the limited space at the intersections.

Beach realized there were two possibilities for moving vehicular passenger traffic away from the streets—a road above ground or one below which would carry a railway train. The young inventor rejected the elevated idea, reasoning that it would be both unsightly and noisy. There was no question in Beach's mind that a subway was the answer. But first he had to find a means of moving rolling stock through a tunnel.

Horses were out of the question. A steam engine would produce too much soot. In 1866, when Beach was ready to put his ideas on the drawing board, practical gasoline and electric motors were not yet available. Pneumatic power seemed the only solution.

To convince skeptics that it was possible to move a small railroad car through a tube by means of air power, Beach constructed a plywood tube, six feet in diameter. He then designed and built a small car, seating ten passengers, which would run inside the tube. For propulsion, Beach proposed to use a Helix fan, ten feet in diameter, which would funnel a blast of air into the tunnel. The air would move the train to the end of the tube and then, with fan reversed, pull it back to its point of origin.

Beach used the 1867 American Institute Fair held in the Fourteenth Street Armory to demonstrate the pneumatic-tube experiment. The armory was packed with spectators who gawked at and cheered the ten-car train as it moved through the tube that linked the 14th Street exit with the 15th Street doors.

The enthusiasm of the crowd during the weeks that the pneumatic train operated convinced Beach that he had himself a winner. But he was realist enough to know that it is one thing to construct a plywood tube and place it on the floor of an armory and quite another task to bore a tunnel under Broadway. Beach went right back to the drawing board to perfect such a tunnel driller. The result was a hydraulic shield which could tunnel seventeen inches with each press into the earth wall. Workers remained inside the shield, bricking the tunnel with comparative security from cave-in. Beach's earth-gouger was flexible enough to move left or right, up or down and, in experiments, proved that it could do the job on a genuine subway construction project.

But hacking through political red tape was a project with which the hydraulic shield could not cope. New York City in 1868 was dominated by the Tammany Hall Democratic machine, the levers of which were controlled by William Marcy Tweed, the boss of all bosses.

Beach realized that, legally, he would require a franchise to build and operate a subway under Broadway. He also knew that Tweed would take as much money from him as could be extracted. During one three-month period following his appointment to the board of the Erie Railroad, Tweed pocketed Erie profits amounting to $650,000. Bribes to Tweed were written off as legal expenses. With this in mind, Beach decided to bypass the Boss. "I won't pay political blackmail," he told his brother. "I say, let's build the subway furtively."

That was extremely dangerous talk, considering Tweed's power and the near impossibility of constructing a full-scale subway in the middle of the metropolis without general public notice. (Some historians insist that many officials *were* aware of the project, but chose to ignore it.)

Beach dismissed the overwhelming obstacles from his mind. He would build the pneumatic tube. He would not inform the public officials about it. It would be warmly received and Tweed, in the end, would not be a problem. He concluded that the subway would be so beautiful, so efficient, indeed unique, so that when it opened public acclaim would erase any objections raised by Tweed or anyone else.

Having convinced his close associates that the subway would overwhelm all opponents, Beach took on the biggest challenge of his life. The first problem was gaining access to Broadway's subterranean depths. This was accomplished by renting the basement of Devlin's Clothing Store at Murray Street and Broadway; then Beach and his men began digging.

The ground under Broadway at that point was sandy and appeared amenable to Beach's hydraulic tunneling shield. In 1868 work commenced when a load of dirt was carried across the cellar of Devlin's Clothing Store and unloaded in a corner.

Beach put his twenty-one-year-old son, Fred, to work on the job as gang foreman. Fred and his crew hacked away at the underground wall of dirt, and gradually they could see that progress was being made, although many of the hired help were frightened off the job by the conditions confronting them under the clothing store.

Claustrophobia was a persistent problem. Fear that the horses galloping overhead, whose hoofbeats were acutely audible in the tunnel, would crash through and expose the project constantly weighed on the workers. Many quit and never returned. Others worked apprehensively in the close tunnel air, guided by lantern light, pecking away at the dirt and sand.

For several nights the work proceeded without formidable obstacles. The sound of iron pick against ever expanding cave was a symphony to Beach's ear. But one night a dissonant noise was heard as a workman's spade struck a piece of stone. Then another and another. Suddenly all forward progress stopped. Instead of sand and dirt, easily penetrated, the laborers had run into a wall of stone.

Beach and his colleagues deduced that the stones were the foundation of an old fort. If a section of the foundation was removed the street might collapse around their heads. Beach had to make a choice; either abandon the project or conquer the obstacle. "Remove it," commanded Beach, "stone by stone!"

One by one, the stones were removed and boring continued while Beach watched the ceiling, hoping against hope that it would hold firm. After several days, during which there was no sign of sagging, Beach was convinced that he had made the right decision. The digging continued. Each night the workers would haul the bags of dirt out of the tunnel, dumping them onto wagons specially fitted with wheels muffled for silence. While these wagons hauled the dirt away, others arrived with tools and bricks for the tunnel walls. "Night after night," wrote Robert Daley in *The World beneath the City*, "gangs of men slipped in and out of the tunnel like thieves."

The project was costing Beach a fortune. By his own estimate some $350,000 of his own money would be needed to complete the subway by its target date of February 1870. A portion of the expense was for lavish fixtures that seemed more appropriate in the Metropolitan Opera House than for an experimental underground railway. But that was part of Beach's plan. A salesman at heart, he believed that an uncertain public had to be wooed with frills as well as efficiency.

To this end, Beach designed a waiting room 120 feet long (the entire tunnel measured 312 feet) and embellished it with a grand piano, a fountain, ornate paintings, and even a goldfish tank. Instead of entering a dank, dreary tunnel, the customers on the proposed Beach pneumatic subway would find themselves in an elegant, airy salon lighted with zircon lamps.

The digging went on without detection or further incident for fifty-eight nights. It was completed according to plan, whereupon Beach began installing the ostentatious trappings, which took longer than the boring and brick work. The walls of the waiting room were adorned with frescoes. Still, the *chef d'oeuvre* would be the subway itself.

Beach designed a single car, which fitted snugly into the cylindrical tube nine feet in diameter. Propulsion would be supplied by a giant fan that the workers nicknamed "the Western Tornado." It was operated by a steam engine, drawing air in through a valve and blowing it forcefully into the tunnel. Thus the single car would be driven from Warren Street to Murray Street, the other end of the line, "like a boat before the wind."

Upon reaching the Murray Street terminus, the lone subway car would trip a wire that ran the length of the tunnel, ringing a bell back at Warren Street and alerting the engineer. The blower would then be reversed, and the train would be sucked right back to its starting point, "like soda through a straw." Air would be conveyed to the tunnel by means of an intake-exhaust grating installed on the surface of the street.

The giant fan, also known as the "Roots Patent Force Blast Blower," was designed to move the train at a top speed of ten miles an hour. The subway was completed, along with the frescoes, the fountain, and the fish tank, in February 1870 without the knowledge of Boss Tweed or, for that matter, nearly any other citizen of New York City.

Alfred Ely Beach, then forty-four years old, was ready to reveal to an unsuspecting public the grand triumph of his life. The pneumatic subway would make its official debut on February 26, 1870. Beach invited the press and assorted dignitaries. His calculated gamble was that the subway would so impress them that potential foes would promptly muffle their opposition.

Beach was right—up to a point. Those who attended came away dazzled by the opulence and impressed by the subway's practicality. "This means the end of street dust of which uptown residents get not only their fill, but more than their fill, so that it runs over and collects on their hair, their beards, their eyebrows and floats in their dress like a vapor on a frosty morning," commented the *Scientific American* (also edited by Beach). "Such discomforts will never be found in the tunnel!"

The twenty-two-seat subway car impressed observers with its rich upholstery and spaciousness, not to mention comfortable ride. Delighted with the initial response, Beach boasted that this subway was merely the forerunner of a line that would run for miles up and down Manhattan Island. "We propose to operate a subway all the way to Central Park," said Beach, "about five miles in all. When it's finished we should be able to carry 20,000 passengers a day at speeds up to a mile a minute." Press comments confirmed Beach's triumph.

The New York *Herald* proclaimed: "Fashionable Reception Held in the Bowels of the Earth!"

The reporter from the New York *Sun* marveled—as Beach had hoped—at the salon. "The waiting room is a large and elegantly furnished apartment, cheerful and attractive throughout."

Nearly everyone of importance was heard from, except the man who counted the most, William Marcy Tweed.

The flunkies at Tammany Hall were already hearing about Beach's subway from the Boss. He had read the papers and it was a toss-up, according to cronies, whether Tweed was more stunned or furious over the surprise subway. One thing was certain: he was not happy, nor was he impressed by the overwhelmingly favorable public opinion generated by Beach's underground.

Already wealthy and the most powerful man in the city, Tweed nevertheless feared Beach on two counts: the inventor had the courage to defy him and, further, his invention would cut into the Boss's profits. It was generally acknowledged that every trolley car company in the city paid tribute to Tweed. A subway of the magnitude proposed by Beach would cut heavily into those profits.

Tweed wasted no time deciding how to handle the upstart Beach; he would go after the fellow the way he'd stalk his most hated political enemy. Across City Hall Park, Beach sat in his office more valorous than discreet. "New York needs a subway," he countered when informed of Tweed's adamant and furious opposition. "I will go before the legislature at Albany."

Beach's single trump card was that his pneumatic tube under Broadway was open and operating; each day a horde of curiosity seekers poured into Devlin's basement to gawk at the grand piano, the fountain and frescoes, and to ride the wind-blown train. Months went by and more passengers paid their quarter a head for the ride, as well as the right to walk through the tunnel when the train was halted.

With public approval on his side, Beach went to the legislature. The Beach Transit bill called for a $5-million expenditure, all to be privately raised. All work would be underground with little or no disruption at street level.

The New York State Senate passed the Beach Transit bill by a 22–5 landslide vote. The State Assembly gave it a 102–11 stamp of approval. There was only one catch: Boss Tweed, who came up with a transit idea to counter the Beach proposal. Dubbed Tweed's Viaduct Plan, the Tammany blueprint called for a series of elevated lines mounted on forty-foot-high stone arches. It would cost $80 million, the monies coming from public funds.

Not surprisingly, Tweed had clout in the state legislature, which also approved his Viaduct Plan. One or the other plan—but not both—would be approved by Governor John T. Hoffman. Since Hoffman and Tweed were political brothers the Beach bill was doomed the moment it reached the governor's desk. Hoffman vetoed the plan and signed the Tweed Viaduct bill. Although the governor's action enraged editorialists who charged Tweed with hanky-panky, the fact remained that Beach was defeated. His only hope was that, somehow, he might marshal enough public support in the next year so that the Hoffman veto might be overcome.

Publicity was the key to Beach's campaign. If he could continue the momentum developed by public opinion in favor of his pneumatic tube the governor's veto would be overcome. Beach redoubled his efforts to lure dignataries down to the tube. But Tweed's influence over politicians of every stripe was so complete that the only official of any stature to accept Beach's invitation was Secretary of the Navy Robeson (who rode December 1870). The cabinet member enjoyed the ride and said so to the press but the publicity was slight compared to what Beach required.

Still, the man-in-the-street liked it and when the Beach Transit bill came up for another vote it passed and then received Hoffman's expected veto. What mattered, of course, was the legislature's attempt to override the veto. A two-thirds majority was needed. When the final tally was in, Beach had lost—by one vote.

A less determined battler would have despaired, but Beach insisted that he still had a chance. He needed a break or two in the political halls and in late 1872 he got it. Tweed's empire showed its first signs of crumbling as the *New York Times* began printing stories of corruption at Tammany Hall. The Boss was indicted and in November 1872 Governor Hoffman was voted out of office.

But Beach himself was showing signs of defeat. The pneumatic tube gradually lost its curiosity value and gate receipts dwindled to a point where Beach decided to close his subway as an economy measure. He hoped, however, to win the big battle in Albany and kept a collection of lobbyists on his payroll for just that purpose.

With Tweed down and Hoffman out, it appeared that Beach finally had the green light he needed for the subway bill. But now foes appeared from nonpolitical quarters. Engineers argued that his hydraulic shield would be an ineffective tunneling device in rocky sections of Manhattan. Other scientists insisted that pneumatic power might be useful on a short subway such as the one Beach operated under Broadway, but certainly not on a five-mile run.

Deciding that if he couldn't beat his critics he'd join them, Beach rewrote the charter of his transit bill. If the pneumatic tube didn't work, he would provide for steam engines to pull the trains. And if his hydraulic shield failed to cut through Manhattan he would switch to the generally acceptable cut-and-fill technique.

Unfortunately, in his enthusiasm for the subway, Beach managed to alienate the millionaire John Jacob Astor, who had become one of New York City's major landlords. Astor and several of his colleagues feared that tunneling under Broadway might endanger the foundation of Trinity Church and its 280-foot tower, then Manhattan's tallest building. Other landlords were concerned about *their* buildings and the damaging effects the subway might have on them.

Despite the opposition the Beach Transit bill won approval from the state legislature in 1873. It then went to the new governor, John A. Dix, who gave it his enthusiastic backing. At last Beach's perseverance and grim determination had paid off, on paper at least. Finding funds to build the subway was another story and a rather grim one. In fact, Beach's victory was a Pyrrhic one of the most traumatic variety. He was physically, monetarily, and emotionally wasted. Inflation had forced a revision in his cost estimate from $5 million to $10 million, all of which had to be raised from financiers such as Astor.

But John Jacob Astor wanted no part of Beach or his subway. Other financiers refused him funds; one after another of Beach's attempts to raise cash failed and later in 1873 Governor Dix withdrew the charter for Beach's pneumatic subway.

New York's first subway remained forgotten until February 1912 when a construction crew—digging for a new Broadway subway, the BMT—chopped through the wall of the Beach tunnel. Unaware of the pneumatic tube, the workers were flabbergasted at the ornate trappings before their eyes.

With the exception of some rotted wooden fixtures, the salon retained its original spendor. The magnificent station arrested the sandhogs' attention. Not only did they delight in the vision of an underground fountain but in the discovery that there had been a subway operating under Manhattan years before they began digging. Beach's tiny railroad car was still on its tracks.

Once the workers' discovery was reported, backers of the new subway decided that some form of acknowledgment should be made to the man who built New York's first underground railway. Their tribute was a plaque in honor of Alfred Ely Beach on a wall of the completed BMT City Hall station.

The Boynton Bicycle Railroad

In 1887, decades before the Brooklyn Rapid Transit and later the Brooklyn Manhattan Transit (BMT) crisscrossed the sands of Coney Island, an experimental railroad of unique proportions threatened to make the traditional rail-and-tie-type railroad obsolete. The brains behind the project was an inventor named Eben Moody Boynton, an irascible, dogmatic individual. Boynton's theory was simplicity itself. The way to run a railroad was *not* to place two rails beneath a train, but to place one track overhead and one track underneath.

Dubbed "the Flying Billboard," Boynton's weird contraption actually was a century-ahead-of-time predecessor of the monorail, with appropriate variations. From the side view, the Boynton train appeared not greatly different from a traditional passenger railroad unit. The key difference, of course, was that the wheels on his train were placed in the middle of the top and bottom of the locomotive, tender, and passenger cars instead of on each side of the bottom of the vehicles.

Boynton's fascination with the bicycle's smoothness and ease of operation provided the inspiration for his train improvement. "A bicycle weighing 25 pounds," wrote Boynton, "can carry a rider weighing ten times as much."

If that was the case, why use a ton of steel and wood to carry a passenger, as was done on the railroads of the day?

Boynton carried his research further. He discovered that a man had once pedaled 334 miles in twenty-four hours on a level track. Boynton figured up the number of ton-miles the man had transported simply by the strength of his two legs applied through the new spindle-type wheel.

Boynton was convinced beyond any doubt that the conventional railroad cars lost power through the sidesway of their four-wheeled design, not to mention the energy wasted through friction and air pressure. By applying bicycle principles to railroading, all of these "four-wheeled failures" would be rendered obsolete.

In its final blueprint form, Boynton's revolutionary bicycle train was, in the words of railroad historian Joseph Harrington, "the most fantastic-looking train ever built in America." Boynton had designed the passenger coach to be *two stories high, and only four feet wide.* It would seat 108 passengers and weigh but five tons. By contrast, railroad coaches of the day averaged in weight one ton to the passenger. "The lightness of Boynton's train," said Harrington, "was phenomenal."

So was the projected speed (100 mph cruising) and fuel savings. Boynton figured he could haul a payload from New York to Boston with a couple of scuttles of coal. After a decade of laborious development, Boynton was ready to lure investors to back his amazing invention. If there was one quality about him that could not be contained it was his enthusiasm. When it came to promoting the Boynton Bicycle Railroad, no press agent was necessary.

Boynton predicted that investors would come away with a company net profit of $80 million to $100 million annually at the start. He added that the railroads themselves would save $400 million a year, even after paying for Boynton's patents.

These projections were based on unusually low construction costs—$7,000 a mile for his heavier model and as little as $3,500 for the economy version. He told New Yorkers that their Sixth and Ninth Avenue elevated lines could be converted to his Boynton Bicycle system for $1 million and not a penny more.

"He said he would carry passengers to their destinations in New York at 100 miles an hour," said Harrington. "And he would go further. He would spin his lacy lines across the Hudson and the East River—for great iron bridges for support were unnecessary to the light Boynton Bicycles."

New York transit experts were fascinated by this inventor and his projections. What was especially appealing to economy-minded rail men was the idea that every single track line would become double track, and double-track lines would become four-track lines. "With the Boynton bicycle locomotives and passenger cars," he said, "the railroad trackage of the nation will be immediately doubled."

Skeptics warned that any vehicle that traveled more than 100 mph inevitably had to be a health hazard. But Boynton would have none of that. "My trains will be healthier than the conventional ones," he countered. "Ventilation will be considerably improved."

What's more, there would be less pollution. His lightweight cars could be pushed by the average human. A pair of strong men, he ventured, could push a Boynton "palace coach" as fast as they could walk. Imagine what could be done with a ton of coal. That is, in the countryside. For New York City use, Boynton promised—far ahead of his time—to design electric motors to move his bicycle coaches. For the moment, however, he would utilize steam to power his twenty-two-ton locomotive.

A train designed to cruise at 100 mph was appealing but engineers questioned what would happen at a curve at such speeds. Boynton replied: "My train will be safer at 100 miles per hour than an ordinary train at 20 miles per hour." His hedge against tipping, of course, was the overhead rail, which would prove its worth during the premiere exhibition. The train won't tip, promised Boynton, and collisions are impossible because each train will operate on its own track.

Since Boynton had an interest in concessions in both the Coney Island and Sea Beach sections of Brooklyn, it was natural for him to gravitate toward that area when he searched for a testing ground. "His prospectus," said one near investor, "had the sound of a Coney Island barker." Those who knew Boynton well contend that his unbridled enthusiasm was his most persistent problem. Boynton thought *too* big. Instead of developing his Bicycle Railroad in New York City and then expanding, he thought on a worldwide basis from the very start and was convinced that he had conquered the world's railroading problems in one swoop.

His first report to his stockholders in 1887 reflected an élan shared by few others when it came to the future of the Bicycle Railroad:

"It will open up inaccessible continents like Africa. . . . With its exceedingly narrow and light trains following a single thread of steel, bracketed to the cliffs and gorges of mountains, it will open up hitherto inaccessible regions, saving a million dollars per mile in the tunnelling of mountains."

When Boynton went so far as to suggest that passengers in his two-story coaches would be able to cross the continent from New York to San Francisco in twenty-four hours, investors thought that was a bit much! The time had come, they said, to see the Bicycle Railroad in action.

Boynton was ready. His locomotive and passenger car were built, and track was laid across a meadow in Coney Island. All he had to do was demonstrate that it worked.

He decided to use a half-mile testing ground for the big day at Coney. A crowd of more than 5,000, including 100 engineers, crossed Brooklyn for the event.

Boynton was ready, and so was his contraption. With a huff and a puff it was underway, moving smartly up to a speed of sixty mph. But that was as fast as it could go, not because it lacked the power, but because it had run out of track.

The reviews were immediately available and, at first, were glowing. "It ran," said one observer, "with incredible smoothness. It was extremely stable. The overhead rail seemed hardly necessary, even on banked turns."

More important, however, were the impressions—and, later, decisions—of professional engineers from New York City's rapid transit lines. One group of onlookers represented the Manhattan

Elevated Railway (MER). They not only watched in awe, but later took a ride and commended Boynton for the silk-smooth ride.

Much as they applauded the project, however, the MER officials were not prepared to scrap their elevated lines for the Boynton Bicycle Railroad.

Typically, Boynton was looking ahead to still another project and virtually ignored the MER snub, since he was busy trying to persuade farmers that they should have a private railroad to bring their produce to market.

"Investors," said historian Harrington, "were repelled rather than attracted by Boynton's ballyhoo. They believed that his dream was impossible to realistically achieve." Those investors who did give Boynton capital soon discovered that it was going no further than the half-mile strip of railroad in Coney Island. "But," said Harrington, "Boynton lost the most, and, in the end, there never was any question of his utter honesty."

Eventually the Boynton Bicycle Railroad crashed in the bankruptcy court. Boynton went to Boston, hopeful of persuading the Massachusetts legislature to provide citizens with perfect, 100-mph train service at a low price. But Boynton kept running into resistance until his death in March 1927.

Monorails—using basic principles of the bicycle—are in use today in Germany, Japan, and even in America's Disneyland and Seattle, Washington. They all suggest that Boynton's ideas were sound.

"There are railroad historians," concluded Joe Harrington, "who have a suspicion that Boynton's chief trouble was that he was born a century too soon!"

BUILDING THE
GREATEST RAILROAD

Planning the First
Subway

Without a doubt the elevated railroads were a smash hit in both
Manhattan and Brooklyn late in the nineteenth century. With each
year an older line was extended and a new route planned; there
seemed to be no end in sight as long as there remained vast areas of
undeveloped land in Brooklyn, Manhattan, the Bronx, and, eventually, parts of Queens. But there remained a vocal and significant bloc
of el critics who harped at its obvious defects. It was loud, smelly,
and frequently a detriment to the neighborhoods over which it rolled.

The earliest elevated lines employed four-wheel steam dummy

locomotives to haul the passenger cars, but the tiny engines were inadequate in terms of power and economy. An improved locomotive, designed by Pennsylvania inventor Matthias Forney, proved infinitely more effective. The Forney model had a small double-end tank engine with a swiveled truck under the tank. Unlike its predecessors, the Forney locomotive could haul seven cars and easily maintain a twelve-miles-per-hour schedule, including stops.

All the el companies in Manhattan and Brooklyn bought Forney engines, and by the early 1890s there were more than 500 in elevated railway service. But even the marvelous little Forney had its drawbacks. It relentlessly spewed smoke and cinders from its smokestack to the ground below, frightening horses, enraging merchants, and inspiring city planners and inventors to come up with something better in the way of transit motive power.

The answer was supplied by two electrical inventors, Frank J. Sprague and Leo Daft, both of whom realized that the most practical method of moving the el cars was by electricity. Daft's offering was a nine-ton electric locomotive called Benjamin Franklin. In 1885 he ran it on the Ninth Avenue line of the Manhattan Railway Company. The Franklin hauled four cars and accelerated to a speed of twenty-five mph. That same year Sprague produced blueprints for the electric operation of the Manhattan el. Like Daft, Sprague developed an experimental car and won the attention of Jay Gould, one of the principal owners of the line.

Sprague persuaded Gould to allow him to run an electric car on the Manhattan Railway and even convinced the renowned financier to take a ride with him. That was Sprague's first mistake. His second was impetuousity. Having lured Gould into the experimental car, Sprague enthusiastically pulled hard on the controller to set the train in motion. But he yanked too abruptly and blew a fuse that sounded to Gould like a bomb exploding. "Gould was so startled by the report," wrote rail historian William D. Middleton, "that he had to be restrained from jumping off the car. After this unnerving experience the financier abandoned all interest in electric traction."

Rebuffed by el interests, Sprague turned his attention to street railways. He originally began with battery-operated cars, but then the Sprague Electric Railway & Motor Company reverted to pure electrification of surface transit. He obtained contracts to work on overhead power systems in Richmond, Virginia, and St. Joseph, Missouri. In 1888 he successfully electrified the Richmond trolleys, proving to the world that it was possible to electrify surface lines. Next in line were the els.

Early electrification experiments on the elevated trains concentrated on development of an electric locomotive which would be capable of pulling a string of as many as eight cars. This system had its drawbacks, especially since some highly successful lines considered use of as many as ten passenger cars on a single run and the electric locomotives of the time simply were not adequate for the job.

Sprague, who had since become involved with elevator experiments, was busy with an installation at the New York Postal Telegraph Building, where he invented a system by which a single master switch could regulate the movement of any elevator in the building or the movement of *all* of them at once. When the elevator experiment proved successful, Sprague decided to apply the same principles to elevated trains. His theory was that if an entire system of elevators could be operated by one master switch, then an entire train of electrified cars could be operated by a main controller. Each elevated car would have a controller and an electric motor but the "multiple-unit system" would be operated from the motorman's cabin in the first car.

By this time Sprague's transit firm had been bought out by burgeoning General Electric, but his ties to GE remained solid. On July 16, 1897 two of Sprague's experimental multiple-unit cars were tested by GE engineers at the company's Schenectady, New York, plant. Before the month was up an entire six-car train was successfully operated and by the end of the year a test train of five cars was running on the Chicago elevated system.

The multiple-unit train worked so well on Chicago's South Side Elevated that in 1898 Brooklyn's steam-operated els began converting to electricity and by 1903 all of New York City's els had disposed of their Forneys and reequipped with Spragues. More important, those who had dismissed the idea of underground trains in Manhattan because of the hazards of smoke and steam now began a reappraisal, and by the turn of the century it had become apparent that New York not only needed but would build the greatest railroad in the world—most of it underground!

Constructing the IRT

While New York City's plans for underground rapid transit remained stalled throughout the latter half of the nineteenth century, other metropoli were developing subways with relative ease. London began the world's first subway in 1863. Another followed in Glasgow in 1886; Budapest, Hungary, unveiled a little underground railway system in 1896; and one year later North America's first subway, the West End Railway, began operating under Tremont Street in Boston, using trolley cars. The Paris Metro made its debut in 1900, whereupon Boston also displayed the first genuine—as opposed to trolley-operated—rapid transit subway in America when the Boston Elevated Railway began operation on el tracks and in subway tubes on June 10, 1901. Finally, the Berliners inaugurated their underground in 1902.

Meanwhile, New Yorkers had endured more than thirty years of subway talk, but no action, when financier August Belmont and Mayor Robert A. Van Wyck broke ground in March 1900 at City Hall, Manhattan. New York's first subway would comprise nearly thirteen miles of underground line and more than three miles of el extensions between Manhattan and the Bronx.

The general plan called for the subway to tunnel northward from City Hall, then up the East Side of the island to Grand Central terminal. It would then turn left and proceed westerly under 42nd Street to Times Square, and then turn right and proceed north again under Broadway to a terminus at Bailey Avenue in the Bronx. The length of the route, of which about two miles were on viaducts, was thirteen and one-half miles.

To build the subway, Belmont's planners had two options: they could copy the techniques used by London's Underground in which deep tubes were bored by shield method deep underground, or they could try Budapest's trench method. Instead of sinking a pit and then driving a bore laterally, as did London and Glasgow engineers, the Hungarians simply cut a huge trench along the route of their subway, built their railroad at the bottom, roofed it with steel girders, and used a few feet of fill and paving on top of the roof. This "cut-and-cover" method was eventually to be universally employed in subway construction. It was infinitely cheaper, easier, and faster than driving a tunnel by the shield method.

While they were borrowing ideas from the Hungarians, American engineers also adopted the Budapest station plan. Unlike the English, the Hungarians did not build surface structures that resembled railroad terminals. Instead they borrowed a design from the gardens of ancient Persia and Turkey, where oddly shaped summerhouses called *kūshks* abounded. New York subway engineers Americanized the *kushk* to kiosk. Thus it happened that the first subway under City Hall had strangely ornamental mosque-like roofs, although New Yorkers constructed the buildings of steel and glass instead of stone and tile. The kiosks also were believed to be functional. It was foreseen, in 1900 when they were planned, that in a heavy rainstorm, without such protection, rain would pour in through an opening and platforms would become sloppy.

The Hungarian cut-and-cover method may have been cheap in dollars but New Yorkers quickly discovered that it was expensive in terms of public opinion. As hundreds of sandhogs ripped the guts out of Broadway, Fourth Avenue, and 42nd Street, business fell flat, storekeepers wailed, and the man-in-the-street wondered when the din would end.

Underground, the men with the digging machines wondered when the variation in earth formations would end. Between 14th and 18th streets, for example, the underground rock protruded almost to the pavement. In other places, work gangs encountered water-bearing loam and sand. At Pearl and Grand streets, this problem was solved by employing a special supporting base for the subway. Confounding the engineers was the labyrinth of sewers, water and gas mains, steam pipes, pneumatic tubes, and electrical conduits. Then there were the elevated railway columns that had to be shored up while underground construction took place. At Columbus Circle, near the entrance to Central Park, great care had to be taken to prevent the undermining of the Columbus Monument, which reached seventy-five feet above street level and weighed 700 tons.

At 110th Street and Lenox Avenue, along the northern border of Central Park, engineers encountered a six-and-a-half-foot circular brick sewer. They had a choice of either removing the sewer completely or subdividing it. They opted for subdivision, and three 42-inch cast-iron pipes were passed under the subway.

In a number of sections of line the road was built in rock tunnel lined with concrete. All of this was executed by construction crews working an eight-hour night shift. Blasting took place early in the morning, with the day gang removing the rubble. All debris was dispatched to the surface in mule-driven cars.

Ironically, some of the most interesting construction took place above ground. Planners had decided that the subway would emerge from its tunnel at Broadway and 120th, climb over Manhattan Valley (125th Street), and then reenter the tunnel under Broadway once more at 135th Street. To span Manhattan Valley, engineers blueprinted a 2,174-foot viaduct that, to this day, is one of the most impressive elevated structures on the system. The span features a two-hinged arch of 168.5 feet. It remains one of the more important stations on the IRT Broadway line.

For two years officials, sandhogs, and sidewalk superintendents managed to avoid what they feared most—an underground explosion. The potential for a sandpick ringing against a stone and igniting escaped gas from a leaky main remained a threat throughout the project.

On January 27, 1902 the threat became a reality, but hardly because of the hazards most feared. Stupidity is the only explanation for powderman Moses Epps lighting a candle just a few feet from 548 pounds of dynamite, just so that he could warm his hands!

The incident took place in an IRT storage shed over the subway cut at 41st Street and Park Avenue, near Grand Central Terminal. After lighting the candle, Epps walked out of the shed for a breather. It was the worst move of his life. In the moments he was gone, Epps's candle had fallen to the floor and set his lunch wrapper ablaze. Thinking he had time to douse the fire, Epps grabbed a bucket of water and poured it on the flames. More water was needed, so the powderman dashed for a refill. Suddenly he wheeled in his tracks to be sure he had time for a second dousing. He didn't. The fire had reached the dynamite and Epps ran from the shanty.

Epps screamed to passersby to run for their lives. In less than a minute, one of the loudest reports ever to be heard in New York City reverberated up and down 41st Street as if several bombs had been dropped in the midtown area. Actually, the effect was as bad, if not worse, than a bombing, for in this case the pedestrians and guests at the nearby Murray Hill Hotel were taken completely unawares and had no opportunity to protect themselves. Those eating lunch in the hotel's restaurant were hurled about, crushed by debris and wounded by flying glass. When the dust had cleared, 5 people were dead and more than 180 injured.

The explosion shook down the plaster at the hotel and broke all the windows in surrounding homes. Even the clocks in the Grand Central Station tower were blown in, while the Manhattan Eye and Ear Hospital had to close its doors to the wounded because of damage to its facility. Ironically, Epps suffered only bruises and the IRT-in-the-making endured the blast with no serious damage at all. However, the blast propelled Mayor Low into action and he immediately appointed a Municipal Explosives Commission, which revised the city regulations governing the storage and use of high explosives in the city limits.

Before the winter was over, the embryonic IRT suffered another trauma just three blocks from the powderhouse disaster. This time a rock slide occurred in the deep tunnel under Park Avenue, between 37th and 38th streets. Fortunately no lives were lost, but the accident delayed construction, as did sporadic labor strikes throughout the contract.

No further mishaps marred work in the midtown area, but a calamitous event took place in October 1903 at the northern sector. To complete tunneling at 195th Street and St. Nicholas Avenue, workmen had to drill through solid rock sixty feet below street level. The tunnel, which was fifty feet wide and fifteen feet high, was pushed forward by workmen who planted sticks of dynamite, cleared the area for the blast, and then returned after the explosion was complete to remove debris and prepare for another move forward.

Dynamiting at 195th Street was under the direction of foreman Timothy Sullivan, who committed as monumental a mistake as Moses Epps had. Sullivan planted the dynamite, cleared the tunnel, okayed the detonation, and then listened for the explosion. The foreman heard the same rumbling noise he had heard so many times before: the sound of exploding dynamite. As if by reflex, he hustled his men back into the tunnel, all thirty of them, with Sullivan in the lead.

But the foreman had moved too fast. As soon as Sullivan and his sandhogs reached the dynamite site, they were greeted with three resounding reports as previously undetonated TNT went off in their faces. Before Sullivan could make a move, the tunnel roof caved in on him. The foreman and nine of his men died in the blasts, while many others were seriously injured. In *The World beneath the City*, Robert Daley detailed the horror of that moment:

"For some, pinned under a boulder estimated to weigh 200 tons, the agony was protracted. Three men hung head downward while rescuers attacked with drills the rock which crushed the lower part of their bodies. A fourth man was caught by the leg. Frantic efforts to pry up a corner of the boulder and free him failed. At last, a doctor amputated the leg. He was rushed to a hospital, but died en route."

Despite such disasters, the 10,000 men who excavated 3,508,000 cubic yards of earth had completed 90 percent of the work by the end of 1903. It was now clear that the subway would be open for business by the end of 1904, so the builders turned their attention to an area that had been considered vital from the start: attractive and practical rolling stock.

Safety was a persistent consideration, and because of this the IRT directors seriously considered all-steel cars, which then were a rarity. In fact, they placed an order for 500 all-steel cars, but were told that it would be impossible to produce so many of a new design in the time allowed. The compromise model was a car constructed of a wooden frame on a steel bottom, with sides sheathed with copper and the electric machinery encased in fireproof material. The car was fifty-one feet long, four feet longer than cars on the Manhattan Elevated Railroad, with a seating capacity for fifty-two passengers. When the first cars were completed in the winter of 1903–4, they were tested on the Second Avenue el and found to be satisfactory, but the IRT moguls continued to push plans for an all-steel car and eventually ordered 200 of the more advanced design. Meanwhile, construction of the line from City Hall to 145th Street and Broadway was nearly finished.

"Fifteen Minutes to Harlem"

The promise of IRT dreamers was that the new subway would whisk passengers from City Hall in the southern portion of Manhattan Island to 145th Street in the northern tier, in less than a half hour. Before the first flaming Tuscan red subway train rolled under Park Avenue, the slogan "fifteen minutes to Harlem" was heard throughout the city. Some thought it was the boast of overzealous subway promoters. To others, especially August Belmont, it was a feat that could be accomplished by his Interborough Rapid Transit Company. Belmont and his colleagues would get the answer on a snappy fall day in 1904 when the green light was flashed for New York's first major subway.

The date was October 27, 1904, a day that rarely has been equaled in the city's long history of major celebrations. Only Armistice Day, V-E Day, V-J Day, and the return of Charles Lindbergh after his solo flight across the Atlantic produced as enthusiastic an explosion of public joy. From the Atlantic Ocean, where foghorns sounded all day, to St. Patrick's Cathedral, which tolled its bells, the town roared its approval, even before the first train left City Hall station.

The official opening was actually launched in the Aldermanic Chamber at City Hall, where a series of speeches and benedictions was delivered by Mayor John McClellan, various politicians, and the city's highest churchmen. Financier Belmont and builder John B. McDonald looked on impatiently as the ceremony droned on. Finally, Archbishop Farley delivered a closing benediction, and Mayor McClellan punctuated the fête with a simple declaration:

"Now I, as mayor, in the name of the people, declare the subway open." Belmont handed the mayor a mahogany case which held the crown jewel of the new IRT—an ornamented, silver controller. Belmont then intoned: "I give you this controller, Mr. Mayor, with the request that you put in operation this great road, and start it on its course of success and, I hope, of safety."

Mayor McClellan gave the officials some nervous moments, however. Instead of simply taking the controller and posing for a few dozen ceremonial photos, McClellan took Belmont literally and began operating the city's first eight-car train as if he intended to be a motorman instead of the mayor. He pulled the train out of City Hall station, while IRT general manager Frank Hedley nervously looked over his shoulder. The trains were built to run thirty miles an hour and McClellan seemed quite willing to make the most of the new motors. At Bleecker Street station, where there was already a "Subway Tavern," opened ten weeks earlier in anticipation of the great event, patrons were at the subway entrance, cheering lustily as the McLellan-operated train rolled by.

When Hedley suggested that perhaps the mayor was ready to allow an IRT professional to take over the controls, McClellan, son of the Civil War general, snapped: *"I'm running this train!"* And run it he did, to Broadway and 103rd Street where he finally surrendered the controller. The trailblazer continued on to its temporary terminus at 145th Street, making the run in twenty-six minutes; not quite as good as the slogan but nearly on time.

Once the mayoral special had run uptown and back to City Hall, the IRT offered free rides to several thousand invited guests until 6 P.M. when the line closed down for a special inspection of its 9.1 miles by Chief Engineer William Barclay Parsons. Exactly one hour later, Parsons gave the signal, and the IRT opened to revenue passengers at 5 cents a ride.

The response was overwhelming. On opening night, more than 150,000 people "tried" the subway. At the 145th Street terminal police used nightsticks to break up the crowd trying to enter. At times the crowds became threatening to life and limb. One young woman suffered a broken leg when she was pushed into the space between the subway car and the platform.

On Friday, October 29, the IRT opened for its first full day of operation and, once again, teeming hordes turned out for the new underground railway. Newspaper headlines told the story: RUSH-HOUR BLOCKADE JAMS SUBWAY.

Inspectors from the Board of Health who toured the first IRT tube in August Belmont's private car, Mineola, rated the underground air "excellent." However, their judgment may have been somewhat influenced by Belmont's two stewards, who served them from a broiler and grill and popped bottles of champagne as the train click-clacked through the "excellent" subway ozone.

Belmont's instinctive knack for selecting the best, be it in wines, station ornamentation, or private rolling stock, also was reflected in his choice of high-level railroad men. As his general manager Belmont hired Frank Hedley, whose great-granduncle had helped build the first steam locomotive near Newcastle-on-Tyne in 1813. Hedley's father was a master mechanic for the London and Southwestern Railway during Queen Victoria's time, and Frank himself was a skilled machinist. "Any fool could be president of a railroad company," quipped Hedley, "but the general manager has to know something!"

Almost immediately after taking command of the IRT, Hedley launched a series of innovations on the city's underground railroad. One of these was a "recorder-coaster," which encouraged his motormen to coast when possible to cut costs. The dynamic general manager also introduced multiple doors in each car to alleviate crowding. A progressive Hedley safety advance was new coupling mechanisms to reduce the danger of telescoping trains in a collision. When it appeared that the IRT was being cheated by its own collectors, he introduced the nickel-in-the-slot turnstile.

The IRT directors acknowledged Hedley's genius with the subway by continually raising his salary until the late twenties when he was earning $75,000 a year. Only the Transit Commission, which was controlled by the state, had jurisdiction over him. Yet, throughout his reign, Hedley cried poverty on behalf of his company and endlessly campaigned, with no luck at all, for a fare raise as the solution to the city's subway problems.

Once, when Hedley was assailed by city officials because his cars were so dirty, the general manager insisted that he could not afford to clean them as long as the fare held at 5 cents. "I saw a car with clean windows today," he said, "and when I got back to the office I raised hell to find out who spent all the money." Hedley was openly contemptuous of the politician's practice of calling a conference or appointing commissions to get all the facts. "I will study the situation," the general manager was fond of saying, "and then do as I please."

But nobody seemed terribly concerned about Frank Hedley or any of his fiscal idiosyncrasies in those first days of the IRT's operation.

New Yorkers found the underground railway as thrilling as a Coney Island roller coaster.

The public enthusiasm seemed to take the IRT directors by surprise. "Nobody knows how many people are going to patronize the road," said Hedley. "But we shall be prepared to increase the number of trains to suit the demand. If it is necessary, we'll run them on a one-minute headway."

At the time, Hedley's eight-car express trains ran on five-minute headways from 6:30 to 7 A.M., four-minute headways from 7 to 9:30 A.M., and at five- to ten-minute intervals during midday. In the evening rush, it was four-minute headways again, with trains running five and six minutes apart until midnight. The five-car locals ran at three-minute headways the entire day, starting at 5:30 A.M. and at five- to ten-minute intervals after midnight.

The IRT's new construction kept pace with public demand for additional lines. Other parts of the first subway were opened for business as follows: Broadway, 145th to 157th streets, November 5, 1904; Lenox Avenue branch in Manhattan, Broadway and 96th Street to 145th Street, November 20, 1904; and from 149th Street and Third Avenue along Westchester Avenue and Boston Road in the Bronx, to the terminus at 180th Street, November 26, 1904. The intervening link from 145th Street under the Harlem River to Westchester Avenue was opened later, and the remainder of the Broadway line, at 157th Street to Kingsbridge, in March 1906.

The IRT had earlier heeded the demand by Brooklynites to extend the subway under the East River and into Kings County, linking the Battery in Manhattan with Joralemon Street in Brooklyn Heights, overlooking New York Bay. In 1905, when the interborough tunnel was being constructed, underwater tunneling lacked the sophistication of later years, and tragedy often lurked behind the next shield.

Serious underwater tunneling for passenger trains dates back to September 1879, when DeWitt Clinton Haskin's Hudson Tunnel Railroad Company began digging a hoped-for tube for trans-Hudson passenger service. The Haskin firm carved 1,200 feet under the huge river and lined the tunnel with brick at the New Jersey shore. But the caisson technique, then employed, caused a "blowout" on July 21, 1880, and twenty lives were lost.

"As with many tragedies," wrote rail historian Brian J. Cudahy in *Rails under the Mighty Hudson*, "this one produced heroism. When men in the airlock realized a blowout was imminent, they started for the pressurized door leading back to safety. Several were through when one Peter Woodland realized the loss of pressure in the tube was about to doom all, even those en route to safety. He closed the door, thereby sealing his own doom and that of the 19 others in the airlock with him, but insuring safety for the men already on the way out. His action is memorialized on his tombstone in New York Bay Cemetery in Jersey City, and the incident itself later formed the basis for a famous story by Theodore Dreiser entitled *St. Columba and the River*."

The Haskin tunnel soon was abandoned, but a British-backed firm resumed the project in 1888, and bored another 1,600 feet toward Manhattan. The new contractor, S. Pearson and Sons, used cast-iron rings instead of bricks and mortar to line the tunnel. In addition, Pearson brought along a major innovation, the Greathead shield, developed by a South African-born British engineer named Sir James Henry Greathead. The shield originally was invented for construction of London's 1880 Tower subway. Pearson erected Greathead shields at the forward positions of each tunnel to reduce the risk of pressure failure in the tubes and speed construction. But money problems applied the brakes until 1901 when William Gibbs McAdoo organized the Hudson and Manhattan (H & M) Railroad. McAdoo's engineer, Charles M. Jacobs, found that the Greathead shields were still in good shape and could be used for the new venture.

Interestingly, work on the H & M tunnel between Manhattan and Jersey City, and construction of the IRT tunnel between Manhattan and Brooklyn, proceeded simultaneously in a race to become the first to launch regular passenger service through a major underwater tunnel in the New York metropolitan area. Belmont's IRT won the race by a month in January 1908. But the IRT's victory was not achieved without mishap.

In 1905, when the Battery-Joralemon Street tunnel had reached the middle of the East River, a blowout developed in the tunnel roof. As the compressed air began escaping a well-disciplined sandhog named Dick Creedon did what he was supposed to do; he snatched one of many available sandbags and rushed to the weak spot, hoping to plug the leak with the sandbag. But Creedon lost his race against time: he was sucked up into the vortex—sandbag still in hand— through thirty feet of riverbed and, finally, up through the East River.

The sandhog was alive and swimming when a tugboat arrived to haul him to safety. As for the hole in the IRT tunnel, it was plugged after scows delivered tons of sand to the leak location and then simply dumped them over the tunnel, where the break soon was repaired.

Another, and this time tragic, IRT accident occurred two years later when four workers were killed in a freak fire that caused a cave-in. The construction men were buried, but still alive and apparently capable of rescue, since their ventilating column had not been obstructed. Firemen arrived too late to douse the blaze before it spread to a load of rubber, and the men were asphixiated by the poison fumes.

Several unsung heroes emerged from these underwater jobs. Once a fire broke out deep in the Joralemon Street tube. A one-armed foreman, "Wingy" Hawkins, hurried to the scene and carried out the dynamite, just seconds before it seemed likely to be set off by the heat or by the change in pressure.

IRT promoters were acutely aware that the public might fear suffocation in the depths of their tunnels. To allay these fears, the subway barons launched a propaganda campaign, distributing timetables which boasted in huge letters: SUBWAY AIR AS PURE AS YOUR OWN HOME. This was followed by more propaganda in the form of an impartial study conducted by Columbia University professor C. F. Chandler, supporting the theory that the air underground was as healthy as surface air.

In fact, the public would not be conned. IRT engineers, determined to waterproof the tunnels, had coated them with asphalt, which prevented any possibility of proper ventilation in hot summer months. Throughout the summer of 1905, complaints about excessive heat and poor air quality poured into the IRT offices. The city's Rapid Transit Commission retained Professor George A. Soper of Columbia University to study the air conditions. Soper reported that, while air in the subway was hotter than air in the streets in summer, it was not deleterious to health and would not have any bad effects if proper sanitary precautions were taken to keep the subway free of dust and odors.

Nevertheless, IRT engineers built fourteen ventilating chambers between Brooklyn Bridge and 59th Street to allow stale air to escape and fresh air to enter the tunnels. In addition, an experimental cooling plant was installed in the Brooklyn Bridge station. Two artesian wells were sunk, and the water from them pumped into a series of pipes installed on each side of the station. Air was pumped through the pipes in counter current to the water, becoming cooled in the passage and then delivered to the station via ducts.

The ventilating improvements all worked; and so did the IRT. Critics then and now agree that it was an engineering masterpiece. "There seems little doubt," said William H. Rudy of the New York *Post* in 1970, "that, for the times, the first IRT was well-built and well-equipped. Robert Ridgway, later chief engineer of the entire system, always thought this was due in great part to the terms: the contractor had to maintain and operate the subway for 50 years."

There were complaints about the original IRT, to be sure— inadequate service was a perennial beef—but, by and large, the city's new subway had scored a big hit on and off Broadway. Socialites thought nothing of donning their finest furs and taking the subway to the theater. When they entered a station, they discovered that colored tiles decorated the walls. Pottery, faience, and marble were used everywhere and, in some stations, glass roofs invited even more light.

But no one added more class and sophistication to the New York underground than the IRT's number one angel, August Belmont himself. One of the wealthiest New Yorkers of his time, Belmont was not the type of person to invest in the subway and then keep it at arm's length. Whenever possible, Belmont rode his rails and did it in a style that has never been equaled.

Belmont commissioned the Wason Manufacturing Company of Brightwood, Massachusetts, to build him a very special director's car. Wason obliged—at a cost of $11,429.40—and in August 1904 the magnificent piece of rolling stock, dubbed the Mineola, made its debut.

The car's appointments included natural mahogany inlay, cut-glass vases, individual pads on windowposts for smokers to scratch their matches, an arched Empire ceiling tinted pistachio green, brass trim, and its own motor and motorman. Belmont had special plate glass fitted to the front and rear ends for easier observation and had twelve special leather chairs built in.

Belmont built the Belmont Hotel at 42nd Street and Park Avenue and saw to it that he had easy access to the Grand Central IRT station below. In the basement of the hotel was a circular bar at subway-track level. It was specifically designed to fit inside the radius of the subway curve. When the spirit moved him, Belmont would hail his subway car, exit through his private passageway, and take his wife and friends for a joy ride. "A private railroad car," wrote Mrs. Belmont, "is not an acquired taste. One takes to it immediately."

In fact, the entire city had taken the IRT to its heart and when visitors came to Manhattan, a trip on the IRT was a must. Even Tin Pan Alley acknowledged its importance in 1912 with a popular song, "The Subway Glide."

By then the IRT had snaked its way to Brooklyn under the East River, and the subway had proven so popular an item in Gotham that there was a clamor from Queens to the Bronx to build more. The public's demand was translated into the most phenomenal growth of any underground railway anywhere. From the 9.1-mile section opened in 1904 at a cost of about $35 million, the system expanded to 239.87 route miles with 726.18 miles of track.

The second, and most energetic, spurt produced a unique bit of rivalry—and teamwork—between the IRT and the Brooklyn Rapid Transit (BRT) Company, which became known as "the Dual System."

Enter the BMT

If the Interborough Rapid Transit (IRT) was the patrician of the New York subway system, the Brooklyn Manhattan Transit (BMT) emerged as the playboy of the underground. It boasted the flashiest rolling stock ever seen in New York, including experimental lightweight cars called Bluebird, Green Hornet, and Zephyr. The BMT (when it was still the Brooklyn Rapid Transit) produced the first sixty-seven-foot-long, ten-foot-wide "standard" car in 1914, setting the criteria for subway cars for decades in the future.

The line was attractive right down to the smallest detail, including its kiosk lamps which, unlike the IRT's round blue-and-white globes, were ornate fifty-pound hexagons, alternately covered with green and white glass and extremely well constructed.

Although the BMT made its initial run from Coney Island to Chambers Street on June 22, 1915, its lineage can be traced to a much earlier date when the city of Brooklyn—later to become one of New York's five boroughs—developed southward to the Atlantic Ocean. The original ancestor of the BMT was a steam line known as the Bath and Coney Island Railroad, which opened in 1864 and reached Coney Island in 1867.

Developers envisioned Brooklyn's resort-by-the-sea in the most romantic terms. It was suggested that someday it might become another Riviera or, at the very least, America's answer to Brighton, England. Instead, Coney Island developed a razzle-dazzle character all its own, and by the turn of the century its image as an amusement paradise for the lower and middle classes was firmly established.

The turn of the century also signaled the consolidation of Brooklyn's elevated lines under the banner of the Brooklyn Rapid Transit Company (BRT). Technically, the BRT was not an operator but, rather, a holding company organized to acquire the security of such earlier corporate acquisitions as the Brooklyn Union Elevated Railroad Company (1899), the Transit Development Company (which ran the BRT's yards and shops and controlled its rolling stock) and the Brooklyn Union Elevated Railroad Company (which operated the elevated trains).

Already mighty but desiring still more power, the BRT watched the development of the IRT with great interest when the city's first subway opened in 1904. The instant success of August Belmont's underground immediately inspired city fathers to propose a web of new routes throughout New York and in 1905 plans were developed for no less than nineteen lines.

The Board of Rapid Transit Railroad Commissioners was largely responsible for the widely acclaimed IRT, but it had been so wonderful a system that New Yorkers demanded to know why the board had not done more, and done it much faster. "Instead of being commended," wrote James Blaine Walker in *Fifty Years of Rapid Transit*, "they [the board] were condemned, not because they had not done well with the first subway, but because it was such a great success that they had not multiplied it fast enough. Because the old board had not ended the crush at the Brooklyn Bridge, because it had not built subways into Brooklyn and Queens and in other parts of Manhattan, it was denounced by the press which clamored for its abolition."

The press got its wish and in 1907 the board was dissolved and replaced by the New York State Public Service Commission (PSC) for the First District, which laid out blueprints for a vast subway system that would make the original IRT look like a mere dot on a map.

The Public Service Commission inherited four different rapid transit projects from the old board. One was a Brooklyn extension of the IRT and another was a Van Cordlandt Park extension of the same line. The others, eventually to become part of the BMT system, included a Fourth Avenue subway in Brooklyn and a Centre Street (Manhattan) line. The PSC decided to push these projects to completion and simultaneously produce still more lines.

On December 31, 1907 the PSC approved a Broadway-Lexington Avenue route and a few months later decided that trains should run over the Williamsburg and Manhattan bridges, spanning the East River, to Brooklyn. In 1908 and 1909 the PSC engineers prepared detailed plans for this system, which would add forty-five miles of new road and cost about $147 million. And still more blueprints were on the way, including lines for Queens, the Bronx, Brooklyn, and, of course, Manhattan.

The IRT, the Long Island Rail Road, the New York Central Railroad, and the Hudson & Manhattan tubes all wanted a piece of the new subway pie, but by 1910 the field had been narrowed down to the IRT. Then the BRT suddenly made an eleventh-hour bid. In its proposal, dated March 2, 1911, the BRT suggested that a new subway be built from the Battery at the southern tip of Manhattan up Church Street northward to Broadway and up Broadway to 42nd Street and thence up Seventh Avenue to 59th Street, with an extension easterly to a connection with the Queensborough Bridge.

The BRT didn't stop there. It offered a number of other suggestions, including the unexpected idea that a tunnel be built under New York Bay to connect the Fourth Avenue subway in Brooklyn with Staten Island, linking with the already operating Staten Island Railway. Surprising as the BRT's last-minute offer may have been, the PSC greeted it with the most serious deliberations. "Probably nothing like the Dual System conferences ever had been held in New York City before," said James Blaine Walker.

In their efforts to expand the subway system and earn a hefty profit for themselves, the transit barons fought with each other as well as with the distinguished members of the PSC. Once Theodore P.

Shonts, president of the IRT, was asked if his company had conceded certain points to the city's representative. "I was fairly well-dressed when I went into that room," replied Shonts, "but they've taken away everything but my shirt, and they would have had that if we hadn't adjourned."

By 1911, within six months after the conferences began, an agreement was hammered out among the PSC, the IRT, and the BRT: the companies would split the proposed routes, as spelled out in what became known as "the Dual (IRT-BMT) Contracts." The contracts themselves were officially signed on March 19, 1913 and Brooklyn, which eventually led the city in subway trackage (87.8 miles), benefited the most. BRT (later BMT) lines snaked over the Manhattan and Williamsburg bridges to such distant points as Jamaica, Flatbush, Bensonhurst, and Borough Park. A tunnel was opened to Astoria, Queens, as the subway sprawl continued.

The four contracts involved were approved by the Board of Estimate and Apportionment on July 21, 1911, and on July 31 ground was broken at 62nd Street and Lexington Avenue.

As fast as the PSC engineers turned out the plans the commission awarded construction contracts for other sections of the work, on the understanding that the Brooklyn company was to be the operator. The Dual Contract ultimately produced much of what today is the vast BMT system, including the Brighton Beach, West End, Sea Beach, and Astoria lines. On June 22, 1915, one of the biggest outgrowths of the Dual Contracts was unveiled when service was launched from Coney Island to Chambers Street via the Fourth Avenue subway and the Manhattan Bridge.

Like its older subway sister, the IRT, the baby BRT suffered severe growing pains. During construction of the Whitehall Street (Manhattan)-Montague Street (Brooklyn) Tunnel in 1916 compressed air escaped from the tube just as it had during work on the IRT's Battery-Joralemon Street tunnel in 1905. This time three sandhogs were trapped under New York Bay when a fierce whistling, then a rush of air, was heard. Before they could make a move the men were sucked into the vortex.

One of them, Marshall Mabey, was lucky. After being vacuumed up through twelve feet of sand and then shot to the surface of the bay on top of a geyser that, onlookers said, appeared to rise forty feet above the water, he had the stamina and presence of mind to swim to a nearby boat. He was pulled safely from the water, but his two companions died in the accident. BRT engineers solved the leakage problem by depositing a large load of clay over the break.

The BRT was enroute to completion without a serious accident until September 25, 1915, when a fault in the rock wall of the excavation at 38th Street set off a landslide that uprooted the supporting timbers. At that precise moment another loaded Broadway trolley approached the sagging street planking. But motorman Malachi Murphy anticipated the danger and, in a split second, threw his electric gears into reverse. Just when it appeared that another streetcar would plunge underground, the wheels stopped skidding and pulled the passengers and Murphy to safety. Less fortunate was a stout female pedestrian who fell to her death. Her male escort was merely bruised.

The only other victim was taxi driver George Sommerer who suffered a temporary case of shock. Sommerer had stopped his cab for a moment and walked to the corner for a few puffs on a cigarette while awaiting a fare. Sommerer did a double take as his cab moved down, down, down until it finally sank out of sight into the subway tunnel.

BRT engineers were bedeveled with another problem in building the 60th Street tunnel to Queens. This time the dilemma was posed by the great depth—107 feet below mean high water—and solved by constructing the tunnel with two-thirds of its diameter above the riverbed. In order to cover the tunnel, contractors dropped a blanket of clay and riprap (large chunks of stone) from scows to the bottom of the river. "It was," said New York *Post* reporter William H. Rudy, "a case of: Don't lower the tunnel, raise the river."

In some cases the BRT found that it had to widen its tunnels to accommodate the new flagship of its fleet, the all-steel, sixty-seven-foot subway car, regarded by some as the single best piece of rapid transit rolling stock ever produced. The "sixty-seven-footers" made their passenger debut on the Sea Beach line on June 22, 1915 and won instant critical acclaim for their design, power, and comfort.

One fatal flaw prevented the BRT from enjoying the full fruits of its new rolling stock. The company was too slow in replacing the rickety wooden cars with the sleek sixty-seven-footers, and even in 1918 the BRT was pockmarked with obsolete cars. One such train filled with wooden cars crashed at Malbone Street in Brooklyn, killing ninety-seven passengers and sending the BRT into receivership. In 1923 it was reorganized as the Brooklyn-Manhattan Transit.

In the years from the Malbone Street disaster (the worst subway disaster ever, causing the name of the street to be changed to Empire Boulevard) until the line's reorganization as the BMT, the New York City mayor, John Hylan, waged a self-declared war against the line, specifically because of his earlier experiences as an el employee (he was fired as a motorman in his younger days). Hylan constantly thwarted BRT attempts at expansion. When the line attempted to construct a massive repair shop and storage yard in Coney Island, Hylan blocked the project. Following the Malbone wreck, Hylan intensified his anti-BRT campaign.

Significantly, Hylan began losing public favor in 1923 and on April 23 of that year he was booed while delivering a speech at groundbreaking ceremonies for an IRT el extension into Flushing, Queens. Hylan, now in his second four-year term, was notorious for his irascible nature, but he had one policy that appealed to his constituents—save the 5-cent fare. The mayor even had hundreds of thousands of silvery pins minted with the inscription in blue lettering: HYLAN FIVE CENT FARE CLUB.

Few of Mayor Hylan's "club members" were aware that he once worked as a motorman while going to law school at night. He was fired from the job when an inspector caught the law student-motorman rounding a curve too quickly. According to one report, he actually had been reading a law school book while operating the train. "To many people," wrote author George Walsh in *Gentleman Jimmy Walker,* "it seemed that he [Hylan] had devoted his entire stay in City Hall to fulminating against the traction interests."

Fortunately for the subway barons, Hylan's term came to a close in 1925 and he was succeeded by one of the most exciting, flamboyant, and lovable mayors in the city's history, James J. "Gentleman Jimmy" Walker. During Walker's administration the BMT filled in marshland near the Coney Island terminal and completed the Coney Island yards and repair shop, to this day the largest in the Transit Authority system. Most of the major work was concluded by November 9, 1927 when yard buildings were finished and put into use. In time the shops were capable of taking a worn-out car and turning it out completely rebuilt mechanically, repainted, and virtually as good as new in eight days. On some days the shops took in nearly 200 cars and turned out the same number.

Under the direction of Gerhard Dahl, chairman of the company, the line adopted a slogan: BMT FOR BETTER METROPOLITAN TRANSIT. Dahl promoted advanced engineering that enabled the BMT to operate a safe, efficient, and expanded subway system. The BMT even ran special trains between Brooklyn and Manhattan for playgoers traveling to the Broadway theater district to see such productions as the Ziegfeld Follies or John Barrymore in *Hamlet.*

The BMT also operated the Brooklyn and Queens Transit Corporation, which boasted an enormous fleet of streetcars. So many streetcars rumbled across Brooklyn that the natives became known as "Trolley Dodgers" and the name of the borough's baseball team (once called the Superbas) was changed to Brooklyn Trolley Dodgers and, ultimately, Brooklyn Dodgers.

BMT became synonymous with advanced transit design. In February 1927 the BMT introduced D-type cars, articulated three-car units which enabled two cars to share one track. The D-type cars permitted passengers to walk freely from any one of the three cars to another without interference by a door.

Late in 1933 the BMT contracted with the Budd Company to build an experimental, lightweight, stainless steel car called the Zephyr or Train 7029. The car featured red leather upholstered seats, bull's-eye lighting, and a fancy braking system. Train 7029 lacked automatic couplers, however, and eventually was confined to the BMT's Franklin Avenue (Brooklyn) line until forced into premature retirement in 1956.

Of all the BMT's experimental trains, two of the most interesting were the Bluebird Special and a Pullman Company-built beauty named the Green Hornet. Pullman constructed the Green Hornet as an articulated lightweight train made up of five sections on six trucks. It also was known as the Blimp because of its rounded look.

The Green Hornet-Blimp was a remarkable hunk of machinery. It was the city's first lightweight, all-aluminum train and featured a number of extras. Whenever the Green Hornet-Blimp entered a tunnel, its lights automatically flashed on and, of course, when it climbed out into daylight the interior lights turned off. Dulcet-toned chimes signaled the closing doors and indirect incandescent lighting made reading easier and more pleasant. Even more enjoyable was the Hornet-Blimp's rapid acceleration and braking powers, not to mention its ability to run both in subways and—because of its light weight—on elevated structures.

The Hornet-Blimp's medium green hue further appealed to straphangers who were fortunate enough to ride it on the Fulton Street (Brooklyn) el or the Franklin Avenue Shuttle to Prospect Park station. Like the other BMT experimental trains, the Hornet-Blimp suffered from a paucity of parts. When a malfunction developed, or a part was needed, the BMT maintenance men had to wait for delivery from the Pullman plant.

In 1941 the Hornet-Blimp was sitting in the 36th Street BMT (Brooklyn) yard waiting for a part to be delivered when scrap bird-dogs from the federal government heard about it. At the time all available aluminum was being collected to help the defense effort, prior to America's entry into World War II. While the Hornet-Blimp was sidetracked, the Feds told the BMT to make do with its standard sixty-seven-footers and other pieces of regular rolling stock.

The Pullman part never arrived and in 1942 the Hornet-Blimp was tossed on the scrap heap.

Resplendent in several shades of blue, with white stripes, the Bluebird Special was odd in every way. It was built by a relative novice in the subway-car field, the Clark Equipment Company of Battle Creek, Michigan. The Bluebird consisted of a single, articulated unit in which three sections were linked together. Instead of traditional subway-el trucks, the Bluebird was fitted with trolley-type wheels and brakes similar to those which had made such a hit on Brooklyn's streamlined PCC streetcars. These were extremely lightweight, streamlined trolley cars designed in the early thirties and called "PCC" (Presidents' Conference Committee) in honor of the streetcar presidents' conference which had been convened to produce an efficient trolley to compete with motor buses. The PCC car boasted spring-suspended motors, eddy-current brakes, magnetic track brakes, not to mention improved heating, lighting, and ventilation systems.

Bluebird went into service on March 30, 1939 and immediately captured the hearts and eyes of straphangers. In March 1941 five more units were added to the Bluebird and it appeared that it could, in time, become the standard of BMT esthetic excellence. The cars featured mohair seats, bull's-eye lighting, and even mirrored walls at the end of each car. August Belmont would have been proud. But the advent of World War II and the eventual standardization of rolling stock (based on the IND's R-1) rendered the articulated-car concept obsolete. "It was a magnificent-looking hunk of subway train," a Transit Authority official conceded, "but it was too hard to maintain." In 1958, the Bluebird died on the scrap heap.

On June 2, 1940 the BMT's era as the most romantic of the city's two privately owned lines ended when the BMT was placed under the control of the New York City Board of Transportation. The IRT joined the BMT as a city-operated line nine days later. Nevertheless, even as a municipally run system, the BMT retained much of its unique, flashy flavor.

In 1949 the BMT Division unveiled a silver streamliner called the R-11. It ran on the Brighton Line to Coney Island and boasted ten cars, a mechanical dust separator, sterile lamps to kill germs, crank-operated windows, and a special braking system. Unfortunately, the braking system proved to be too special and in 1957 the R-11 was taken out of service and placed alongside the Zephyr in the Coney Island yard. Thus, two of the prettiest subway trains ever to grace a railroad were left rusting on the BMT tracks.

The Last Big Line— the IND

The third and final golden era of subway construction in New York City spanned the mid-twenties and thirties when more than fifty additional miles of underground railroad were opened in Manhattan, Brooklyn, Queens, and the Bronx. Unlike its predecessors, the newer Independent Subway (IND) was city-owned and -operated from the start.

Like the IRT and the BMT, the Independent, for years known simply as the Eighth Avenue subway, was built to satisfy the commuting needs of a still-growing city. Ground-breaking took place on March 14, 1925. "It is," said the *New York Times,* "Father Knickerbocker's latest and most gigantic effort to improve his sluggish circulation. It promises the subway rider more room to breathe and more safety for his corns."

Safety was a major concern in construction of the IND and such catastrophes as befell the IRT during earlier projects were avoided. One pedestrian was killed when he fell into an excavation, and the death of one workman on the job was reported to have been due to heart disease. In addition two men were killed by a cave-in at 53rd Street and two others were fatally hurt when struck by cranes, but these tragedies were few in number compared with the serious accidents that occurred during construction of the IRT and the BMT.

While safety was a high-priority item in the construction of the IND subway, frugality was not. Development of the Eighth Avenue subway was the Walker administration's single important improvement, but New York paid dearly for its third major line. The cost of building the IND was $800 million—approximately twice what many transit experts believed should have been the true cost. "The city did not get what it paid for," said Fusion Party financial expert Joseph D. McGoldrick. "Although it certainly paid for what it got!"

Despite his questionable behavior, Walker was a popular official. New Yorkers loved their smiling, goodhearted mayor and didn't seem to mind the fact that he was two-timing his wife or that he was dipping into the public treasury. "One thing about Jimmy," his cronies would say, "he may steal a dime, but he'll always let you take a penny!" A few of those dimes apparently were taken from the new Eighth Avenue line.

Nevertheless, New Yorkers were appropriately proud of their new subway, which encompassed five basic units with a sixth added to service the World's Fair at Flushing Meadow in 1939. The units were: (1) Washington Heights to East New York; (2) Bronx-Grand Concourse; (3) Queens-Manhattan; (4) Sixth Avenue-Houston Street; (5) Brooklyn-Queens crosstown. Construction was, of course, more advanced in concept than methods used in building the IRT and BMT, although many of the earlier features were included in the IND's development.

Wherever possible the cut-and-cover system was used rather than the shield method of boring laterally underground. While this minimized the problems, in a great congested city like New York no construction project is simple. The contractors had to cut through the underground ganglia that supply Manhattan with water, steam, electricity, gas, and telephone lines without interrupting these necessary services. They also had to see to it that no buildings fell into their big holes.

In places the line ran too deep for open cutting and hard-rock men had to be brought in to tunnel. At 191st Street and Fort Washington Avenue, they cut through the rock 165 feet below the surface. The job throughout, as in other parts of the new system, was marked by increased use of machinery wherever it could be substituted for hand work, and by short cuts to reduce unnecessary operations. In former days, dirt and rock were usually lifted out by the bucket method.

Most observers probably thought that steam shovels were being used. As a matter of fact, they were gasoline-operated shovels, introduced because steam engines made too much smoke. In the deep-rock work the older type of drilling machinery was largely replaced by the so-called Jap hammers, which received their name because they were smaller as well as more efficient. In general, however, this was just one more job of boring, blasting, and digging, heroic in its magnitude, calling for daily risk of life and limb (although there were surprisingly few accidents in proportion to the number of men employed), calling upon every resource of modern large-scale engineering.

The digging was not everything, as the cost of equipment, running to nearly one-third of the construction cost, testifies. The open cuts had to be roofed over, the whole tube sealed and lined, the roadway ballasted, the tracks laid, power and signaling systems installed, a lighting system put in, stations built and equipped, yards provided, repair shops built . . . .

Engineers, sandhogs, and contractors had learned a lot from the earlier IRT and BMT (BRT) experiences and applied them to construction of the new subway. In some cases the amount of matériel required was staggering.

About thirteen miles of pipe, ranging from six to twelve inches in diameter, were required for drainage of trackways. Sump chambers with a capacity of from 4,000 to 7,000 gallons were constructed for drainage purposes.

For the walls of the twenty-eight stations, 750,000 square feet of glazed tile were required—enough to decorate 5,500 average-sized bathrooms. There were 142,000 square feet, or about thirty-three and one-third acres, of ventilating gratings in the sidewalks over the structure.

Engineers expected the momentum of trains to change the air in the tunnel every fifteen minutes. There were fifty large ventilating fans, requiring motors furnishing 2,500 horsepower, or enough to operate 40,000 fans of office or home size.

Some 22 million cubic yards of earth and rock were excavated. This material if spread evenly in Central Park would raise its level four feet. It would take 198,000 freight cars, comprising a train 1,400 miles long or the distance from New York to New Orleans, to haul this material away.

The new subway contained one million cubic yards of concrete, or enough to build a new highway such as the Bronx River Parkway from New York to Albany. The same concrete if cast into blocks one foot square and placed end to end would extend from New York to Buenos Aires.

The work required 6,700,000 bags of cement. They would fill a freight train fifty miles in length or if laid out on a highway thirty feet wide would extend from the Battery to Albany. It would take a fleet of barges forty-eight miles in length to carry the stone, gravel, and sand used in making the concrete.

The steel used in the tunnels weighed 150,000 tons, or three times as much as that in the Empire State Building. That is enough steel to build fifteen first-class cruisers for the navy or five ships the size of the *Queen Elizabeth II*. It would girdle the earth if drawn into a bar one inch in thickness.

The waterproof fiber in the structure would cover 480 acres if spread out in a single layer. If laid out in a sheet 100 feet in width it would extend from the Battery to Bear Mountain.

The timber in the track ties would cover a floor one inch thick, 100 feet wide, and ten miles long. The power ducts totaled in length 3,200,000 feet. If placed end to end they would reach from New York to Cleveland.

The material used in construction was shipped from 248 plants in 139 cities in thirteen states. The construction work required seven million man-days of labor, as compared with one million man-days for the George Washington Bridge. Construction involved relocation of 26 miles of water and gas pipes, 350 miles of electric conduits, and 18 miles of sewers. It was necessary to rebuild gas and electric service connections to 3,100 houses along the 12-mile route.

Another "item" that would be constructed for the new IND was a prototype subway car. The design ultimately selected proved to be not unlike the BMT's all-steel, sixty-seven-foot gem of 1914. Both models employed large, exposed overhead fans and featured both longitudinal and latitudinal seating. While the BMT offered three sets of doors on each side, the newer IND had four sets.

Subway buffs were disappointed when they learned that the new sixty-foot IND car (soon to be labeled R-1) utilized a large front windowpane that significantly differed from its BMT counterpart in that it could *not* be opened, thus depriving "second motormen" from enjoying the speed-produced breezes as the A train roared through the tunnel. But the new R-1 was not speedier, more attractive, or in any way outwardly more magnetic than its counterparts on the BMT, although according to some rail fans it did look better than the IRT's standard car design. However, the R-1, underneath its relatively standard-looking exterior, did offer some innovations.

The doors themselves were designed to permit loading and unloading in the least possible time and with the least possible wear and tear on the passengers. Each car had four double doors on each side, each doorway being three feet ten inches wide. They differed from the IRT car doors in one important respect, however. When they encountered a passenger or other obstruction in closing they did not reopen to their full extent, but stopped where they were. Jocular individuals who held up trains by playing with the doors would thus be thwarted to a considerable degree. On test runs it was found that the station stops, with allowances for loading and unloading under rush-hour conditions, ranged from thirty-seven seconds at Times Square to twenty-two seconds at 145th Street and nineteen seconds at West 4th Street. On an average, the new cars could be loaded and unloaded in about two-thirds the time required for the older-type car.

A small detail which became important in the course of time: the lights in each car were fitted with left-handed threads so that they could not be used in ordinary light sockets and were therefore unprofitable to steal. The heating of the cars in cold weather was directly under control of the motorman. Trains were plainly marked by letters to indicate whether they were expresses or locals. Identification of stations was made easy by the use of five different colors in the lettering and patterns on the platforms, so that once a passenger had mastered the color sequences he knew at a glance about where he was.

As construction of the Eighth Avenue subway sped to its conclusion in the summer of 1932, it had become apparent that its planners had succeeded in handling the mammoth project with a minimum of complaints from merchants and property owners and a low accident and mortality rate.

"One of the greatest sources of annoyances which the contractors had to contend with was that of 'inspired' accidents," said James W. Danahy, managing director of the West Side Association of Commerce. "A nail sticking up in a board was sufficient inspiration for some persons to rip their clothes and scratch their hands and then demand payments.

"Merchants generally along the avenue took their losses, which were heavy, with a degree of stoicism which was amazing to the contractors. Fewer than twenty merchants or property owners, out of some 1,500 involved, actually brought suits in court against the contractors. In no small way this situation was due to the willingness of the contractors to adjust cases where there was a reasonable degree of evidence that they were morally or legally to blame for the loss."

At last the IND was ready for its world premiere. A total of 300 spanking new cars were delivered for the opening on the twelve-mile stretch from Chambers Street up Eighth Avenue to 207th Street. Before the first passenger dropped a nickel into the turnstile, grand promises were made about the IND's prospects. The new system, in its first year, was expected to carry 114 million passengers and within ten years more than 300 million annually.

The Eighth Avenue system, although only twelve miles long, already was being designed to ramify like a nerve system far into the Bronx, Queens, and Brooklyn. All methods of connecting it with the existing BMT and IRT subways had been made and numerous attempts at effecting a permanent unification of the three major systems already was under way. But, for the moment, all eyes were on the IND as its creators and leaders went through the final dry runs prior to the official debut.

The Eighth Avenue subway was opened to the public at midnight on September 10, 1932. There was no ceremony to mark the opening, and there was no first train. At 12:01 A.M. platform guards simply removed barrier chains from the turnstiles, the crowds which had been gathering all evening had free entry until 6 A.M. when they then dropped their nickels in the slots and the new line took its place as the third of the city's great rapid transit systems.

Sixteen trains—eight expresses and eight locals—were somewhere in the twelve-mile stretch between the temporary southern terminal at Chambers Street and the permanent northernmost station at 207th Street. Whichever train happened along first at each station became the first train for the passengers at that station.

The nearest approach to ceremony was a gathering at the dispatcher's office in the 42nd Street station of the three members of the Board of Transportation and the highest operating officials of the Independent system. In the group were John H. Delaney, chairman of the Board of Transportation; Commissioner Daniel L. Ryan, member of the board in executive charge of the system; Commissioner Frank X. Sullivan; Colonel John R. Slattery, general manager of the Independent system and deputy chief engineer of the Board of Transportation; Robert Ridgway, chief engineer of the board; and William O. Fullen, chairman of the Transit Commission.

Watch in hand, Mr. Delaney stood by one of the turnstiles, simultaneously trying to talk to the official party around him and to peer at the growing throng outside the gates. He almost forgot to look at his watch, and it may have been 12:02 or 12:03 when he waved to the guards at the gates and said: "Open up."

The crowd surged in, led by seven-year-old William Reilly of 406 West 46th Street, who was born on March 14, 1925, the day ground was broken for the new project. Mr. Delaney, having learned of this, made sure that young William was the first in.

It was a cheerful, noisy throng that pushed through the turnstiles. When they heard the roar of the first train and saw it slip into the brilliantly lighted station, a volume of cheers and shouts went up that all but drowned the rumble of the wheels.

As the train pulled out, northbound, it was loaded to rush-hour capacity, the passengers still venting their enthusiasm with whistles and cheers that would have been most unusual had they been riding home from work. But the strangest spectacle of all, on this first train out of 42nd Street, was the absence of newspaper readers, the chronic occupation of most subway straphangers.

A single pair of eyes, those of a middle-aged gentleman, were directed to the pages of a morning newspaper. The rest of the passengers were far too busy inspecting the train, from ceiling ventilators to floor coverings.

In the first hour after the turnstiles were opened at the 42nd Street station, a total of 2,808 paid admissions were registered on the automatic counters. Except for the cheering and whistling and the large crowds at every station, the opening of the line was uneventful.

The *New York Times* reported the IND's debut this way:

"The new Eighth Avenue subway, which was thrown open to the public at 12:01 o'clock yesterday morning, passed its first real operating test successfully by handling smoothly and efficiently its first rush-hour traffic.

"Members of the Board of Transportation, General Manager John R. Slattery and Superintendent Philip E. Pfeifer declared that they were satisfied with the initial operation and confident that the new line would be more than adequate to meet the demands of the traveling public.

"The rush hour local service began on a four-minute headway promptly at 7 A.M. At 9:28 A.M a five-minute headway prevailed, to be replaced at 11:28 A.M. by a four-minute headway which lasted until noon, when longer headways became effective.

"The express service went on a four-minute headway after 6:56 A.M., with a five-minute headway after 9:28 A.M. This prevailed until 11:28 A.M., when it was replaced by another four-minute headway period lasting until 2 P.M.

"During the rush hour, express trains, according to Colonel Slattery, were comfortably filled, with fair-sized standing crowds. On the local trains there were, with few exceptions, seats for all riders.

"Colonel Slattery was especially pleased with the way the car doors helped to expedite the loading and unloading of passengers. There are four doors on each side of every car, affording quick access or exit for riders. The conductors were able to open and close their doors in strict accordance with the brief time allotments fixed by the schedule.

"The first operating problem on the new line occurred soon after 2 P.M., when a compressed air coupling broke on a south-bound local leaving the Fifty-ninth Street station. It caused a delay of about twelve minutes, but normal service was re-established soon afterward."

Unlike the Victorian IRT with its mosaics and nineteenth-century kiosks or the BMT's mélange of subways, els, and trolley cars, the IND represented the very acme of modern subway engineering. Its bright, new stations were, as a rule, long and spacious. Instead of mosaics, IND designers resorted to simpler, yet colorful, tiles to spell out the station name. Express lines, such as the A (under Central Park West from 59th Street to 125th Street) and the E and F (from Roosevelt Avenue to Continental Avenue), were among the speediest, lengthiest, and best-planned express runs in the world.

Once the Eighth Avenue line was completed, IND workmen then turned their pickaxes and drills on Sixth Avenue, Manhattan, where the last—and in some ways most trying—stretch of digging took place. According to Groff Conklin, author of *All about Subways,* the building of the Sixth Avenue subway at Herald Square (34th Street) was unique in the annals of underground planning. "It was," he wrote, "the most difficult piece of subway construction which has ever been attempted."

Because of the labyrinth of tunnels and pipes under the intersection of 34th Street, Broadway, and Sixth Avenue, special precautions had to be taken. The Sixth Avenue (IND) line was built *over* the Pennsylvania Railroad tubes and the Long Island Rail Road tubes and *under* the Broadway BMT subway and the Hudson and Manhattan tubes. At the time a Sixth Avenue elevated line operated overhead, which meant that it had to be supported during the construction. Meanwhile, the usually heavy vehicular and streetcar traffic had to be maintained and, finally, exceptional care had to be taken not to disturb a huge, high-pressure water main which carried water from the Catskill Mountain reservoirs to New York City. The deep-lying main was buried 200 feet below the surface but was a threat should blasts or low-digging unsettle the water tunnel.

The mammoth Herald Square maze finally was completed in 1940, and on December 15 of that year the IND began operating trains under Sixth Avenue from 50th Street to West 4th Street. It was the last major opening on the IND although a smattering of extensions were built later, including a two-mile route for the GG local to the 1939–40 World's Fair in Flushing Meadow.

In 1946 the A line was extended from its former terminus at Rockaway Avenue, Brooklyn, to a new station called Broadway-East New York. Less than two years later another extension was finished to Euclid Avenue, Brooklyn. Pushing ahead in Queens, the IND extended its route from 169th Street to 179th Street on December 10, 1950.

Except for some minor changes here and there, the IND completed New York's subway triumvirate. "It was," said Groff Conklin, "one of the greatest engineering feats man has ever accomplished."

Post–World War II Growth

Since the turn of the century the New York subway's growth has been significantly unsteady. The underground system was built in spurts of activity; the original line constructed by August Belmont was followed in the second decade of the century by the Dual (IRT-BMT) system, which more than doubled all that had been built before. Then came a third spurt with the building of the city's own Independent line, the IND.

The IND began operating prior to World War II, at which point all major subway construction was halted "for the duration." Once hostilities had ended in the Pacific, city planners got back to the drawing board and concluded that more subways were needed; the sooner the better. In Brooklyn it was agreed that the IRT Flatbush Avenue line, which terminated at Nostrand and Flatbush avenues, should be extended all the way to the sea along Nostrand Avenue, winding down at Sheepshead Bay. Real-estate interests in Manhattan clamored for the razing of the Third Avenue el. It would be replaced by a *new* subway under Second Avenue. Still other routes were suggested.

However, not until 1951 were the hopes of transit planners and straphangers given realistic encouragement. In November of that year a $500-million transit bond issue was put on the ballot. Promoters of the bond issue clearly indicated that its approval would mean construction of the long-awaited Second Avenue subway, at a cost of $446 million, as well as a number of other improvements and extensions.

As expected, the bond issue was approved, and the Board of

Transportation authorized the line in 1952 for completion in 1957–58. It was to be a four-track line with connections to the Bronx and Queens. The $500-million bond issue was sold through the banks, and New Yorkers eagerly awaited the start of construction. They waited and waited and waited. Finally, it became apparent that voter approval or not, the Second Avenue subway would exist in blueprints only.

The culprit, in this case, was the newly created New York City Transit Authority (TA), which replaced the old Board of Transportation in 1953. Before expediting the Second Avenue project as everyone had expected the new agency to do, the TA decided to review the bond issue. When the review was completed, the TA insisted that the money would be better spent for other purposes, namely, the rehabilitation of existing lines. Mayor Robert Wagner supported the TA's assertion that the subway system had so deteriorated that the funds from the bond issue were needed for rehabilitation. To which a TA official added: "If we had used the $500 million as originally planned, we might have had a very fine Second Avenue subway and the rest of the system wouldn't be worth the powder to blow it to hell with."

But many respected critics believed that the TA and especially Wagner had knuckled under to the then powerful Robert Moses, a strident champion of highways over rapid transit. Moses, who was chairman of the Triborough Bridge and Tunnel Authority, among other agencies he headed, had managed to build ribbons of highways from the late thirties on while the subways stagnated, and was known to have Wagner's ear.

A large portion of the $500-million bond issue was used for the improvement of existing lines, but to this day critics argue that failure to launch the Second Avenue subway was a crucial mistake and one that has had long-range damaging effects on New York City. Unquestionably the Second Avenue subway *should* have been built in 1953 but Moses's influence on Wagner and the Board of Estimate appears to have been too strong to permit widespread improvements in the city's rapid transit system. What growth there was on the system came in the form of improvements in subway car design (although there was some retrogression in this department, too) with the ultimate goal realized: air-conditioned cars.

The mere thought of air conditioning the city's subway rolling stock was regarded as a pipe dream in the days following World War

II, when new cars were again available. The 1946 model (R-10) offered a cooling system that, practically speaking, was no better than the overhead fans featured on the 1914 BRT sixty-seven-foot standard car. If anything, the R-10's smaller fans made ventilation even worse.

But a few years later an advanced subway car called the R-15 made its appearance. Featuring a turtle-back roof, fluorescent lights, multicolored tiles on the floor, and soft seats, the R-15 boasted a more sophisticated ventilating system. When the car temperature passed 65 degrees Fahrenheit, the cars automatically changed over from the heating to the ventilating system, and the dampers opened. As the temperature in the air increased, the speed of the fans (embedded behind louvers in the ceiling) increased. If the car temperature fell below 65 degrees, the heat increased accordingly.

On September 9, 1964 the TA displayed the first of an order of 600 stainless-steel cars, R-32 Brightliners. The order, the largest ever placed in the United States, cost $68,820,000. Apart from their attractive appearance, the new R-32s were 4,000 pounds lighter than their predecessors and saved considerable amounts of power. However, the stainless-steel Brightliners relied on thermostat-motivated fans and still there was no air conditioning.

Actually, the TA had been testing air-conditioning equipment on the system since 1955. The first experiment involved an IRT R-15 car. TA engineers outfitted Car No. 6239 with four packaged air-conditioning units of one-and-one-half tons capacity each. (In a packaged unit the compressor and evaporator are mounted together in an integrated unit.) A year later ten IRT R-17 cars, Nos. 6800-6809, were received from the St. Louis Car Company equipped with six units of one-and-one-half tons capacity. After a relatively short period of time these packaged units were replaced with two-ton units, increasing the air-conditioning capacity of the cars to twelve tons.

Every experiment failed. The air conditioners broke down but were left in the subway cars that remained in service, and eventually were removed and replaced with traditional axiflow ceiling fans. The early air conditioners failed because of a combination of inadequate capacity and car-ceiling mounting, where they were inaccessible for maintenance purposes and yet caused noise and vibration that were at intolerable levels.

By this time TA officials believed they had proven to the public that the subways simply could not be air conditioned. They argued that there was no way to avoid the loss of cooled air though opened doors at the frequent station stops or the high humidity generated by heavy rush-hour crowding. But the public was not convinced. Demands for air-conditioned subways continued and became even more pressing after the receiver of the Hudson and Manhattan Railroad Company, Herman T. Stitchman, then operating the Hudson tubes connecting New York City with Hoboken, Jersey City, and Newark, began a series of successful experiments with railroad-type air-conditioning equipment. When the Hudson tubes were acquired by the Port Authority-Trans Hudson Corporation it ordered 206 air-conditioned rapid transit cars and, suddenly, New York City's TA was again on the spot.

Back to the drawing board went the TA engineers, who concluded that air conditioning *could* work if the machinery were better designed. To test their theory ten R-38 cars with air conditioning were ordered and placed in service on July 19, 1967. "If these tests prove successful," said Mayor John Lindsay, "the City will put a top priority on orders for several hundred more so that air conditioned trains will be moving on nearly all subway lines in the next few years."

The tests were a success and in 1968 the city ordered 600 air-conditioned subway cars (200 R-40's plus 400 new R-42's). From that point on the TA had irrevocably decided that air conditioning would be standard equipment on all subway cars ordered in the future.

Inevitably, a "lemon" would emerge from time to time among the shiny new designs. One of the worst was the R-40, styled by the industrial design firm of Raymond Loewy-William Snaith, Incorporated. The design was an attempt to provide a more esthetically pleasing vehicle and, in some ways, it succeeded.

The R-40's most distinguishing feature was a sharply sloped front end that gave it a sleek, ultra modern look, a distinct contrast to the TA's generally austere rolling stock. But no sooner did the R-40 go into operation than it became the butt of heavy criticism. In November 1968 the TA admitted that the R-40's design was unacceptable, and an additional $200,000 would have to be spent to rectify the flaws.

While more attractive than previous rolling stock, the R-40 clearly was less safe for passengers. The sharply sloped ends produced a "lip" which seemed to invite youths to ride in hazardous fashion on the outside of the train. The new car also was conspicuously lacking safety devices to protect passengers walking from one car to another. Following a spate of criticism, the TA installed pantograph gates and safety stanchions adjacent to the body's end-door openings to permit riders to walk between cars without hazard from the sharply sloped ends. In its final concession that the Loewy-Snaith design was impractical, the TA ordered the industrial design firm of Sundberg-Ferar to revise the styling of the last 100 R-40 cars on order to make them similar to the R-42 then under design.

Throughout the postwar years one anachronism survived on the system. In the distant Canarsie section of Brooklyn a grade crossing reminiscent of an Iowa farm village survived the growth and modernization of the BMT 14th Street line. Located at East 105th Street, the crossing gate and a small wooden station building originally served an area of small truck farms. But by the end of World War II Canarsie was becoming heavily populated and the bucolic flavor of the old community disappeared. Finally in August 1973 the BMT submitted to "progress" and closed the grade crossing. A new and very unattractive station was built at a cost of $400,000, which included an overpass above the tracks. Eliminating the grade crossing meant the loss of jobs for four towermen, including one beloved gatekeeper who was accustomed to keeping the gates up when people were running toward the station to catch a train.

Genuine progress was made in the area of train communications when, in 1968, the TA installed two-way radios in the motorman's cabs. Now, when a motorman wants to contact someone over his radio, all he has to do is step on a footswitch and talk into a microphone while keeping his hands on the controls.

One of the most dramatic, not to mention controversial, changes made in the TA's rolling stock was the Authority's decision in the early seventies to increase the length of trains from what had become the standard sixty feet to a record seventy-five feet from front to back. Heretofore the longest cars had been the sixty-seven foot "standards" introduced by the BRT in 1914 and used regularly on BMT lines until they were eased out of service in the sixties.

The new rolling stock was designed for operation on the IND and BMT where tunnels originally had been designed for trains no longer than seventy feet. The TA's assistant general superintendent, Harold J. McLaughlin, was aware of the intrinsic dangers and ordered TA engineers to devise a machine to detect potential obstructions. The result was a bizarre looking car over 75 feet long—with whiskers!

TA crews at the Coney Island yard constructed the hirsute train from a battered R-1 subway car, No. 192, that dated back thirty-nine years to the first days of the IND line. Mechanics first cut the old car in half and then welded in what appeared to be an Erector Set midsection, extending the standard sixty-footer to seventy-five feet, the length of the projected new cars.

To probe the subway tunnels for obstructions in much the same way a cat uses its whiskers to gauge whether it can squeeze through a narrow space, the TA mounted wire "whiskers" at the front, center, and back of the old R-1 car. When the "whiskers" touched an obstruction anywhere at the top or sides of the tunnel an electrical circuit closed, causing a buzzer to sound and a bulb to light on a panel board. This enabled the test-car crew to pinpoint the obstruction. On its first two predawn runs the bewhiskered train discovered clearance problems at the upper and lower corners of the car. Most of the difficulties involved concrete catwalks on curves as well as columns, light fixtures, and wires. Old No. 192 had done its job well. A list of 119 obstructions were compiled, which meant that the TA had to spend $400,000 for tunnel modifications to accommodate the seventy-five-foot cars.

Built by the St. Louis Car Company—just before the firm permanently closed its factory—the new R-44 cars cost $211,850 each and immediately caught the fancy of New Yorkers because of their comparative opulence. Seats were three different shades of orange. Fluorescent lights ran down the middle of the ceiling and at each end of the car the panels were made of an attractive imitation wood.

The shiny, clean new trains were equipped with bells that warned when the doors were closing and an interior that was remarkably quiet. Gone were the straphangers' straps. Instead there were five-foot eight-inch high bars above the seats. There were also eight vertical poles in each car, well away from the doors to avoid jams at the entrances. "The spectacular thing about the new cars," commented the *New York Times*, "is their silence, which is due to new methods of insulation."

Not everyone was enthusiastic about the new rolling stock. One of the most vocal antagonists was Carol Greitzer, head of the City Council's Mass Transportation Committee. On December 4, 1975 Councilperson Greitzer charged that the city's new subway cars were "unsafe, impractical and overly costly to maintain." Ms. Greitzer based her charges on a report by a consultant engineer, Dr. Martin Huss, professor of transportation engineering at the Polytechnic Institute of New York. Dr. Huss contended that a design problem in the electric circuitry of the cars could lead to fires and darkened cars and pointed out that there had been a number of fires in these cars while they were standing in the yards. He recommended several changes, including emergency brake-pull cords at each end of the cars; a fire extinguisher at each end of the cars; an automatic lock on end doors to function when trains took a curve (included in original plans but not built in), and installation of safety glass between cars.

The TA, which was amassing a fleet of more than 1,000 new cars—R-44 and a newer model, R-46—was predictably furious over the criticism. John G. deRoos, who had become the senior executive officer of the TA, replied that the new cars were "the best and safest railroad cars of their kind anywhere." DeRoos acknowledged that the cars had problems in the electric circuitry but maintained they were being eliminated.

While the new rolling stock was immediately pleasing to the eye, the commuters in distant areas of Queens and Brooklyn as well as residents of Manhattan's East Side still clamored for more extensions and new lines. Although many New Yorkers had long forgotten the $500-million bond issue for the Second Avenue subway, others did remember and demanded that the line be built. The IRT's East Side subway was the city's most crowded line in 1970, though the densest traffic was on the Flushing-Times Square line at peak periods when thirty-six trains ran each hour at a headway of only 100 seconds. Only a Second Avenue addition could relieve East Side congestion.

"You just can't go on doing what the city's done," said Metropolitan Transportation Authority (MTA) chairman, William Ronan. "You can't go on building office buildings, apartment buildings, without planning for adequate transit. You ought to require that there be transportation just as there must be water, light, sewage and so forth."

Responding to the public pressure, the MTA, supported by Governor Nelson Rockefeller (significantly, a close friend of Ronan) and

Mayor Lindsay, produced the most comprehensive plan for subway expansion in more than forty years. It included the following projects:

1. A high-speed rapid transit line along Second Avenue connecting the Bronx to midtown and downtown Manhattan.
2. A superexpress line in Queens connecting Forest Hills and Long Island City, feeding into the new 63rd Street tunnel.
3. A crosstown link in Manhattan along 48th Street between First and Twelfth avenues.
4. A line along the Long Island Expressway to serve northeast Queens.
5. A line to serve southeast Queens, using the Long Island Rail Road Atlantic Branch right-of-way, including the demolition of the Jamaica Avenue elevated train in the Jamaica business district.
6. Extension of the Second Avenue subway into the northeast Bronx connecting to the Dyre Avenue and Pelham Bay lines.
7. Extension of the Nostrand Avenue line in Brooklyn to Avenue W.
8. A subway extension along Utica Avenue in Brooklyn to Avenue U.
9. A line in the Bronx to replace the Third Avenue elevated.
10. Relocation and extension of the 14th Street Canarsie line.

Construction actually began up and down Second Avenue and by 1973 the route from the lower East Side of Manhattan to East Harlem was pockmarked with trenches and the thick wood planks that characterized subway building in the second decade of the century.

But this subway was never to be. The fiscal crisis that brought New York City to its knees in the autumn of 1975 also forced construction of the Second Avenue subway to a dead stop. Mayor Abraham Beame, who had succeeded the more aggressive, subway-oriented John Lindsay, ruled that the city's proposed Second Avenue underground was not *that* essential. All work was halted "for the duration," as City Hall put it, but the more cynical New Yorkers feared that it would be forever. "No," insisted Edward Silberfarb, the former *Herald-Tribune* subway expert now turned TA public relations officer, "Second Avenue subway work is merely *DEFERRED!*"

Fortunately, not all construction on subway extensions was halted because of the city's monetary mania. Throughout the early seventies the clangorous symphony of jackhammers was heard in and around the southern tip of Central Park in Manhattan where workmen tunneled through porous rock, starting in 1971, to produce two new underground connections from existing lines. One extension continued the BMT's tracks past 57th Street station (Central Park South) on Seventh Avenue, northward through the park, and then, abruptly, eastward to 63rd Street. The second extension moved the IND line northward from 57th Street station on Avenue of the Americas (Sixth Avenue) under Central Park where it eventually linked with the BMT tunnel at a point immediately south of the zoo. The two routes continue eastward under 63rd Street and then in a double-deck tunnel under the East River to Queens.

The TA eventually expects to run its subways to Queens. The two projects still in progress (as of 1976) include:

1.   A superexpress line to bypass the Queens IND line. It will run from Seventy-first Avenue and Continental Avenue in Forest Hills through the new 63rd Street tunnel and connect to the BMT 57th Street station in Manhattan. Completion is expected in the early 1980s.

2.   A southeast Queens line to connect that area to both the Queens Boulevard and Jamaica lines. The new line will follow the Long Island Rail Road Atlantic Branch right-of-way and calls for the demolition of the Jamaica el in the Jamaica business district.

DISASTERS

The Malbone Street BRT Wreck

At 6:45 P.M. on the evening of November 1, 1918 Irving Melton, a tailor who lived in the Brighton Beach section of Brooklyn, picked up his evening newspaper and scanned the headlines. Melton was sitting in the front coach of the five-car Brighton Beach local-express which was taking on passengers in the Park Row terminus of the Brooklyn Rapid Transit Company at City Hall in Manhattan.

It had been an exciting day and Melton didn't know where to turn first for his reading. The Allied offensive in France was crushing the Kaiser's armies and it appeared that, any moment, World War I would come to an end. Soon, the sons of Irving Melton's friends would return from overseas. But another story on page one furrowed his brow.

Motormen and train guards of the Brooklyn Rapid Transit Com-

pany had walked off their jobs and were on strike. In order to maintain service on the heavily traveled lines, the BRT said it would
recruit employees from other positions and give them instant training
as motormen. The company assured riders that there would be no interference with schedules. Melton glanced up from his newspaper
and everything seemed normal. Commuters were pouring into the
rickety wooden cars. Conductor Michael Turner and train guard
Samuel Rosoff watched as the more than 900 passengers came
aboard. Turner jerked the handle and the gate swung closed with a
loud report.

The route of the Brighton Beach local-express traced the spectacular growth of New York City since the turn of the twentieth century. The train would roll over the Brooklyn Bridge and on to Fulton
Street in the downtown shopping area of Brooklyn. It would eventually switch to southbound tracks at Franklin Avenue in the posh
Bedford-Stuyvesant area and cut a swath through the newly
developed communities of Flatbush and the fishing village of Sheepshead. Finally, it would end its long run at Brighton Beach at the
southern tip of the city.

A series of intricate curves along the route bedeviled motormen.
One in particular traumatized even the most competent motorman—
the approach to the Malbone Street tunnel in Flatbush. Engineers had
designed the Brighton Beach line so that it dipped from an elevated
run at the Franklin Avenue and Dean Street stations south to a
street-level station at Consumer Park, and dipped still further until it
reached the Malbone Street tunnel less than a quarter-mile away.

About twenty feet from the mouth of the concrete tunnel the tracks
lurch sharply to the right, and fifty feet later swerve just as
dramatically to the left, carrying the trains into the Prospect Park station. As S-curves go, there were few sharper or more perilous in the
world—a fact that was quite evident to the management of the BRT.
To neutralize the danger, they emphasized to all motormen that the
train's speed along the tunnel approach must be limited to six miles
per hour. A sign posted well in advance of the tunnel underlined the
regulation.

For motorman Edward Luciano (identified in some dispatches as
Edward Lewis) the Brighton Beach local-express represented a formidable challenge and a threat. Dark, slender, and ambitious, the
twenty-three-year-old Luciano had worked for the BRT for three

years, first as a train guard and then as a dispatcher. When he reported to the dispatcher's office at 5 A.M., he learned that only minutes earlier the Brotherhood of Locomotive Engineers had called its strike. Luciano was ordered to act as a motorman.

He had mixed emotions. On the one hand, he sympathized with his colleagues and their aspirations, but on the other hand, he realized that the BRT had vowed to break the strike and would recruit inexperienced men like himself to run the trains at a considerably higher salary than he was making as a dispatcher. The death of Luciano's three-year-old daughter a week earlier, from influenza, and the unpaid funeral bills, coupled with the threat of reprisals against workers who didn't help break the strike, convinced him to go along with the company's demand.

The BRT, whose motto was "Safety Always," normally required that its motormen undergo a minimum of sixty hours of training before they pilot a train on a regular run. But in this case the railroad barons were willing to overlook the rules if it meant crushing the strike. When Edward Luciano jerked the controller to start his first official solo trip as a motorman, his experience consisted of two hours' instruction, one-thirtieth of the minimum requirement.

Luciano's first trip was the BRT's Culver line. As routes went, it was relatively easy, even for a novice. And since Luciano had been a dispatcher along the line, he was more than casually aware of its pitfalls. But when his ten-hour stint was finished and he was preparing to head home, he was told to switch over to the Brighton Beach local-express and guide the train from City Hall to the shore.

The Brighton Beach line was a mystery to Luciano. What's more it was nightfall, and he did not have time to study maps of the line or consult with veteran motormen who could have warned him about its dozens of switches, hairpin curves, the new tunnel construction at Malbone Street and the dreadful S-curve. As he waited in his cab at the Park Row station, all Luciano could think about was the end of the day and the moment he could go home and unwind.

Rush-hour passengers, confounded by strike delays, were anxious to get home for a weekend's rest. And the signalmen were just as anxious to get the Brighton Beach local-express back on schedule. "Take her out quick, you're ten minutes late," the station master bellowed at the already jittery Luciano. He tugged hard on the bulbous wooden handle of the controller. The motors groaned and the wheels screeched as they brushed against the curved steel rails that swung onto the Brooklyn Bridge.

The first stop would be Sands Street in Brooklyn at the other end of the span. Darkness had enveloped the city on this balmy November evening and fatigue was disrupting Luciano's concentration as the train reached the crest of the bridge and approached the long descent to Sands Street station. It was a descent that required sensitive braking to prevent the wooden trains from speeding out of control. Luciano tried to use the brake handle but the complicated formula for air pressure baffled him. The click-clacks of the wheels against the rail openings accelerated far beyond the normal speed. Irving Melton, who was scanning his newspaper, stopped reading as he realized the train was plummeting down the incline.

An abnormally sharp right-hand curve awaited the local-express at the entrance to the Sands Street station. By now, Luciano had lost control of the train but it managed to whip around the curve with the confidence of a speeding roller coaster. Before the motorman could regain control of his machine and bring it to a terrifyingly abrupt halt, two cars had overshot the station.

It was now 6:50 P.M. Luciano had been working for fourteen consecutive hours, but he knew he had only to reach the Brighton Beach terminal and his stint would be complete. The tracks curved on to Fulton Street and, this time, Luciano's confidence returned. The braking system was coming to him. He put the controller on high and, in the distance, he could see the Franklin Avenue station switch tower.

A switchman awaited the Brighton local-express. When it rolled into full view, he would pull the long wooden handle in his tower and the rails would swing into place allowing the train to switch off the main line and turn right in the direction of Brighton Beach.

Suddenly the switchman noticed the train was thundering down the track at an abnormally high speed. Thinking it was a City Line train, he did not pull the lever and, no doubt, saved the train from disaster at that juncture. Having temporarily lost control of the local-express once again, Luciano finally brought it to a stop far past the cut-off.

By now riders were either paralyzed with fear or furious with the motorman. When the train was backed up to the Franklin Avenue station, they eagerly alighted. Before it reached the Malbone Street tunnel, more than half of the 1,000 passengers left the train rather than gamble on the motorman's ability.

George Horn, a husky marble cutter, was leaning against the iron gate on the end platform of the train and recalling his wife's premonition ("I dreamed you'd be in a bad accident today," she had told him), but he decided to stay on the train. When Horn related his wife's words to a companion, the other laughed. "What the hell do you think can happen to you on the el?" Horn refused to enter the subway car. "I feel safer out here," he said remaining on the open-end platform and watching his friend walk inside—to his doom.

Irving Melton found it difficult to concentrate on his newspaper. He gazed up at an advertisement hanging over the front window: TRY GRAPE NUTS, THE FOOD THAT YOU'VE HEARD SO MUCH ABOUT. IT SAVES WHEAT, SUGAR, FUEL, AND WOOD. A REAL WAR TIME FOOD. SOLD BY GROCERIES.

Less than six feet from Melton, inside the motorman's cab, Luciano looked at his watch. He was ten minutes late. Obsessed by a desire to make up lost time, he disregarded caution and barreled the train at top speed into the next station, Dean Street, then crashed on the air pressure with such volume that the train nearly swayed off the tracks. Ironically, he actually stopped the train too soon, forcing some riders to trudge from rear cars forward to the station platform. A few people screamed hysterically and conductor Michael Turner began walking toward the cab to warn Luciano. But too many passengers were exiting to allow him to leave his post, so Turner remained at the gates and hoped for the best.

By now, everyone on the train was aware that the Brighton Beach local-express was not in competent hands. At Dean Street the train was still plying a straightaway along the elevated tracks but soon it would descend toward the tunnel. Dozens of passengers refused to continue the journey. When the motorman started the train before all departing passengers had alighted at the Dean Street station, several men vaulted the iron gates and fell to safety on the wooden station platform.

Those who hadn't learned their lesson at Dean Street had one last chance at Park Place, where the train once again overshot the platform. Despite attempts to make up for the lost time Luciano was fighting a losing battle. He could see the lights of a train behind him and he was worried. As far as he knew, there was a straightaway before him. But it was dark and Luciano, a Culver Line man, was ignorant of the Brighton system. The hill leading down from Park Place would bring him to the Consumer's Park station, which was so small trains stopped only by request, and then the sudden turn right into the blackness of the Malbone Street tunnel and the S-curve.

The long leather straps hanging from the ceiling began to dance crazily inside the car as the train moved down the incline. Irving Melton had made up his mind. "Tell him I want to get off at Consumer's Park," he ordered train guard Samuel Rosoff.

Without hesitation, Rosoff tugged on the overhead cord three times, ringing a warning bell in Luciano's cabin. But it was too late. Before he realized it, Luciano had permitted his train to surge out of control toward Malbone Street below. With each yard of track, the wood-and-steel caravan gained speed until it rocked past Consumer's Park station so fast its platform signs and lights melted into a blur to the passengers.

A woman leaped from her seat and smashed her fist against the thick wooden cab door, pleading with Luciano to slow down. It was no use. He played with the brakes but the complicated braking system eluded him in his panic. The train was now doing forty-five miles per hour as it passed a tiny yellow light that reflected a sign: SIX MILES AN HOUR.

Those who remembered how the train managed to negotiate the Sands Street curve off the Brooklyn Bridge prayed that another miracle would save the Brighton Beach local-express. And for a couple of seconds it appeared that just such a miracle would occur. The front wheels of the first car clung tenaciously to the tracks as the train screeched around the first curve. Dozens of standing passengers were hurled to the floor.

When the lights of Luciano's front car picked up the threatening curve, he hit the brakes again with all the energy at his command, but the mounting speed proved too much for the old cars and the brakes lost all hold on the wheels. While the front truck of the lead car managed to survive the gravity pull of the swerve, it was too much for the rear wheels. They surmounted the tracks, plunging the rear platform into the side of the tunnel with a deafening report. Passengers were catapulted off the train and thrown against the new concrete wall.

Once the first car jumped the track, it carried the second with it. The front of the second car leaped upward, smashing its roof against the tunnel ceiling while its wood frame crumbled into thousands of splinters. Amid frenzied cries from the 400 passengers, the train still plunged forward to its ultimate doom.

Deafening crash followed upon crash as the second car was decapitated from its floor up. Plate-glass windows turned into bayonets, impaling the helpless passengers. The third car had so much velocity behind it, it fused with the second. The fourth smashed its front against the tunnel wall with such force it ripped its coupling off the fifth car, which miraculously came to a halt without a scratch.

In a matter of seconds the Malbone Street tunnel had become a cave of horror and death. Fresh crimson covered the faded dark red paint of the cars. Agonizing shrieks pierced the air and carried out to Malbone Street where a ticket seller at Prospect Park station heard them and bellowed for police and firemen.

When the police arrived they were confronted with chaos. The train had wiped all lights off the tunnel walls. Automobiles were requisitioned and driven to the tunnel where their lights at least partially illuminated the disaster. But they arrived too late to save those who at first had escaped injury only to be felled minutes later by an ironic mistake.

When the train crashed it uprooted the third rail, shorting out the circuit. Electricians in the BRT powerhouse spotted the short circuit, but mistakenly suspected it was the work of union saboteurs. They were ordered to restore current in such emergencies. The juice was revived on the third rail as countless survivors made their way over the tracks toward salvation. Without warning, the current electrocuted dozens of survivors in an eerie lightning-blue flash of light. Within minutes, the rails shorted out again, but this time the electricians suspected more than foul play and kept the power off.

Sitting at the head of the front car over the wheels that held the track, Irving Melton survived the pulverization of the train. When the shock of the impact had abated, he got to his feet and remembered he had a small flashlight in his pocket. It still was working but he wondered whether it made sense to keep it on. Wherever he turned, the beam picked up dismembered bodies and several passengers still alive but trapped beneath debris.

Melton tugged at a survivor. Soon others joined in the desperate rescue operation, until 250 of the most seriously injured were carried to safety on Malbone Street where they awaited transportation to hospitals. Within the hour, relatives descended upon the site from all points of the borough. The curious drifted down, some to offer aid, others to capitalize on the disaster. Human jackals invaded the tunnel and corpses were later found with their ring fingers chopped off.

Doctors and ambulances were hard to find because the city already was in the grip of an influenza epidemic. George Horn, whose wife had had a premonition of the disaster, lay on blood-stained Malbone Street awaiting help. He had suffered a fractured skull in the disaster. His friend, who had insisted upon sitting inside the train, was dead.

In lieu of ambulances, private cars and fifty volunteers from the Women's Motor Corps helped transport the most seriously wounded to hospitals. The ninety-seven dead were lined up in the Snyder Avenue police station and in the lobby of the Ebbets Field baseball stadium, three blocks away.

When Luciano's train plowed into the concrete tunnel wall, the motorman, like Irving Melton, was saved by the front truck which somehow clung to the tracks. The motorman's cab further protected him from the flying wooden flak. Finally Luciano staggered from his cab, physically unscathed. But the shock held him in a vise. Unable to release his grip on the brake and motor handles, he clutched them tightly as he fumbled his way through the carnage toward the mouth of the tunnel.

Slowly, the intensity of the disaster penetrated through to him. He began a hysterical trot, then a run toward his house. When he arrived home, he sobbed in his wife's arms: "Today is All Saints' Day. They must have spared me."

Unaware of the full extent of the disaster, Luciano's wife prodded him. "What about the other people?" He told her everything, but when she urged him to give himself up to the authorities he refused. Through the night they argued until, finally, he relented.

He surrendered himself and was subsequently indicted for manslaughter. Similar indictments were brought against top BRT officials. Brooklyn's district attorney sought to prove that the men who had ordered the inept Luciano to pilot the train had sentenced 97 people to death. Some reports had the number of dead at 102 or more. It marked the first time a railroad management was brought to account for a fatal accident.

Luciano insisted throughout his trial that the brakes had failed. BRT officials contended that the young motorman was incompetent. After six months of legal wrangling, the trial ended and all of the accused were acquitted.

The Malbone Street crash gave rise to demands for more safety measures. The BRT responded by coming up with an automatic time tripping device by which a thick metal arm activates the braking system of a train that runs through a red light or similar cautionary signal, over the prescribed speed limit. Should the train exceed the desired speed, the trippers swing into action, activating the brakes, a system long in use on the IRT.

Just such a system is in operation now along the route of the old Brighton Beach local-express. Today they call the line the Franklin Avenue Shuttle. It begins its run at the Franklin Avenue station, with short hops to Dean Street, Park Place, Eastern Parkway, Botanic Gardens (then Consumer's Park) and, finally, the S-curve into Prospect Park.

The only thing missing is Malbone Street. That's not there anymore. The name conjured up such fear in New Yorkers, it was changed to Empire Boulevard.

The Times Square IRT Mystery Crash

As always, the Times Square station was a maelstrom of activity in late afternoon on August 24, 1928. IRT locals and expresses plied the four-track main line up and down Broadway. Rubbing shoulders underground were the heavily trafficked Brooklyn Manhattan Transit's Brighton, Sea Beach, West End, and Montague Street (tunnel) trains, each of which stopped at Times Square.

An underground arcade, extending from Broadway and 43rd Street to Seventh Avenue and 40th Street linked the main IRT and BMT routes as well as the IRT's 42nd Street shuttle that bounced between Grand Central station and Times Square. Through these portals thousands of commuters were funneled at 4:55 P.M. that summer afternoon when the IRT southbound express from Van Cortlandt Park in the Bronx lurched through a mild curve and into the complex station called Times Square.

Motorman William McCormick applied the brakes on the steel cars. The ten-car train screeched its way to a normal halt and as soon as the doors opened passengers dashed for the few available wicker seats.

At that precise moment Mounted Patrolman John F. Ward of the New York City Police Traffic Division was riding his horse southbound down Seventh Avenue from 42nd Street toward the corner of 40th Street and Seventh Avenue, then the site of the Metropolitan Opera House.

Patrolman Ward was accustomed to hearing the incessant starting and stopping of the subway beneath him. His ear was trained to detect the unusual but there was, at 4:58 P.M., nothing especially strange about the sounds emanating from the checkerboard steel subway grating alongside him at the curb. Nothing, except the fact that the IRT downtown express from Van Cortlandt Park had *not* pulled out of the station. Considering the rush hour and the urgency to maintain headway, it was highly unusual for a train carrying 1,800 passengers, as was the case with the downtown express, to remain sitting in the Times Square station.

Underground, and unknown to Patrolman Ward, IRT maintenance men had held the express at the terminal because of a problem that appeared aggravated by the hour. A switch in the tunnel eighty-five feet south of where the express tracks reenter darkness beyond the station had been betraying defects as successive trains thundered over the tracks. At this point several individuals became involved in determining the fate of the downtown express.

Harry King, an IRT towerman, was on duty in the signal tower immediately south of the Times Square station at 40th Street under Seventh Avenue. The tower contained an interlocking machine of twenty-three switch and signal levers, but King was concerned with only three of the levers. One was the switch on the downtown express track, eighty-five feet south of the platform. King actuated the switch by operating Lever 17.

Of the many switches on the IRT system the one south of the Times Square station was among the most strategic and therefore potentially hazardous. Its prime function was to shunt extra rush-hour trains uptown from Times Square. The transfer was accomplished in this manner:

A rush-hour extra—a "gap train"—would complete its southbound run to Times Square. It then would proceed past the station and approach the switch operated by Lever 17. The towerman would activate the switch, shunting the train to the left off the express track and onto a special "gap" lay-up track from where it would then be switched onto the uptown express track and resume operation.

One such gap train had preceded the Broadway express into Times Square station that fateful Friday. After its passengers were discharged the train was to proceed to the switch and then cross over to the lay-up track. Towerman King activated Lever 17 but it would not work.

When King was certain that the switch had failed, he immediately notified his superior, IRT maintenance foreman William S. Baldwin. Baldwin was stationed at 34th Street and Seventh Avenue at the time. Accompanied by his assistant, signalman Joseph Carr, Baldwin arrived at the Times Square tower in a few minutes. Meanwhile, the gap train was held at the platform until the switch could be repaired. Immediately behind the gap train sat the regular Broadway express, waiting for a red stop light to turn yellow, signaling "proceed with caution."

Having inspected the defective switch, Baldwin determined that the gap train could be shunted over to the lay-up track if he himself manually operated the switch from track level. Baldwin warned King not to touch Lever 17. "I did not touch the switch," towerman King later insisted. Baldwin then ordered his aide, Carr, to go to the emergency box and manually crank the switch and "key" the waiting gap train, which was to be shunted into the northbound service.

Having concluded that it would be safe to manually dispatch the gap train leftward on the switch, Baldwin shouted to Carr that the procedure could begin. At this point Carr held the switch key down as the train moved forward. The flanged steel wheels hissed and screeched as they rolled out of the station toward the troublesome switch now locked into the turn-left position. Baldwin and Carr peered through the semidarkness of the tunnel, their eyes riveted on the precise point where the curved switch rail hugged the straightaway and prayed that it would hold.

Moving at approximately five miles per hour, the train heaved on-to the switch, its two foremost right wheels leaning against the curved rail. Carr heaved a sigh of relief while keeping his hand firm-ly on the key. The train easily negotiated the defective switch and moved onto the lay-up track.

The red signal which had halted the southbound main line Broad-way express at the entrance to Times Square station flashed to amber as the gap train swerved left out of sight at the other end of the sta-tion. Motorman William McCormick pushed his brake handle for-ward to its release position, pressed down on the controller (ac-celerator), and pulled it one notch, so that the train softly rolled into the Times Square station.

By this time, Mounted Patrolman Ward had ridden his horse into the shadows of the Metropolitan Opera House. Almost directly beneath him the southbound express had pulled to a halt and discharged and ingested its passengers. Once again Baldwin had to take command and make a decision; either continue the practice of manual operation of the switch and hope that it would hold fast as it had for the previous train, or take another option by "spiking" the defective switch.

Spiking (driving a regular railroad spike into the wooden tie alongside the switch, thereby locking it into place) was common railroad practice and ensured that the switch would not drift from its proper position. It would have been a feasible alternative in this situation were it not for the need to continue switching gap trains back to the uptown tracks. Baldwin was persuaded that the manual system, having worked for one train, would continue to operate safely—at least for the southbound express, and probably for trains that would follow—until repair crews arrived.

Motorman McCormick leaned forward in his cab. He saw that all the block signals ahead of him were in red lights; he could not pro-ceed until they changed to amber or he received hand signals at track level from Baldwin.

Carr looked to his boss and got the order without hesitation. Baldwin told him to key the waiting southbound express past the switch. They beckoned to Motorman McCormick. Given the go-ahead hand signal, McCormick again tugged on his controller, gathering speed as the express moved toward the station portal.

Towerman King and a motorman, Michael O'Connor, were in the

40th Street switch room at the time. O'Connor had entered the tower waiting to take charge of the gap train for the northbound (uptown) rush-hour run. Mounted Policeman Ward was heading south along Seventh Avenue toward 39th Street.

Motorman McCormick's train lumbered out of the well-lit station into the black portal. As it approached the switch, the express had gathered momentum and was moving from ten to fifteen miles per hour. Less anxious than before, Baldwin and Carr waited at the crossover where Carr held down the switch key.

Less than a half-mile ahead, the lights of the Pennsylvania Station-34th Street express stop flickered as McCormick tugged his controller another notch faster. To his right was the downtown local track. In front and to the left gleamed the switch connecting with the layover track. Just beyond the switch was a concrete and steel barrier which separated the downtown express tracks from the layover area.

Satisfied that the gap train ahead of him had cleared the switch without incident, McCormick confidently worked his express toward the twenty mph mark as he reached Baldwin and Carr. The wheels on the front truck of the first car did a thundering *paradiddle* as they rolled safely through the switch toward 34th Street. The pattern was repeated by the rear trucks and then the front trucks of the second car. Baldwin and Carr were noticeably relieved as car after car of McCormick's express negotiated the switch and roared southward. As the eighth car thunked over the switch the train was doing twenty mph. Baldwin couldn't wait until the last two pieces of rolling stock cleared the switch, so he could make another attempt at getting it back into normal working order.

He trained his eyes on the intersection of straightaway and curved switch rails as the front truck of the ninth car spun ahead. In the two seconds between the crossing of the first truck and the arrival of the second truck on the ninth car a faint but fearsome noise assailed Baldwin's ears. It was a hissing sound, like the exhale of a giant. To a trained railroad man such as Baldwin, the hiss was the unmistakable sound of escaping air from the switch valve. Horrified, Baldwin realized that the switch was moving from straightaway position to curve (over to the layover track) as the rear truck of the ninth car approached it.

"I knew what was going to happen," Baldwin later said, "but I was powerless to prevent it."

Baldwin's worst fears were justified. The switch had completely moved from straight to curved position as the rear trucks approached. While eight cars of the express continued to plow ahead through the tunnel, and *half* of the ninth car lunged forward, the rear of the ninth car drunkenly swerved left over the curved portion of the switch.

For an agonizing split second, the ninth car was engaged in a tug-of-war with itself; one half pulled south on the downtown tracks while the other half swerved east on the switch curve. The strain was unbearable and, finally, the rear trucks leaped the curved switch track with a horrific jolt. Its wheels now cutting an ugly swath across the wooden ties and uprooting the rails, the rear truck seemed not to want to give. Suddenly there was a terrific jolt, whereupon the front quarter of the ninth car was torn from the rest of the car.

Remarkably, the wild-swinging front quarter of Car Nine remained coupled to the eighth car, but only for the briefest agonizing moment. Then it was flung against the concrete-and-stone partition immediately beyond the switch. Its passengers already shrieking in horror, the severed section was pulverized as it crashed into the twenty-foot-high abutment separating the north and southbound tracks. Simultaneously the lights had gone out in the rear three-quarters of Car Nine, which whipped left, throwing itself against several steel supporting pillars.

Immobilized by the horror before their eyes, Baldwin and Carr watched helplessly as the tenth car, pulled forward by the train's momentum, crashed into the tangled rubble of the ninth car. The uprooting of the third rail instantly created a bizarre succession of lightning-like flashes as the tenth car buckled and bent like a bow. Amid a crescendo of screams, the last car of the doomed express finally sagged over to become a mass of ruins.

The scene thirty seconds after impact was grotesque. Looking like a battered piece of tin, the ninth car was scattered in bits and pieces along the track. Its forward part was lying sideways, a few airpipes and valves sticking out of the corridor. "It had been twisted," said one early viewer, "as one would twist a piece of paper. Its interior was diminished to a space through which a small man could hardly crawl. The center was only a foot or two in width."

So vicious was the blow of steel car against steel pillars that two twenty-foot vertical barriers were sheared from their base by the impact and bent in a wide curve where the front of the derailed ninth car had hit them. Leaning against the partition, the rear of the ninth car only partially survived. One side of it was intact; the other was scattered somewhere in the tunnel.

Convulsed by the explosion of its forces, the subway tunnel was alternately pierced by excruciating screams, glowing with eerie flashes from the third rail, and obscured by swirling dust and dirt as if a volcanic eruption had begun to subside. Were it not for the carnage that accompanied the derailment, an objective viewer would have been arrested by the awesome beauty of the underground pyrotechnical display.

Aboveground Mounted Patrolman Ward heard the thud and crash of the ninth car as he rode his horse past Seventh Avenue and 40th Street. He wheeled his horse around and raced to the subway entrance at the southbound corner to the rear of the Metropolitan Opera House. Leaping off his horse, he raced down the subway steps. Ward surmised that an accident had taken place, but he had no idea of the extent of damage until he tried to get onto the station platform.

Panicked by the thunder and lightning in the tunnel, passengers waiting on the Times Square station platform stampeded toward the exits. The scene at the wreck site inside the tunnel was a distillation of agony, panic, confusion, and infinite heroism. The earliest rescuers reported that the victims were so badly crushed that, in many cases, identification was impossible. Several of the survivors on impact were killed during the ensuing panic over escape routes. Several bodies in Car Nine were found wedged at one window, indicating that the victims had struggled one against the other to escape through the small opening at the top of the window.

One of the first to reach the scene was Magistrate Hyman Bushel, who heard the dull roar of the smashing cars while walking along Seventh Avenue. He rushed down into the subway entrance at 40th Street only to be confronted by chaos. "The sight was so terrible," said Bushel, "that I stood for a time in awe. I was incapable of doing anything. There were horrible cries, all lights were out, and there was the pungent smell of smoke.

"I saw people hurry over to the wrecked cars and take out persons who were dead and others who seemed to be dying. It was a terrible sight."

If there was any solace for rescuers, it was in the absence of a major conflagration. "There was no fire, thank God," said Assistant Fire Chief "Smokey Joe" Martin, "although there was a flare or flash at the start. We did not have to fight flames, and this enabled our men to get right to work helping to get passengers who were hurt or frightened out of the place."

Mounted Policeman Ward, who at first assisted passengers off the station platform, now rushed to the scene of the collision. Using his flashlight, Ward searched for victims, pulling out dead and injured from the wreckage of the crumpled ninth and tenth cars. He guided those who still were mobile through the darkened subway to the south end of the Times Square platform and to the street.

By this time the first batch of ambulances from Bellevue, St. Vincent's and New York hospitals were on their way to the scene. Ward was immediately aided by Detective John J. Broderick, head of the Police Department's Industrial Squad. In his first trip to the street with the injured, Broderick carried an injured girl under one arm and a man under the other, while another girl clung desperately to his neck as he struggled onto the street.

A phalanx of taxis were already at hand to help the wounded, and in no time at all the Police and Fire departments had coordinated their rescue efforts. Less than ten minutes after the initial impact of the ninth car against the concrete wall, Lieutenant John O'Grady was on the scene with the first Police Department Emergency Squad. He sent an alarm for all reserves and every available ambulance. Within fifteen minutes police lines had been established from 35th Street to 42nd Street and Seventh Avenue, and a short time later 200 policemen were on duty at the scene.

Less than fifteen minutes after the wreck had taken place, Mayor Jimmy Walker was escorted into the tunnel where he comforted the injured and conferred with IRT officials. Forsaking dinner, the mayor then went to the hospitals to visit with survivors of the crash.

Meanwhile, reporters from the city's dailies combed through the Times Square station, interviewing passengers who survived the wreck and other witnesses. Many of the most coherent statements were offered by passengers in the forward cars, immediately brought to a halt by Motorman McCormick, who sensed the calamity as soon as he felt a reverberating thud in his compartment. Some of the on-the-spot observations of onlookers follow:

An Interborough guard, who declined to disclose his name, said:

"It was horrible. I was hurled almost the entire length of my car and knocked out. When I came to I found a woman lying dead beside me."

Lawrence Kerney, who was on the third car of the southbound express, said: "There was something wrong with the train all the way down from Seventy-second Street. There was a heavy, constant grinding and the train was lurching from side to side. Some of the passengers thought something was wrong, but none of the Interborough people took any notice of it.

"Suddenly there was a terrible smash. Lights went out. The train shook like a leaf. There was some screaming and a rush began toward the windows. But on the whole most people kept their heads. The women were cooler than the men.

"I was one of the last to leave the train, helping as much as I could in lifting dazed passengers down so they could be taken out of the emergency exits. On my way out I saw three dead men near each other."

According to Lillian Harvey, of Eastern Parkway in Brooklyn, "We were riding only a short while when I heard a great noise and then the car I was in turned over. A man grabbed me by the arm and pulled me out through the fifth car."

Thomas Guilfoyle, U.S. Treasury agent, was passing the subway entrance at 40th Street and Seventh Avenue when he heard the crash and raced down the stairs.

"I could make out the car forms in the darkness. I ran over to one of the cars, broke a window, and began taking passengers out to the platform. It seemed to me that at least two of those I helped pull out of the car windows died on the platform.

"In all I assisted fifteen passengers, men and women. Most of them seemed badly hurt. Those who were capable of limping or being helped up stairs I got in the open air.

"By the time I arrived on Seventh Avenue with the first two or three passengers the police and others were commandeering automobiles to send the injured ones to the various hospitals.

"From what I heard some of the passengers say, the train they were on was traveling fast. They said there was a sudden crash, followed by several explosions and then darkness.

"Passengers who were frightened but not hurt added to the confusion by shouting and attempting to push their way out. It was more than half an hour after I ran down the stairs that there was anything like order.

"I drove three children to the Polyclinic Hospital. As I was carrying a little boy, he suddenly went limp in my arms, and I realized that he was dead. About thirty injured people were driven in private cars and commandeered taxis to the hospitals before ambulances reached the scene."

Mounted Patrolman John F. Ward said:

"I realized the accident was a bad one and knew that an alarm had already been sent in. I got to work trying to get out the living as quickly as possible. From every window as near as I could make out were protruding hands and arms. Some of the windows contained wedged forms of two or three, none able to move.

"Everyone seemed to be shouting as loud as possible. Wherever I saw an arm or head I pulled. In most cases, I am glad to say, those I succeeded in getting out of the train were alive.

"After most of the injured were removed from the cars came the work of getting out those who were unconscious or dead. It looked to me as if some had been killed by being crushed.

"It seems like a miracle that more were not killed. When you realize that the sudden crash and the extinguished lights added terror and maddened those trapped in the cars, I wonder that the list of dead did not have hundreds of names."

Dave Oliver, a newspaper cameraman, was standing in the Times Square platform at the time of the crash.

"I was on my way to the Pennsylvania Station and I was just cursing my luck for missing the train which was first pulling out. I was watching the train disappear, when suddenly I heard a screeching of what sounded like a train's brakes. Then there was an explosion. Everything went dark. I heard a women scream and then groans. Smoke and overpowering fumes began to fill the station. Several women fainted on the platform.

"My first thought was pictures. I fought my way as close to the downtown end of the platform as possible. By the time I got there the lights were on again on the platform and down the track. I was able to get a little room and set my camera up long enough to photograph the wreckage.

"Most of the smoke had cleared away. I guess they turned the power off. I could see the train down the tracks. It was bent and twisted. One car was broken in two like a stick of wood. The pillars supporting the subway roof were torn down. The whole scene was a tangle of twisted steel."

Peter Molitor, a twenty-four-year-old chauffeur, was in the seventh car of the doomed train. Although suffering from a sprained ankle, he remained in the train, helping the passengers to safety. As he sat on the curb waiting for an ambulance, he said: "The crash and stopping of the car was so sudden that everyone in the car must have been either injured or badly shaken up. It was like a madhouse when the lights went out. Everywhere I could hear shrieks. Those who were not shouting for help were sobbing. There were a number of children in the car and their cries could be heard above the others.

"I was near a window, and taking out a wrench from my hip pocket, smashed the window glass. We were near the platform and I managed to push out those nearest me. It was very difficult working in the dark. Now and then someone would strike a match, and the tiny flare showed a struggling, heaping, milling crowd in the car. I never saw anything like it in all my life, and never want to again."

The chief medical examiner, Dr. Charles Norris, was on the scene fifteen minutes after the accident. He was one of the first to go into the subway.

"I don't know how many were killed," Dr. Norris said soon after the crash, "but I know it's a nasty accident, one of the worst in the city's history."

Police, firemen, and bystanders were so involved in rescue operations that few took time to determine precisely what caused the accident. IRT President Frank T. Hedley conferred with company employes and inspectors of the New York City Transit Commission and, for the moment at least, announced that the cause of the wreck was a defective switch.

Colonel John F. Slattery, a commissioner of the Transit Commission, was more precise. He said that presumably *the switch had been thrown too swiftly or had been defective.* Commissioner Slattery didn't realize it at the time but he had carefully delineated what soon would be the major mystery to be solved by the IRT, the Transit Commission, and the district attorney.

The immediate response was to blame the IRT official nearest to the accident. Acting in advance of any findings, District Attorney Banton placed responsibility for the accident upon maintenance foreman Baldwin. Charged with homicide, Baldwin was released on $10,000 bail. However, there was evidence that he might be innocent of any culpability in the accident. For Baldwin, the first ray of hope came from the Transit Commission, itself, which released an official finding on August 25, suggesting that the derailment might have been caused by the switch being thrown as the train was passing over it.

Towerman King maintained that he had no control over the train once Baldwin, his superior, appeared. "I've been told not to talk," King told a reporter, "but I will say that I did not touch the switch."

It seemed unlikely that Baldwin had erred. He had thirty years of railroading experience, fourteen on the IRT. His future would be determined by District Attorney Banton's investigation to fix responsibilities for the 16 deaths and 100 injuries to passengers in the disaster. Steadfastly, Baldwin insisted that he never threw the switch. The district attorney's task was to determine first whether the switch was thrown and, if so, which of the three suspects—Baldwin, Carr, and King—did it.

The first witnesses were called on August 29. Baldwin denied that he or Carr had done anything that would have caused the switch to shift. King and motorman Michael O'Connor acknowledged being in the switch tower at the time of the crash and within reach of the switch levers, but they denied having touched any of the levers.

Within twenty-four hours Banton revealed that he had made several definite determinations. One was that the switch had *not* been thrown by manipulation of the switch lever in the tower. He added, however, that on the wall back of the levers was a row of buttons, pressure on which would operate the switches by compressed air. Signal experts agreed that it would have been possible to throw the switch, even with the weight of the train on the crossover, by use of the proper button.

The investigation suggested two possible causes of the crash:

1. Someone may have tampered with the emergency button in the tower.

2. The entire electrical or mechanical system controlling the switch may have been out of order.

"A third possibility," Banton said, "is that some one may have taken the twenty-five-pound drum covering off the switch mechanism at trackside. But there is little likelihood that the third possibility occurred."

On August 31 an anonymous letter to the district attorney revealed that King was, according to the technical IRT job description, a train clerk, not a towerman. IRT President Hedley explained: "King is a train clerk but he is also a fully qualified towerman. Part of the time he works as a train clerk in the tower and part of the time he acts as towerman."

Testifying on September 17, King admitted that he never had received special instruction in the handling of the switches, but pointed out that Baldwin, who was on the scene, warned him not to touch the switch lever.

King described the heavy roar he heard when the ninth car jumped the switch and crashed into the partition, then added an extremely pertinent piece of evidence. Minutes after the accident, Baldwin ran into the tower and exclaimed: *"Someone must have touched that lever!"*

King insisted that he had not done so. Nevertheless, he came under further scrutiny on September 18, when Gilbert Whitney, signal engineer of the Transit Commission, who had inspected the wreck site two hours after the collision, testified that it was "extremely doubtful" that Baldwin could have operated the switch. He added that the probability was that the switch was thrown by someone in the signal tower. Whitney further testified that someone in the switch tower would have required *only five seconds* to throw the switch lever and push the emergency button after Baldwin's hand signal to the motorman had been given. While the switch lever was in proper position when Whitney examined it after the wreck, it could have been placed there after having been wrongly operated.

Recalled to the stand, King argued in his defense that he had not touched the switch lever. On September 21 King was called to the stand for the third time. His testimony, though abbreviated, was crucial.

King testified that he had been in New York since November 1926 when he left Baltimore where he had lived for five years after coming east from Iowa. When his statements were found to be inaccurate Homicide Court Magistrate Corrigan ordered King's arrest on October 4, charging second-degree manslaughter in connection with the Times Square subway wreck. At the same time the magistrate dismissed the homicide charge against Baldwin.

At his grand jury hearing King admitted that he had lied about his name. It was not King but, rather, Harry C. Stocksdale. He also revealed that he had once been convicted in Baltimore for cutting another man with a knife. Magistrate Corrigan told the court:

"I am forced to the conclusion that the switch was moved by someone throwing the lever and pressing the emergency button in the tower. The only people in the tower at the time of the accident were Harry King, the towerman, and O'Connor, the motorman who was waiting to take the 'gap' train. . . .

"The testimony proves that the only way in which the switch could possibly have been moved at the time of the accident was by the use of the lever plus the emergency button in the tower. It follows that someone in the tower house must have caused the movement. There is no reason to suppose that O'Connor interfered in any way with the lever. King swore that O'Connor did not do so.

"If O'Connor did not do it, King did. Moreover, King's demeanor and his testimony were not satisfactory. His cross-examination based upon investigation conducted by Inspector Valentine of the Police Department shows that King's testimony before me was false in many particulars. His name is not King, but Stocksdale. He was not born where he said he was; he did not live the life he described. He was convicted in Baltimore of stabbing a man with a butcher knife.

"I am forced to the conclusion that in defiance of Baldwin's order he moved the lever, pushed the emergency button and caused this wreck."

It now was up to the grand jury to confirm or deny Corrigan's theory. The indicted towerman held firm in his denial that he had defied Baldwin's order, and no evidence could be obtained to prove otherwise. Finally, on November 19, 1928, nearly three months after the fatal throwing of the switch, the grand jury made the decisive move to dismiss the complaint of second-degree manslaughter against the towerman.

To this day, railroaders debate the cause of the accident. One school of thought endorsed by a local transit expert is that the problem was not in the tower but at trackside. "A disaster would have been averted," he said "if the switch had, as the rules stipulate, been spiked." But it was not and no further evidence was forthcoming. All that was definitively known was that the switch did move and, on Friday afternoon, August 27, 1928, more than 100 passengers were injured and 16 were killed in New York City's second worst subway disaster.

The Astor Place Flood

The old, abandoned John Wanamaker department store buildings sat like overblown mausoleums in Manhattan's Greenwich Village area on a hot Saturday, July 14, 1956. Adorned with cast iron, the New York City landmark was built in 1862 by A. J. Stewart.

The two Wanamaker buildings dominated Astor Place. They reached only five stories but spread over a whole block—9th and 10th streets and Fourth Avenue and Broadway—with the store actually comprising a north and a south building, connected by a bridge. The plot of land itself was steeped in history, most of it turbulent. At the building site, Broadway takes an abrupt westward turn. The bend occurred because a stubborn New Yorker named Hendrick Brevoort wouldn't allow city planners to cut down his favorite shade tree that stood in the line laid out for Broadway in 1807.

Old Brevoort kept making trouble for the city fathers, which explains why there is no 11th Street between Broadway and Fourth Avenue. Brevoort adamantly refused to allow any cuts through his farm. Hence, a portion of 11th Street never was opened.

More controversy erupted at the eventual site of the Wanamaker store in May 1849 when two rival actors—Edwin Forrest and William Charles Macready—became embroiled in a dispute over which of the pair was the better Hamlet! The argument escalated into a bloody riot, and when the dust had cleared Astor Place was strewn with 200 dead and dying.

In 1876 A. J. Stewart sold the building he had erected to a firm called Hilton, Hughes and Company. John Wanamaker bought the store in 1896 and developed it into one of Manhattan's most successful department stores, which included a newer annex. But business sagged in the years following World War II, and in late December 1954 the Wanamakers abandoned the buildings, which were bought from the Wanamaker family in January 1955 by a syndicate headed by David Rapoport, a lawyer. Rapoport decided to raze the old landmark and erect an apartment development.

This seemed like a splendid idea because the prospective tenants would not only be adjacent to Greenwich Village, which was enjoying a renaissance, but also be conveniently close to two of the city's main subway lines. The IRT Lexington Avenue line, a four-track express-local route, operated in a tunnel under Fourth Avenue, while the BMT Broadway line, a similar four-track run, flowed in a north-south direction under Broadway. The IRT Astor Place station was within shouting distance of the Wanamaker building, as was the BMT's 8th Street local stop.

Late in the winter of 1956 demolition work on the original Wanamaker building was begun by Lipsett, Inc., a New York-based firm. On Friday afternoon, July 13, 1956, Lipsett's wreckers had completed scaffolding around the building and were cutting up pipe in the subcellar. Julius Lipsett, the company's vice president, later would tell questioners that the building had been inspected at 4 P.M. on Friday, and basement areas, where acetylene torches had been used to cut up pipe, had been wetted down to prevent fires.

Lipsett maintained a full-time watchman service at the site. Nothing of a suspicious nature was reported during Saturday morning or afternoon. Sam Piparo, an employee of the United Service Detective Corporation, was on duty outside the Wanamaker building that morning. According to Piparo, he noticed a peculiar smell emanating from the onetime department store. Piparo did nothing, theorizing that the odor came from burned articles on the floor left behind by workers the previous day. His job, he insisted, was to watch the *outside* of the building. "I had nothing to do with the inside," he later said.

Precisely what happened inside the abandoned department store will remain a moot question forever. Fire Commissioner Edward F. Cavanagh, Jr., theorized that a spark from an acetylene torch ignited a piece of flammable material minutes before closing time on Friday afternoon. The smoldering material went unnoticed by the workers, who then left the structure for the weekend. "It is very likely," said Cavanagh, "that the fire was going all Friday night and Saturday."

At 5:46 P.M. on Saturday the flames became visible and the first fire alarm was sounded by an unnamed passerby. By that time the subcellar and basement areas were, as Commissioner Cavanagh described it, "a raging fire." As hook-and-ladder companies arrived at the scene, it soon became apparent that more than two alarms would be required to extinguish the rapidly increasing blaze. By 9 P.M. the conflagration was so intense that firemen were ordered out of the building.

The immediate strategy was to confine the fire, but it had spread too rapidly and was generating a crippling amount of smoke, especially from the basement. Before midnight thick smoke rolling out of the lower reaches of the structure had caused five firemen and a radio reporter to be taken to hospitals while others were treated at the scene.

The quarter-inch glass windows of the old store sometimes resisted a single hose for as much as ten minutes, with other jet streams being necessary to break them. Eventually almost all the arched windows—twenty-one in a row from the avenue sides, thirty on the side streets—were broken out.

There were other problems. The old store was full of spaces concealed by partitions, where the fire would lurk and then make a surprise breakout. There was a 40,000-gallon fuel oil tank, with some oil inside.

There was also the need to defend the surrounding area. Besides a bridge linking the northern and southern buildings of the store, there was a tunnel at the cellar level. Firemen inside the southern structure successfully held the blaze away from the northern end with the help of double steel fire doors.

Danger from smoke inhalation and the possibility of a wall collapse led to evacuation of a nearby rooming house. Thirty-four occupants of the building at 57 Fourth Avenue, at 9th Street, were ordered out by the police on advice from the Building Department at 4 A.M.

During the early hours of the fire little concern was given to the state of the two nearby subway lines, the IRT and the BMT. Both had been operating normally in the early evening. But as firemen poured millions of gallons of water on the Wanamaker building it began to seep through to the tracks. The underground seepage to the Lexington Avenue line grew to hazardous proportions at 11:50 P.M., as a five-car southbound Pelham local approached the Astor Place station. At that moment the roadbed at the station dropped four feet.

Fortunately, the motorman detected the dip in the tracks seconds before he brought the train to the platform. He pulled his brake to emergency position and stopped the local before pulling all the way into the station. Since the train was adjacent to the platform—although a considerable distance from its normal stopping point—the conductor opened the doors to permit the passengers to exit. This they did without panic, despite the fact that four feet of water now covered the tracks and was rising rapidly to station-platform height.

Moments later the ground beneath the third and fourth cars of the Lexington Avenue local caved in, dropping the end of each car four feet and leaving them in a semijacknifed position. The time was 11:55 P.M. Twenty minutes later, at 12:15 A.M. Sunday, the Transit Authority ordered all traffic on the IRT Lexington Avenue line halted between Grand Central Station and Brooklyn Bridge.

The Wanamaker building still was blazing and there was no indication when the fire would be brought under control. What troubled TA engineers most of all in the early hours of Sunday morning was the imminent flooding of the BMT's 8th Street station. Water was rapidly filling the two underground basements next to the station. Two double-opening glass doors provided an entrance to the platform from the old building. In a desperate effort to bolster the barrier, TA workers lugged sandbags and timbering, improvising a second "wall" behind the glass doors. They then waited and hoped that it would hold until the fire was extinguished.

As long as the barrier held fast, the BMT trains could continue running. The TA dispatched two pump cars to the BMT station. They sucked out 2,400 gallons of water a minute and were effective as long as the glass-door barrier remained solid.

At 8 P.M. on Sunday the heavy timbers began creaking under the strain, and soon the water, which had reached a height of five feet behind the glass doors, smashed down the portals and spilled a torrent of water onto the BMT platform where workmen had been busy with the pumps. The water spilled over the platform and hit a live third rail, causing a cloud of steam. Service in both directions on the BMT Broadway line between Canal Street and 34th Street was discontinued at 8:20 P.M. Now two of the busiest subway lines in the world were completely halted by the cascading effects of the millions of gallons of water poured on the fire.

Nevertheless, the tide had turned. Arthur J. Massett, acting chief of the Fire Department, announced on Sunday night that the fire was under control, twenty-five hours after it had first been reported. By that time more than 600 firemen of the department's entire complement of 11,000 men had fought the blaze. They worked in three shifts and 187 of them had been treated for smoke poisoning.

By early morning, Monday, July 16, the legion of firemen knew that they had won their battle. Now the TA faced one of its most awesome challenges: the rehabilitation of the flooded stations and undermined roadbeds and the restoration of service on the eight affected tracks, four on the IRT and four on the BMT. Officials at City Hall told Mayor Robert Wagner that it would take at least one month before full service could be restored on the IRT Lexington Avenue line. The BMT line, which suffered considerably less damage, was expected to be ready sooner.

Now that the water from the 50 million gallons poured on the fire had stopped flowing onto the tracks, TA engineers tackled their first major problem on Monday afternoon—removal of the stranded IRT Pelham local cars from the Lexington Avenue tracks.

To hasten the job, the TA crew took several gambles. At 3:30 P.M. the TA requested that a ten-car train be brought up from the south to attempt to pull out the first two stranded cars, which had remained on the level, and the third car, which had dived into the washout. Its motors straining under the pressure, the rescue train gradually pulled the three cars to safety. Nathan Brodkin, chief engineer with the TA, examined the remaining IRT car, No. 6554. Its front was down in about seven feet of water, while its rear had risen to about six inches away from the tunnel roof with its eighteen-inch cross beams.

After sizing up the situation, Brodkin ordered a work train, powered by four motor cars, down from the north. A huge chain, thirty feet long, was rigged to the 85,000-pound car. The final rescue operation began at 5:19 P.M. when the motorman in the work car turned on the juice and the chain tightened. Would it hold? Would the $105,000 subway car remain on the warped tracks or would it derail, further complicating the salvage operation?

"Go ahead," shouted Brodkin, "take her away!"

Engines groaned as the work train slowly but relentlessly pulled at the half-drowned IRT car. It crunched and squeaked, but within fifteen seconds it was out of the morass and back on the level rails. "We've won the battle," the gray-haired Brodkin cheered.

But there were other battles to be fought. As soon as Car No. 6554 was rescued, ten men began carrying away loosened rails past the pool of mucky water while chanting the "Song of the Volga Boatmen."

Next, the TA had to strengthen the station foundation weakened during the ordeal. At 8 P.M. workers completed cutting a six-by-four-foot hole through the paving on Fourth Avenue near 9th Street to allow concrete and timber to be passed into the tunnel for the underpinning job. Meanwhile, tracks had been cleared on the BMT, and limited service was resumed.

On Tuesday, July 17, at 9 A.M., the Fire Department officially declared that the Wanamaker fire was extinguished, although it was not called "closed" because a dozen firemen remained as a watch line and three engines still were pumping water from the building. Nevertheless, TA workmen were readying concrete for a Wednesday pouring operation.

Before this could be done excavation of a hole eighty feet by thirty feet, averaging five feet in depth, was necessary under the steel ledges supporting the first and second rows of subway columns. Mechanical screw jacks, were installed beneath the most critical columns. Drills and shovels broke up debris, which was removed by a work train and by a crane that reached down with a clamshell bucket from a hole dug into Fourth Avenue and 9th Street, eight feet by four-and-a-half feet.

On Wednesday, July 18, 500 cubic yards of concrete were poured down a chute from the street access hole. Workmen shoveled it under the column benches for the new foundation, encasing the jacks as well. Then the TA crews installed ties, rails, and a crushed-stone roadbed, as well as new signaling equipment.

Late Wednesday afternoon Brodkin and his boss, TA Chairman Charles Patterson, stood on the flood site and confidently predicted that full IRT service would resume by 8 A.M. on Friday, July 20, nearly a month before many believed possible. Early the next morning (Thursday) new tracks were installed on the new roadbed.

Sure enough, on Friday morning the first train, led by Car No. 6643, rolled into the Astor Place station. It had headed south from Grand Central at 12:02 A.M., five days and twelve minutes after the undermined roadbed of the Lexington Avenue line had crumpled gently beneath the local.

It was one of the Transit Authority's finest hours. "About the time an ordinary railroad would be deciding when to call a conference to decide what to do about it—about that time, we had it done!" said a proud TA worker.

The Roosevelt Avenue IND Mixup

By New York City subway standards the GG (Brooklyn-Queens crosstown) line is an oddity. Unlike other routes on the IND division, all of which enter Manhattan at some point in their runs, the curious GG wends a circuitous trail from its starting point in middle-class Forest Hills, Queens, to its other terminus in Flatbush in a deteriorating section of Brooklyn, without entering Manhattan. The line had opened in part in 1933 and was fully completed in 1937. The GG carries its passengers on local tracks alongside the speedy E and F express trains at the start of its journey at 71st Street-Continental Avenue. The expresses, enroute to Manhattan, exchange passengers with the GG at two important junctions: Roosevelt Avenue in Jackson Heights (Queens) and Queens Plaza in Long Island City. Since the E and F lines are the most heavily traveled New York subway lines, a considerable number of passengers cross the platform at Roosevelt Avenue where local and express meet.

The GG picks up and discharges another large passenger load at Queens Plaza, where the local then turns away from the main express run. Both E and F continue on under the East River to Manhattan while the GG plunges beneath Newtown Creek, swerving southward to Brooklyn. The crosstown local moves through such old Brooklyn communities as Greenpoint, Williamsburg, Bedford-

Stuyvesant, Clinton Hill, and Fort Greene before reaching another major local-express junction at Hoyt and Schermerhorn streets near the Fulton Street downtown shopping center. Then, a few stations beyond, in an oddity for the IND system, the GG moves up and outside for a short but thrilling climb along the highest elevated run (87½ feet) of any line—the concrete viaduct over Brooklyn's Gowanus Canal. The Smith-9th Street station sits perched atop the viaduct. From there the local slopes downward to Fourth Avenue and reenters the tunnel before reaching its last stop at Church and McDonald avenues.

From the Transit Authority's fiscal viewpoint, the most vital section of the GG operation is the densely packed rush-hour run from the local's starting point at 71st Street-Continental Avenue to Queens Plaza, where it splits off from the expresses. After leaving Continental Avenue, the local picks up large numbers of passengers at such Queens stations as Sixty-seventh Avenue, Sixty-third Drive, Woodhaven Boulevard, Grand Avenue, and Elmhurst Avenue before reaching the express stop at Roosevelt Avenue. These were stations that a passenger like Anna Bovino passed every workday enroute to her office at the CBS building in Rockefeller Center.

Anna Bovino was a typical GG passenger on the morning of May 20, 1970. Her husband, Frank, drove her to the 71st Street-Continental Avenue station, where she boarded a GG local. On this morning Ms. Bovino, thirty-six, thought she would take the leisurely local run all the way to Queens Plaza and then catch the express to Manhattan.

Anthony Haynes and Abraham Williams, Jr., comprised a typical GG crew. Haynes, fifty, was the motorman in charge of piloting the train to Brooklyn, while Williams, thirty-seven, a conductor, opened and closed the doors and maintained a safety vigil for his motorman and passengers.

Haynes and Williams began their workday at the IND's Jamaica yard, where they climbed aboard the GG for the rush-hour run. Their first passengers poured in at 71st Street-Continental Avenue. It was 7:13 A.M. By Woodhaven Boulevard, three stops later, the local was crowded with passengers, among whom was one Timothy Cronin. A regular passenger, Cronin was disturbed when he noticed the GG was remaining with its doors open at Woodhaven Boulevard station for an abnormally long time.

At the Woodhaven Boulevard station motorman Haynes had encountered a malfunctioning of the brakes on his first and second cars (a "married" pair set of 4501-4500 R40s). A road-car inspector, Francis Farmer, forty-five, happened to be on the disabled train. After Haynes conferred with Farmer, it was decided to cut the brakes out of the first two cars and operate the train from the third car. Car inspector Farmer told motorman Haynes to contact the desk trainmaster at the command center later. Haynes decided the local train would have to be taken out of service. This meant that all passengers were to be discharged, after which the train would be shunted along the local tracks to a siding and then to the repair shop.

Conductor Williams informed the passengers that they must vacate the disabled train and wait for the next GG. All riders but one heeded the order. Timothy Cronin remained on the local, assuming that it would have to stop at Roosevelt Avenue, which is where he wanted to get off. There he would catch the Manhattan-bound express.

Meanwhile motorman Haynes and conductor Williams worked out strategy for piloting their wounded local to the IND infirmary. Car inspector Farmer cut the brakes out on the first and second cars, a procedure often used by the Transit Authority when the lead car was disabled and a train had to be shunted out of service. Farmer also told Williams to stand at the front car and use his flashlight to signal Haynes the condition of the signals ahead. A wave of the flashlight was the only means of communication used by this train crew. Farmer remained on the train to assist the motorman if further mechanical difficulties were encountered.

Once its doors were closed, the local lurched forward and rolled westward toward Roosevelt Avenue. At this point, stowaway passenger Cronin approached Farmer and asked him to have the motorman drop him off at Roosevelt Avenue. Farmer reluctantly agreed; he couldn't, after all, leave Cronin alone in the train as it made its way to a siding track. The car inspector opened the third-car motorman cab door where Haynes was operating the train. "I was surprised to see the motorman running the train from the third car going at the normal rate of speed for trains operated from the first car," Cronin said later.

Before the crippled train was moving again TA dispatchers had quickly arranged to prevent a major jam of locals behind the disabled GG. In cases where a stalled local blocks the tracks the following locals are rerouted onto the express tracks. In this case the operation took place at a switch at the west end of the 71st Street-Continental Avenue station. The rerouting operation enabled the locals to continue moving westward on express tracks until the disabled train cleared the regular local tracks. Rerouted locals would be switched from express tracks back to the local tracks just west of the Roosevelt Avenue express station.

This meant that all rerouted westbound locals would bypass the Sixty-seventh Avenue, Sixty-third Drive, Woodhaven Boulevard, Grand Avenue, and Elmhurst Avenue stations. They would stop at the Roosevelt Avenue station on the express track and then proceed over the switch in order to return to the local track enroute to Brooklyn.

Motorman Haynes guided the disabled GG along the local tracks to Roosevelt Avenue without obstruction, since all other trains ahead of him had cleared the track. As the train lumbered toward Roosevelt Avenue station, Williams kept his eyes on the tracks ahead of the train. Farmer soon opened Haynes's cabin door and asked him to allow Cronin to get off at Roosevelt Avenue.

Once Cronin had alighted, the disabled local was set in motion again and rumbled toward the darkened tunnel ahead. Approximately 50 to 100 feet beyond the end of the platform lay a crossover enabling trains to switch from express to local tracks. At this point a new and disturbing element complicated Haynes's operation.

Unknown to the motorman, who lacked communication with the TA's central command center, a rerouted local had pulled into Roosevelt Avenue on the express tracks. It discharged its passengers, took on new ones, closed its doors, and then proceeded according to the command center instructions to the switch where it would cross over to the local track.

Precisely why Haynes was unaware of the switching local remains a question. The Transit Authority later established that all signals were operating properly and that the motorman ignored a double-red (red-over-red) "stop-and-stay" signal at the west end of the station. This signal protected movements over the crossover just ahead.

Haynes pulled on his controller in the third car and the local moved forward out of Roosevelt Avenue station toward the switch. Suddenly conductor Williams, up front, saw the local train swerving right from the express track, directly into the path of the disabled GG. Williams rushed behind the empty motorman's cab in the first car and reached for a red wooden knob attached to the emergency cord. He yanked the cord downward with all his might. Normally such a maneuver automatically set the train's brakes in "emergency" position, thereby bumping the local to a quick stop. But this time the cord had no effect at all, for the brakes in the first two cars had been cut out and were inoperable. Conductor Williams watched helplessly while his local bore down on the GG ahead as it rocked over the cross-switch, veering onto the local track.

Haynes's local rammed the fifth car of the passenger-filled GG with a horrible force before it completed the turn onto the local track. The impact was so severe that the rammed steel car leaped from the tracks and hit the tunnel's concrete wall that separates local and express tracks. Anna Bovino was sitting next to the window of the smashed train when the crash occurred.

"I went flying in the air," said Ms. Bovino. "It was like dreamland. I think I must have been unconscious, but not too long."

She had been lifted from her seat and hurled into the aisle against a pole. Her glasses were ripped from her face as she fell to the floor in the darkness that enveloped the scene. Meanwhile, the fifth car had been split open at the middle, as if struck with a giant ax. One side of the car was almost completely ripped away.

"Witnesses said the scene in the tunnel just after the crash was one of twisted metal and shattered glass," according to a dispatch in the *New York Times.* "The only sounds were the cries and moans of the injured and the hiss of escaping air from broken brake hoses."

Motorman Haynes's train had gathered enough speed by the moment of impact that the two cars were fused together following the collision. Hours later, even after workmen had begun to use acetylene torches to cut away sections of the contorted cars, it was difficult to tell one train from the other. The crash killed two persons and injured approximately seventy others.

Service on the line was spotty for the remainder of the day while TA crews removed the tangled mass of metal from the tracks. By the next morning the tracks were usable and normal service was restored in time for the rush hour. But the question of why it had happened remained unanswered. "The main thing," said Mayor John Lindsay, "is to make sure that the public gets every fact in this tragedy so that we can know why the safety mechanisms—the mechanisms that are supposed to keep this sort of thing from happening—why these safety mechanisms failed."

Probers began at the beginning. They investigated the disabled braking system. They questioned car inspector Farmer's role in having motorman Haynes move the train from Woodhaven Boulevard station. They wondered why there was such poor communication between conductor Williams and his motorman in the third car.

David Lubash, attorney for the Rank and File, a dissident group of largely black and Puerto Rican transit workers, blamed the TA's emergency procedures for the accident. "Permitting the operation of that train out of the third car was just asking for trouble," said Lubash. Equally bitter was Bronx Borough President Robert Abrams who charged the TA with "abandonment of preventive maintenance."

Mayor Lindsay immediately organized a Subway Service Watchdog Commission, an unpaid group of fifteen city residents. The commission launched an independent study, which concluded that "bad engineering and poor maintenance" were responsible for the collision. However, differing views were offered by the Metropolitan Transportation Authority's probe and another conducted by the Queens grand jury.

While the Queens grand jury deliberated the case for more than two months, the MTA's investigative panel made its decision with minimum delay. On May 24, four days after the crash, and before conductor Williams appeared before the grand jury, the MTA panel officially blamed Haynes, Williams, and Farmer for the accident, attributing the disaster to human failure rather than mechanical mishap. Haynes, who the MTA said had acted irresponsibly in operating the train from the third car without proper supervision, and Farmer, who ordered Haynes to do so, were suspended. Williams was not.

"Motorman Haynes, in starting his train without any signal from his conductor at the head end of the train clearly violated rules governing such emergency procedures," the MTA concluded. "This was the immediate and principal cause of the accident." In addition, the board said, Haynes had operated the train through a red signal. That was the key to the disaster.

As for inspector Farmer, the board said he "had exercised improper authority over the motorman in directing the motorman to call the trainmaster at the command center at a later time and to proceed with the movement of the disabled train."

The findings of the seven-member panel were criticized by the Transport Workers' Union, which accused the MTA of going for a "hasty" report in order to get headlines. Instead, said the union leaders, it was "inexcusable neglect in maintenance and operating procedures" by the MTA in general that caused the accident and was responsible for generally poor subway service.

The mayor's panel largely agreed with the union. "The MTA, and its subsidiary, the Transit Authority, tried to cover up their own negligence by issuing white-wash press releases," the panel charged. The specific charges issued by the commission included the fact that the braking system of the disabled GG local was inadequate.

Just eight days later, on July 8, the Queens grand jury released its findings, charging that both sides were equally to blame, but refusing to indict anyone for criminal negligence. The grand jury's thirty-three-page report, based upon testimony of twenty witnesses, pinpointed several causes of the collision:

1. Employees who "have repeatedly demonstrated manifest disregard for standards of safety," creating "a substantial and unjustifiable risk of harm."

2. Failure by the three-man crew—Haynes, Williams, and Farmer—to communicate effectively.

3. Inherently dangerous automatic braking equipment. The accident would not have occurred, said the grand jury, if the train had not broken down in the first place.

Now the ball was in the court of Metropolitan Transportation Authority chairman, Dr. William J. Ronan. The man in charge of the new superagency which oversaw the Transit Authority had been accused by many of being insensitive to the problems of subway riders.

At a news conference following the release of the grand jury's report, Ronan assured the press and the public that the Transit Authority would take quick and proper action to rectify the faults in the system as spelled out in the report.

The manufacturers of the car braking system, Ronan said, had been told to redesign the brakes so that the malfunction that led to the accident would no longer be possible. In addition, all TA trains were being immediately supplied with two-way radios to ensure better communication between motorman and conductor. New rules on operating from other than the first car were instituted.

And finally, the MTA chairman said, there would be a review made of the hiring practices of the MTA and the Transit Authority, as well as a thorough check of the personnel records of people assigned to such crucial jobs as motorman and conductor. It was disclosed by the grand jury that Haynes, the motorman, had violated safety rules on twelve previous occasions in his nine years with the Transit Authority.

"With any accident, except for one caused by an act of God," Ronan concluded, "I assume it could have been prevented. I am never satisfied that everything is being done to make the subway reliable and safe," Ronan said, closing the incident.

There is, however, one footnote to the crash. On the day a GG local crashed into another one, killing two passengers and injuring seventy-one, MTA Chairman Ronan *was* doing something to make the subway more reliable and safe.

He was in England, inspecting a newly designed train.

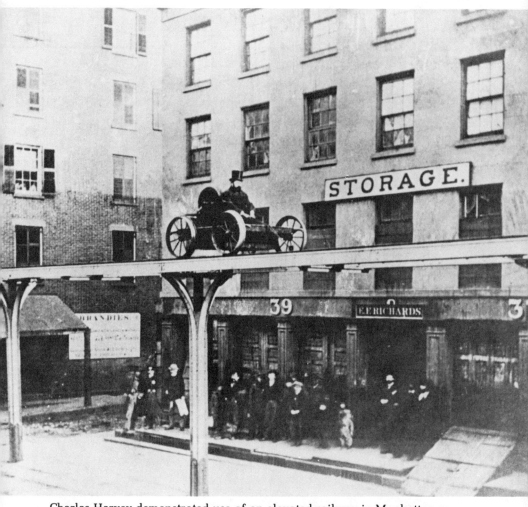

Charles Harvey demonstrated use of an elevated railway in Manhattan on December 7, 1867. *New York City Transit Authority Photo File*

IRT construction along Fulton Street in Brooklyn did not stop the trolley, elevated train, or pedestrian traffic. (BELOW) *New York City Transit Authority Photo File;* (FACING PAGE) *Sprague Library, Electric Railroaders Association, Inc.*

This congested scene at Broadway and Fifth Avenue in 1893 was as persuasive as any in convincing New York City planners to build a subway. *Collection of Library of Congress*

A steam engine puffing its way along a Manhattan elevated line, prior to electrification. *Sprague Library, Electric Railroaders Association, Inc.*

No transit treat could beat a summer ride on an elevated open bench car around Manhattan. *Sprague Library, Electric Railroaders Association, Inc.*

The original Third Avenue el in Manhattan was a two-track line that later added a center track for expresses. *New York City Transit Authority Photo File*

Mayor John McClellan and a group of dignitaries on a pre-opening inspection tour of the first IRT subway in 1904. *New York City Transit Authority Photo File*

Looking north along IRT tunnel construction under Lexington Avenue in 1904. *New York City Transit Authority Photo File*

Pipes snaked their way around Columbus Circle in Manhattan as workmen began digging for the IRT's first subway. *New York City Transit Authority Photo File*

The original Interborough Rapid Transit Company's City Hall station, which opened in 1904, no longer is in use in this form. *Sprague Library, Electric Railroaders Association, Inc.*

The center (express) track is empty on the Third Avenue el as a pair of locals arrive at the 67th Street station in Manhattan. *Sprague Library, Electric Railroaders Association, Inc.*

Then, as now, Herald Square (34th Street and Broadway) was sprinkled with trains and trolleys. The Sixth Avenue el is seen at the left. *Sprague Library, Electric Railroaders Association, Inc.*

Every imaginable vehicle traveled on or above the Bowery at the turn of the century, including the electrified Third Avenue el and electric street-cars utilizing a power source under the middle aperture. *New York City Transit Authority Photo File*

The last horsecar line in Manhattan was the Bleecker Street-Broadway run which ceased operation July 26, 1917. *Sprague Library, Electric Railroaders Association, Inc.*

The Brooklyn Rapid Transit Company (later the BMT) sported every conceivable style of streetcar including this track sweeper. *New York City Transit Authority Photo File*

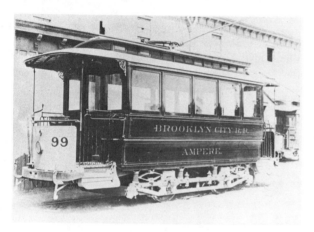

Brooklyn trolley riders were occasionally lucky to get a ride in one of these beautifully appointed parlor cars. *New York City Transit Authority Photo File*

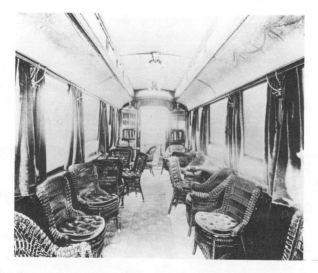

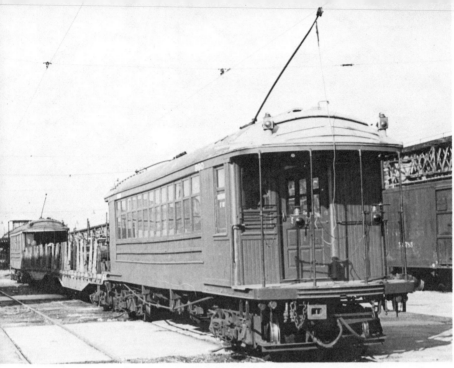

This 1000 series convertible car, built in 1903, put in many years of passenger service before being sent to the yards for work detail. *Sprague Library, Electric Railroaders Association, Inc.*

The Brooklyn & Queens Transit Corporation (part of the BMT) bought the first truly futuristic trolley cars in 1935. They were swift, silent, and extremely comfortable. *New York City Transit Authority Photo File*

The early elevated lines of Manhattan frequently traversed a labyrinth of steel linking one el to another. Here, a steam engine click-clacks through a crossover. *New York City Transit Authority Photo File*

To assist passengers boarding and alighting from Brooklyn trolleys, a metal plate, located under the folding wooden doors, would drop into position when the trolley stopped and the door opened. *New York City Transit Authority Photo File*

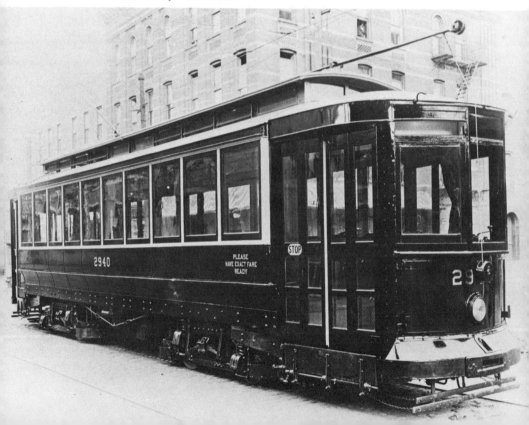

A Sunday by the sea was the height of summer living thanks to the convertible trolley cars that converged on Coney Island. *New York City Transit Authority Photo File*

Rolling stock victims of the
Malbone Street (Brooklyn)
disaster on the BRT Brighton line were stored in the
Coney Island yards after the
crash in November 1918.
*New York City Transit
\uthority Photo File*

124

The Transit Authority's
most colorful chairman was
Charles L. "Big Charlie"
Patterson, seen here inspecting the TA's short-lived
robot train at its testing
track on the Sea Beach line.
*New York City Transit
Authority Photo File*

For years the mainstay of
the Interborough Rapid
Transit subway and the
elevated routes, the "Low
V" cars got their name from
"Low Voltage." *Sprague
Library, Electric Railroaders
Association, Inc.*

One of the most remarkable repair jobs in transit history occured in
1956 when torrents of water used to extinguish the fire in the abandoned
Wanamaker department store near Astor Place in Manhattan flooded
both the IRT and BMT stations nearby. Although experts predicted that it
would take more than a month to get the tracks operable, the Transit
Authority completed the job in less than a week. *New York City Transit
Authority Photo File*

One of Brooklyn's oldest elevated lines ran along Myrtle Avenue. At first it featured open-gated cars. Before being razed the Myrtle el sported cars refurbished for the 1939 World's Fair. *Sprague Library, Electric Railroaders Association, Inc.*

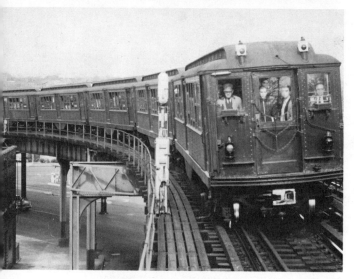

In their last years, the "Low V" IRT cars groaned from straining motors but remained a favorite of subway buffs. Its "extra" front viewing window always was a treat. *Sprague Library, Electric Railroaders Association, Inc.*

The saddest sight a BMT buff ever could see—the scrapping of the famed "67-foot" standards that served Brooklyn and Manhattan from 1914 until the early seventies. *Sprague Library, Electric Railroaders Association, Inc.*

The BMT boasted the classiest rolling stock in the city, including the beautiful, experimental *Bluebird*, a three-car articulated train. *Sprague Library, Electric Railroaders Association, Inc.*

In the late fifties, the Transit Authority opted for stainless steel cars, model R-38, manufactured by the St. Louis Car Company. *New York City Transit Authority Photo File*

One of the Transit Authority's "lemons" was the R-40, elegantly designed but, in the opinion of some experts, hazardous because of sloping ends. *New York City Transit Authority Photo File*

In the sixties, the model R-42 car offered riders uncomfortable
longitudinal seats but lots of standing room. *New York City Transit
Authority Photo File*

PATH trains, New York's other subway, shuttle passengers to terminals in
the World Trade Center and Gimbel's basement. *The Port of New York
Authority.*

The East New York
storage yard is rarely
completely jammed, but
the 1966 transit strike
sent every piece of roll-
ing stock back to the
base. *Sprague Library,
Electric Railroaders
Association, Inc.*

A subway car production
line at the St. Louis Car
Company plant. The out-
fit is no longer in the
car-making business.
*Sprague Library, Electric
Railroaders Association,
Inc.*

Construction is moving
along at full throttle on
the Hudson-Manhattan
tubes. *The Port of New
York Authority*

Demolition of the rapid transit tracks on the Brooklyn Bridge in 1944, south of the Sands Street station. *Sprague Library, Electric Railroaders Association, Inc.*

One of New York's busiest stations is at Grand Central station where the IRT Lexington Avenue route meets the 42nd Street shuttle and the Flushing line that runs to Queens. *Sprague Library, Electric Railroaders Association, Inc.*

OFF THE
BEATEN TRACK

Art in the Subway

One January morning in 1957 a woman telephoned the Transit Authority public relations office at Jay Street in Brooklyn and told publicity man Joe Harrington that she had been admiring the beautiful mosaics in the subway systems.

"What do they mean?" she asked. "Why do you use them?"

Harrington, a former newspaperman who usually had an answer, was dumfounded. "What mosaics?" he replied with a mixture of concern and curiosity. "In our subway?"

Once he was assured that the caller was hardly a prankster, Harrington said he would immediately get on the case. He contacted Walter Cozzolino, the TA's senior architect, who confirmed that mosaics existed on the subways. "But," said Harrington, "he didn't know what they represented and why they were installed."

133

Joe next approached Adolph Bergbom, assistant secretary of the TA, who pored through his files and unearthed further clues. Bergbom's search revealed that the first contract for the first subway (IRT) specified that each station was to be embellished with a landmark of the neighborhood. But he had no further details.

Harrington checked with George Horn, then an IND motorman who, in his spare time, made special studies of practically everything connected with the subway system. Horn had no definite information, nor did Irving Finkel, the TA's chief of designs. After contacting a host of IRT employees and passengers, most of whom were not even aware the mosaics existed, Harrington concluded that this simply must be recorded as "the Great Subway Art Mystery" and eventually turned his attention to more mundane publicity work.

No official records had been kept of the handsome bas-reliefs and mosaics that grace both IRT and BMT stations, but transit—and art—specialists combined on their own to decipher the picturesque symbols and offer several conclusions.

This much is known. When the city's first subway, the IRT line from Broadway to upper Manhattan, was planned its financial backer, August Belmont, ordered $500,000 spent to decorate the new stations. The ceilings were separated into panels by wide ornamental moldings and rosettes. Norman brick was used on the wall bases, above which was glass tile or glazed tile followed by a faience or terra-cotta cornice. Ceramic mosaic was used for the decorative panels, friezes, pilasters, and name-tablets.

The panels adorned at least sixteen stations. "They are," said an IRT brochure issued when the subway was opened, "instructive and decorative, as well as practical, and will have their effect on public taste just the same as anything else that tends to uplift and refine." According to John Tauranac in *Historic Preservation* magazine (1973), some outstanding examples of subway art include:

1. *Canal Street, IRT Seventh Avenue line: Mosaic, Spire of St. John's Chapel.* Renowned for its 215-foot spire, St. John's Chapel was opened in 1807 as part of Trinity Parish and located on Varick Street near what was to be the Canal Street subway station. During the first half of the nineteenth century, St. John's boasted a large parish. But in 1865 Commodore Cornelius Vanderbilt, president of the New York Central Railroad, bought land in the area. He erected a freight depot in 1867, and the neighborhood spun into rapid decline. In time St. John's lost its congregation and was razed in 1918.

2. *Fulton Street, IRT Lexington Avenue line: Bas-relief, Robert Fulton's 150-foot Steamship* Clermont. Although a Connecticut Yankee named John Fitch actually invented the steamship twenty years before Fulton built the *Clermont,* Fitch encountered money problems that sank his project. In contrast, Fulton persuaded Robert Livingstone to give an advance for the *Clermont* and, in return, named the steamship after the Livingstone estate on the Hudson River.

3. *Grand Central Station, IRT Lexington Avenue line: Mosaic, Bell-stacked Locomotive, New York Central Railroad.* When the IRT Lexington Avenue line was extended northward in 1918 the train mosaic was installed in the then new station.

4. *Columbus Circle, IRT Broadway West Side line: Bas-relief Christopher Columbus's Caravel Santa Maria.* The great Italian navigator's flagship was featured in the IRT's original promotional brochure in 1904 after the mosaic was completed at the 59th Street-Columbus Circle station.

5. *116th Street, IRT Broadway West Side line: Bas-relief, Seal of Columbia University.* The Columbia University emblem features a woman, symbolizing Columbia, sitting on a throne with three children at her feet, symbolizing her students. The Hebrew word for Jehovah is above her head and within the circle of the seal is Columbia's Latin motto which, translated, reads: "In Thy light shall we see light."

6. *Borough Hall, Brooklyn, IRT Seventh Avenue-Broadway line: Mosaic, The Hall of Records.* In this handsome work a spire of what once was Brooklyn's City Hall pierces the clouds. The building was completed in 1848 and was the site of ceremonies marking Brooklyn's transfer from an independent community to one of the five New York City boroughs.

7. *Chambers Street, IRT Seventh Avenue-Broadway line: Mosaic, King's College (Columbia University) 1760–1857.* The institution then was located between Murray and Barclay streets and stretched from Church to Chapel streets. The mosaic depicts the academic garb introduced to the colonies by Myles Cooper, King's second president. Chambers Street, after which the station is named, itself was named for John Chambers, the first lawyer admitted to the bar in the province of New York.

8. *Brooklyn Bridge, BMT Chambers Street: Bas-relief, Brooklyn Bridge.* The subway version of the bridge must have caused designer

John Roebling to turn over in his grave. The bas-relief shows cables from the bridge running vertically to the roadway. Actually, the Brooklyn Bridge cables emanate fanlike from the towers to the roadway, not vertically as in the subway picture.

9. *Astor Place, IRT Lexington Avenue line: Bas-relief of a Beaver.* John Jacob Astor, who made his fortune out of furs, mostly beaver, was once the richest man in America. Born Jacob Ashdour, Astor started life in America as a baker's boy. He later sold pianofortes and soon entered the fur business. In time he was to be called "Landlord of New York."

10. *Clark Street, Brooklyn, IRT Broadway-Seventh Avenue line: Mosaic, Brooklyn Heights Waterfront, circa 1900.* Bustling now as it was then, the Brooklyn wharves were just a stone's throw from the Clark Street station. The especially colorful mosaic depicts two steamships, a church spire, several trees, and what appears to be the outline of the massive St. George Hotel.

11. *Canal Street, BMT Broadway line: Mosaic, Aaron Burr's Old Homestead* (no longer visible). The mosaic reveals a little waterway flowing beneath a bridge adjacent to Burr's house. The waterway is the canal after which Canal Street was named.

12. *South Ferry, IRT Broadway-Seventh Avenue line: Bas-relief of a Sloop.* In presteamship times, the vessels were dubbed Hudson River sloops and were the workhorses of the New York City port, carrying both freight and passengers. The sloops were about seventy feet long with a large mainsail well forward, a small jib, and sometimes a topsail. They were fast and seaworthy and one captained by Stewart Dean of Albany sailed all the way to Canton, China, in 1785.

13. *Court Street, Brooklyn, IRT Lexington Avenue line: Mosaic, Kings County Courthouse.* Built in 1865, the Brooklyn courthouse was directly across the street from Borough Hall. It was the scene of a famous trial pitting Theodore Tilton, editor of the New York *Independent,* against Dr. Henry Ward Beecher, the abolitionist brother of Harriet Beecher Stowe and pastor of Plymouth Church on Orange Street. The courthouse was vacated in 1958 and razed three years later.

14. *Whitehall Street, BMT Broadway local: Mosaic, Peter Stuyvesant's House, White Hall.* In colonial Dutch times, the area around what is now Whitehall Street was called Schreijer's Hook. Stuyvesant built his house at the beginning of a street called Het Marckvelt.

Originally, the residence was known as the Great House. However, the building was whitewashed and became known as the White Hall. Boasting an unobstructed view of the harbor, the house stood until 1776, when it burned down along with a quarter of the city in a mighty fire.

15. *Broadway-137th Street, IRT Broadway-Seventh Avenue line: Mosaic, Seal of City College of New York.* The first site of City College was a building at Fourth Avenue and 23rd Street. At the turn of the twentieth century CCNY moved to 137th Street and Convent Avenue. The seal is a variation on the Janus theme: three female heads facing different directions, with the Latin inscription *Respice, Adspice, Prospice* (Past, Present, Future). It has been said that some of the rock excavated in construction of the Broadway subway was transferred to the CCNY site and used for buildings on the north campus.

16. *City Hall, BMT Broadway line: Mosaic, City Hall.* Fully utilized to this day, New York's City Hall was opened in 1812. At the time the city had a competition for the design of its new municipal building, offering $350 to the winners. The team of John McComb, Jr., and Joseph Mangin won the award. McComb, Jr., a Scot, and Mangin, a Frenchman, designed the structure, which went up on the site of the old almshouse. It was covered with white marble on the south, west, and east sides, with cheaper sandstone used on the north side. At that time no one expected the city to expand northward enough for people to have occasion to see the north side of the building. A restoration job in 1956 included a covering of Alabama gray-veined limestone and Missouri red granite on *all* sides.

The use of mosaics was abandoned when the third and last major subway, the Independent system (IND), was constructed in the thirties. "Instead," said Irving Finkel, "on the IND they worked out a system of using colored tiles to acquaint passengers who couldn't read with their whereabouts. The system is fully keyed."

However, hardly anyone on the Transit Authority staff has been able to decipher the key! Senior architect Walter Cozzolino simply called the idea "a noble experiment." Finkel wouldn't even go *that* far. He admitted that he didn't know the color of the tile at his home station. "But," he added, "I'm sure I'd sense something wrong if I got off at a station with different tile!"

Graffiti: Art or Ugliness?

Using an assortment of writing implements from felt-tipped pens to spray cans, subway graffiti artists launched full-scale activities in 1970 and soon became ubiquitous on the IRT, BMT, and IND lines. The scrawls were first noticed on the Broadway (No. 1) local on Manhattan's upper West Side.

Whatever the causes and whatever the messages, municipal leaders were concerned enough about the problem to call it an epidemic and to inspire then mayor, John Lindsay, to organize an antigraffiti task force.

"The ugliness of graffiti," said Lindsay, "and the ugly message—often obscene or racist—has generated widespread support for the city's campaign to end this epidemic of thoughtless behavior."

In 1971 the city's Transit Authority spent $800,000 to remove the eyesores from its buses and subways. A year later the figure leaped to $1.3 million.

The classic example of Manhattan's graffiti problems is the 91st Street station on the Broadway line. Although the station has been abandoned and closed for more than a decade, almost every foot of the platform has been covered with scrawls applied in the early seventies.

"I know the problem is complex," said Lindsay at the time. "But we have to roll up our sleeves and stop it. The assault on our senses, and our pocketbooks, as we pay the cleanup costs, must be stopped."

The nature of graffiti is less complex than the means of stopping it. More than 90 percent of the scrawls are first names accompanied by a street number or Roman numeral. "Bing 170" is typical of the signees.

"Bing 170," "Joe 145," and "Pipilo 105" among the graffiti armada are believed to have been inspired to their destructive tendencies originally by a seventeen-year-old high school graduate from Manhattan, whose signature was "Taki 183."

Taki, whose real first name is Demetrius—he refused to divulge his last name—spawned the graffiti school of scrawl during the summer of 1970. He began by writing "Taki 183" on neighborhood ice cream trucks, but soon expanded his operation to such distant locations as Kennedy Airport and across the state line into Connecticut and New Jersey.

"I just did it everywhere," he said. "I didn't have a job then and it was a way of passing the time."

Within a year, Taki's style was imitated and enlarged upon. Today the scrawls are larger, and instead of using a felt-tipped pen the culprits resort to cans of spray paint, or, in extreme cases, regular paint and paintbrush. The late Robert Reisner, an authority on graffiti, explained the wall scrawl as "a twilight means of communication between the anonymous man and the world."

A few New York City police officers have been able to do something about the graffiti problem. One of them is thirty-one-year-old Transit Patrolman Stephen Schwartz, who was personally honored by Lindsay in August of 1971 for his antigraffiti campaign.

Patrolman Schwartz began his crusade by keeping a record of the most likely time scrawlers would go to work—usually during the late-night hours when the subway cars are in the yards. He then arrested the suspects on the spot.

But, as most every other New Yorker discovered, Patrolman Schwartz fought an uphill battle. The *New York Times* wrote an editorial on the subject, suggesting that the Transit Authority "be induced to run a Graffiti Special once a week or so, equipped with markers and spray paint."

Proof that the scrawlniks ultimately triumphed is on nearly every one of the city's 7,000 subway cars, and new confirmation, in the form of fresh defacement, appears daily.

"Star III" or "Bob 148" or "Superbad" and thousands of other signatures, epithets, slogans, and drawings cover the trains and buses in garish color. Occasionally, the entire side of a car will become a mural.

Ever since the graffiti guerrillas began attacking Transit Authority rolling stock, the TA general staff underestimated the enemy and, subsequently, has been defeated at every station. Transit officials view the facilities of other cities such as Toronto, with envy, because of the almost sterile cleanliness.

Captured scrawlers have been forced to scrub down cars and stations they have illegally painted, the theory being that such seemingly onerous work would deter them in the future. But the strategy has failed.

"Instead of being a pain to the kids," said the late Frank Berry, who was the TA's graffiti-control official, "the cleanup turns into a lark. Meanwhile, we have to provide supervisors to watch them and it costs us even more money." Berry said the deterrent should be more severe, but not everyone agreed with him. Such personalities as Andy Warhol, Norman Mailer, and columnist Shana Alexander applaud the scrawlers.

"If I were chairman of the Transit Authority," said pop artist Warhol, "I'd leave the graffiti on the subways. I love graffiti."

So does Mailer, the best-selling author who published the book *The Faith of Graffiti,* and *Esquire* magazine, which featured a scrawlnik on the cover of its May 1974 issue. *Esquire* described graffiti as "the great art of the '70's."

Such testimonials infuriate the antigraffiti forces of the TA, which spends an annual $5 million cleaning up graffiti. "The average rider doesn't think graffiti is so nice. It's no different than if I came into somebody's house and defaced it," said the TA's Berry.

But the apparently growing numbers in the pro-graffiti camp affirm the importance of self-expression—even on subway cars—and the esthetic values of a good train mural. More doctrinaire scrawlniks like to quote pop art sculptor Claes Oldenburg in defense of their art: "You're standing in the subway station, everything is gray and gloomy and all of a sudden one of those graffiti trains slides in and brightens the place like a big bouquet from Latin America."

Others point to respected establishment columnists such as Shana Alexander, who wrote in favor of scrawlniks: "The last time I took the subway, I rode in a car spray-painted with a host of angels. Today's graffitists have cleaner minds than some of our politicians."

There are inconveniences to be sure. Graffiti frequently make subway maps illegible and often cover train windows, thereby obliterating station signs.

For a time the city believed it would win the graffiti war by attrition. Officials hoped the scrawlniks would weary of the effort, especially since there appears to be so little drawing space left on the cars.

140

"They fooled me," said a subway official. "The kids keep coming back with more paint and more expressions. There's no question they've defeated us."

This transit executive said that he realized the war was lost when a clean, freshly painted A express once made its first run after leaving the TA's antigraffiti shops. "By the time it got to 42nd Street," said the official, "a slogan was painted on it."

The scribble read: HELP STAMP OUT GRAFFITI.

Is the end of the graffiti epidemic in sight? One encouraging sign was the offer by thirty members of Bronx youth gangs to clean graffiti off a subway train.

Civic leaders are hopeful, but they agree that the laws are futile because of enforcement difficulties. "The only way the epidemic will end," said a transit official, "will be with cultural change. That's how it came and that's how it will go. Like so many moods, it will eventually pass away."

The other possibility is a new paint that the TA has developed. The paint is capable of withstanding the most potent solvents. "After repainting in the shops," a TA official explained, "any graffiti can be removed quickly and cheaply with the more powerful solvents."

Smelly Kelly, Kass the Con Man, and Other Subway Characters

While the subway alternately is a menace, an annoyance, and a general pain in the ears to many riders, it nevertheless has remained a love object to a small but ardent segment of the population. To them, the ultimate joy is the simple act of standing at the front window of an IRT Seventh Avenue express as it careens along the rails at 55 mph (it seems like 155 mph) through the tunnel between 14th Street and Chambers Street stations. The distillation of magnified speed, doubled decibels, and a sensation of the train about to jump track is not unlike the thrill of riding a Coney Island roller coaster.

Most subway buffs are paying customers, who have to ante up their tokens before savoring the many nuances of tunnel and track. But there always have been a select few who have had the pleasure of *being paid* while enjoying their transit hobby. These, of course, are the assorted employees of the subway system.

There are absolutely no bounds to their ardor, no limits to their pursuit of the ultimate train ride. Nobody carried this passion further than Harold Wright, a public relations official in the Transit Authority's Brooklyn offices during the early sixties. The extremely bald and often whimsical Wright had a lifelong passion to take the world's longest subway ride.

"Childe" Harold's dream was realized when the TA bought a fleet of new subway cars from the St. Louis Car Company in St. Louis, Missouri. "This," said Wright, "is the chance I've waited for."

Wright had some vacation time coming to him so he bought a one-way plane ticket to St. Louis. Then, using his TA credentials, Wright arranged to shepherd the train over the 961 miles from St. Louis to New York City. "I knew," Wright boasted, "that nobody had ever ridden a subway car 961 consecutive miles and I knew that I was well-equipped to do so."

His "equipment" included an overwhelming desire to have his name inscribed in the *Guinness Book of Records,* as well as several cardboard boxes filled with egg salad sandwiches and Thermos bottles of coffee, milk, and tea. The trip took three days.

"It wasn't exactly what you'd call a Pullman car," said Wright. "I had to sleep on the hard, plastic longitudinal benches that pass for seats in a subway car."

The subway car was part of a fleet that was pulled by a standard diesel freight engine over the Pennsylvania Railroad tracks to New York. "On the whole," Wright concluded, "it was a rather bumpy ride but, then again, comfort was not my object."

Wright received the ultimate accolade upon his return when the New York *Journal-American* carried a six-column banner headline: WRIGHT RAILROADS TO A RECORD.

No less passionate than Wright was one George Horn, who began his professional career in 1947 as a trolley car motorman in Brooklyn. Horn was twenty-nine years old at the time but he had already put in more than twenty years of unofficial rapid transit study. When George was only seven he knew the number of every trolley on the Gates Avenue line in Brooklyn. He could tell by the clank, as it passed his door, which trolley it was.

This was quite natural for Horn. His grandfather had been a motorman on the Third Avenue line and died in a powerhouse accident. His grandmother was a ticket agent for the Brooklyn Rapid Transit until she died, and his mother was in the transfer department. She couldn't look after George, but Aunt Lucy could. At the time, Aunt Lucy was a ticket agent on the Fifth Avenue and Fulton Street lines.

When little George got tired, he crept underneath the money board in the change booth and was rocked to sleep by the passing cars. Even then it was quite obvious to family and friends that George loved the enchanting world of banging wheels, trolley bells, hissing subway brakes, and percussive switches.

Horn became both a transit employee and a record seeker. He paid the last fare on the old Sixth Avenue el. He piloted the last of the Vanderbilt Avenue trolley cars over Brooklyn Bridge and presided at the controls of the last Smith Street (Brooklyn) trolley car, the last 86th Street car, and the last Bay Ridge Avenue car. George paid the first nickel to ride the IND train that opened the Jamaica line. He also was a firster at the openings of the 23rd Street-Ely Avenue subway station, the Sixth Avenue line at 34th Street, and the Euclid Avenue station of the Fulton Street line.

George waited forty hours to be the first to drive through the Brooklyn-Battery tunnel, but he dismisses the feat as ersatz record breaking. "You've got to have rails under you to get the real feel of the thing."

In 1951 Horn switched from trolley motorman to rapid transit as a motorman on the BMT and later the IND. "The TA people only let him work an eight-hour shift," said Joe Harrington, then a member of the Authority's public relations department, "but they didn't mind if he poked around an additional seven hours. He had a movie camera by then and recorded the operations of every elevated line and thirty-five streetcar lines. Then, he moved on to the subways."

George's heart really wasn't in his work once the New York City TA decided to eliminate all trolley car operations. After he retired as a yardmaster in 1970, he grabbed the first jet to San Francisco where he took a job as a motorman on the Market Street trolley! "George," said his pal Don Harold of the New York TA, "simply returned to his transit roots." He's still there, as happy as he was on that day in 1947 when he drove his first trolley car.

Equally passionate about trolleys and trains was Gilbert Reiter, a smallish Brooklynite who once had dreams of being a frozen-custard king and wound up becoming one of the most distinguished motormen in the TA. After graduating from high school, Reiter began selling frozen desserts at Coney Island. He became manager, then owner, of a stand that proved so popular that Reiter established a second frozen-custard place at Rockaway. Having acquired the beginning of a chain, Reiter saw his hopes dashed by the Depression. Too few people were buying the frosty fluff so he got a job in 1941 as a trolley operator. He enjoyed streetcars but not as much as subways. Finally, four years later he graduated to the BMT underground, piloting the Brighton local between Coney Island and Manhattan.

About this time Reiter was also developing into an avid artist. "I would get terribly absorbed in my work," said Reiter. "Once I spent three months in an art class that had a nude in front of the room. Not once did I look at the nude. I kept concentrating on a painting of a subway scene that *I* had in mind."

That's where Reiter's subway passion temporarily rolled out of control. He was obsessed with doing a painting of the inside of a tunnel as seen from his motorman's cab. Gil was particularly enthusiastic about the view in the Brighton local's run from Prospect Park station in Brooklyn to Seventh Avenue.

There was only one problem: Reiter realized that it would be necessary to do a series of pencil sketches before beginning the actual painting. But he couldn't very well sketch with his left hand on the controller and his right hand on the brake handle. Eureka! Reiter had the solution. He would take the Brighton local out of Prospect Park station, bring it to a point equidistant between Prospect Park and Seventh Avenue, stop his train for a minute, and knock off a quick sketch on his pad. And that is precisely what he did.

For about one week, riders on the Brighton local were perplexed by the unexpected screeching of the brakes inside the tunnel after leaving Prospect Park station and the mysterious stop. Little did they know that motorman Reiter was busily drafting what would become a prize-winning painting.

The finished product, titled *Brighton Local*, was the Brighton tunnel seen in brave reds and yellows. Reiter sold the painting for $250, proving that the murky, forbidding subway tunnel could be attractive and profitable.

Another subway fan was Kassel "Kass" Pollock, one of the TA's legendary and lovable public relations officers. Among Pollock's jobs was trying to explain to newsmen and the public precisely why trains such as Gil Reiter's Brighton local were late. Built like a fire hydrant, Kass was a delightful character whose popularity was at its height in the late fifties.

The longer Pollock worked for the TA, the fonder he became of its rolling stock and its employees. And the fonder he became, the less able he was to recognize its blemishes. Pollock's loyalty eventually reached absurd proportions. He began denying that the subways system suffered (a) derailments, (b) fires, and (c) crashes.

"Kass," said former colleague Joe Spaulding, "had his own particular vocabulary. Instead of admitting that there was a derailment, he could call it 'a misaligned wheel.' When there was a fire, he wouldn't call it a fire but rather 'rapid oxidation.' And small crashes were defined by Kass as 'hard couplings.' "

Pollock was at his PR peak the day a collision took place. When a reporter phoned Pollock's office and demanded details of the crash, Kass insisted, "They *didn't* crash. One train sort of kissed the other"!

Kass Pollock's devotion to duty was matched only by Irish-born James Patrick "Smelly" Kelly, who, in his sniffing heyday during the forties and fifties, was officially known as the superintendent of subway structures. Actually, Kelly's job was to patrol the 300 miles of IND-line tracks sniffing for strange odors (potential gas leaks), eyeing leaky tunnels (he also was known as "Leaky" Kelly), and testing rock or soil on which the tracks rested.

On a good day, Kelly would find at least one malevolent odor and a couple of leaks, and nobody was prouder of his ability to detect them than James Patrick himself. "Quick ears, good nose, better feet— those are the requirements of my job."

Kelly patrolled the TA's tracks for more than thirty years and established several subway records. His biggest accomplishment, in more ways than one, occurred at the IND's 42nd Street station at Sixth Avenue. Kelly was summoned there because of bizarre reports that an elephantine odor was permeating the entire length of the underground station.

"I had heard elephant jokes in my time," said Kelly, "but this story was on the level."

Well, not quite on the level. Several feet under ground level Kelly discovered that there was, in fact, a distinctly zoological aroma covering both the express and local tracks. "In a word," said Kelly, "it smelled like elephants. But how could elephants get into the subway?"

With Sherlock Holmesian fervor, Kelly launched his investigations. He walked back and forth through the tunnel several times. Next he covered the same footage above ground, carefully eyeing the surface structures. Then he recalled a bit of history—and solved the mystery.

"I remembered that the old Hippodrome arena was at the corner of 43rd Street and Sixth Avenue. They had circuses there and used to bury the elephant dung somewhere in the subbasement garbage bins. That was fine until one day years later a water main busted and we had a whole new ball game."

When the water main burst it soaked the long-buried elephant dung and the fumes permeated the IND station.

Kelly was only one of several TA employees who have patrolled the tracks in search of sagging pavement, stained walls, and dangerous odors, but none ever has approached his record for accuracy and reliability. "In thirty years in the railroad business," said TA chairman Charles Patterson, "I have never encountered a man with the peculiar talents of Mr. Kelly."

Describing his job, Smelly once put it this way: "Mostly you walk. You make regular inspection trips beneath gasoline storage tanks of service stations, beneath raw chemical factories, beneath storage areas for manufactured gas. You check areas known to form pockets of sewer gas, and areas beneath new construction jobs where a steam shovel might scrape gas mains.

"Sometimes a guy calls in and says he smelled something on a certain train which made him dizzy. You intercept the train and find some guy sitting in the corner with a ten-gallon jug of gasoline. You get characters like that up into the street fast. You'd be surprised how many people think nothing of riding the subways with explosive liquids."

In his book *The World beneath the City*, Robert Daley wrote, "If

Smelly Kelly did not exist he would have to be invented. . . . Only a Smelly Kelly, following his nose along the track, can find, identify and obviate fumes before they attain lethal concentrations."

Before his retirement Kelly broke in more than sixty qualified sniffers, saved at least two workers' lives in the tunnels, caught a two-and-a-half-foot eel, a ten-inch trout, forty killifish ("always dead when caught"), and a pack of rats.

Less well known than Smelly but no less ardent was another TA employee, Frank Turdik, who worked for the IRT division, supplying motor cars for maintenance trains. Turdik had a special affection for the IRT's passenger cars known in the transit trade as the "Low Vs," (for low voltage). By the mid-sixties the TA had decided that the ancient Low Vs were ready for the scrapheap. Turdik strongly objected and was determined to save as many of the Low Vs as possible. The question was how to hide a full-sized subway car, let alone a dozen of them coupled together.

Turdik had the answer. A veteran of the system, he knew every mile of track and remembered that there were unused storage tracks in the tunnel under the Esplanade on the IRT Dyre Avenue line, in a distant area of the Bronx. "What made these tracks even more useful," said Don Harold of the TA public relations department, "was the fact that they were in a tunnel, with a wall separating the storage tracks from the platform."

Turdik maneuvered several Low-V cars up to the Pelham Parkway tunnel where they were safe for the moment. But there was one catch. The missing cars remained on the TA's master inventory list.

A TA supervisor in charge of chasing down potential scrap noticed the cars on the inventory one day and wondered why they hadn't been scrapped. "You can't scrap what you can't find," he was told.

At this point the supervisor decided to check out every single track on the system. A week later he had not found the missing rolling stock. Then it dawned on him that he had forgotten to search out one piece of track on the IRT division.

"I'm off to the Dyre Avenue line tunnel," he told an aide.

That was a crucial mistake. The aide was a close friend and ally of Turdik in the surreptitious "Save the Low Vs" campaign. The minute the supervisor left his office at Jay Street in Brooklyn, the aide phoned Turdik. "You better move the Low Vs," he warned, "because You Know Who is on the way to the Dyre Avenue tunnel."

147

Turdik sped to the rescue of his hidden train and deftly arranged to move the Low Vs to the IRT's 180th Street storage yard where they were placed, unnoticed, in a remote location.

In the meantime, the supervisor arrived at the Dyre Avenue line tunnel only to find an empty tunnel, and returned to Brooklyn thoroughly perplexed about the disappearance of the Low Vs. Turdik persevered with his juggling act. Then one day in the mid-sixties the Transit Authority sent out a memorandum to employees to find a few cars that would be useful as a "Museum Train."

To the amazement of TA officials, Turdik moved a five-car train comprised of "Museum" Low-V cars to the 207th Street yard. "That wasn't all," Don Harold recalled. "Turdik managed to save all his Low Vs in one way or another. He realized that the TA didn't have much money for the repair of work cars so he made sure that whenever an old work car broke down, one of his beloved, functioning Low Vs would turn up as its replacement."

One of the most unusual railroaders is the Reverend Francis J. Cosgrove, probably the only priest who is also a qualified motorman.

Cosgrove, Jesuit associate pastor of St. Ignatius Loyola Church, 84th Street and Park Avenue, is also chaplain for many Catholic groups in the Transit Authority. He became interested in the subways in the late 1940s when he lived in the Bronx and used the old Third Avenue el to commute to Fordham University.

"A classmate's father was in charge of training motormen on the el," explained Cosgrove, "and one day he invited me down for the grand tour."

One thing led to another, and soon Cosgrove was getting private instruction and practicing on empty trains. "It was the greatest training," he said. "The old el cars had primitive air brakes, nothing like today's equipment. It was like learning to drive on a car with manual shift. We had to use extreme caution. Except in certain areas, like around curves, there were no signals. You just had to eyeball the train in front of you."

Later, transit employees on their own time ran Cosgrove through the official motorman's course. He passed with flying colors. Several times a year he sharpens his skills by operating a work train or an empty train enroute to the yards.

He remembers an incident at the 86th Street station near his church.

Cosgrove was there to pick up a work train and take it to the yard. He was not wearing his clerical clothing and the token seller, who knew him, asked him to watch the booth for a while.

"I was in there pushing tokens and a fellow came down who works in a store in the neighborhood. He stared at me without saying anything but I could see a big question mark on his face."

A few minutes later Cosgrove took out his train and operated it to the 125th Street station, where he had to lean out a window to press a button alerting a dispatcher to his destination. "The same fellow was waiting on the platform there. Instead of a question mark this time I saw a giant exclamation point. It was like the legend, in the Koran, of Mohammed looking in all directions and seeing the face of the angel Gabriel. If he had a guilty conscience about anything he probably thought he was being haunted by this face of a priest."

Another time, Father Cosgrove piloted a work train into a station in the early morning hours, brought the cars to a stop, and called out to a passenger on the platform: "Come aboard, rabbi, this is the clergy special!" With the rabbi aboard, the train pulled out, leaving an astonished group of passengers on the platform.

Cosgrove is a native New Yorker and has spent most of his life in the city. A few years ago, however, he was assigned to a mission in the Caroline Islands in the South Pacific.

"Some friends of mine sent me a few subway kerosene marker lanterns. At night, when I was out on the water, I'd have them hung on the fish trap off shore. The IRT signal took me straight to my house."

For all he knows, the old IRT lights are still guiding the islanders to port. "During typhoons, when every other lamp blew out, they always stayed lit."

Cosgrove considers the entire subway system his parish and is well liked up and down the line. "He's the kind of friend who's always there when you need him and religion doesn't matter," said one long time TA employee.

Cosgrove has held special masses in the TA building during a strike, when employees were on twenty-four-hour duty and could not go to church. He's often gone to the side of transit policemen shot while on duty.

But it's the lighter moments he likes to recall. Like the time he was with a crew taking a string of derelict cars to the yard for scrapping and the yardmaster had not been told of their arrival.

"He saw this thing coming down the track—a train of old wrecks pulled by a diesel—and he knew one thing: he didn't want it cluttering up his yard. He started swearing a blue streak. One of the men told him there was a priest on board, but he didn't believe it and swore even louder."

When cars are transferred from one place to another, the process requires a pink form. "The crew prevailed on me to put on my clerical clothing and take the pink slip to the yardmaster," Cosgrove said.

Upon seeing Father Cosgrove, the yardmaster politely turned his blue streak to cautious amber and, finally, a healthy full-speed-ahead green. Father Cosgrove continued on his merry way, enjoying, like all subway buffs, his favorite set of electric trains, the New York City subway system.

The Biggest Bust
and Bargain of All

It costs approximately $200 million to build just one mile of subway in contemporary New York. But in 1940 New York City paid only $1,783,577.03 for a four-and-a-quarter-mile stretch of existing four-track right-of-way that ranks even today as one of the most magnificent rapid transit runs in the world, boasting station buildings constructed of concrete in renaissance, mission, and classic style.

To thousands of New Yorkers it is known as the Dyre Avenue (Bronx) line, but old-timers still refer to the IRT route as "the old Westchester run" because in its youth the tracks belonged to the New York, Westchester & Boston Railway Company, an offshoot of the New York, New Haven & Hartford. Needless to say, the N.Y., W. & B. never was intended to be part of the city's subway system.

Soon after the beginning of the twentieth century, directors of the successful New York, New Haven & Hartford Railroad were on the lookout for more and better ways of turning a profit. New York City comprised five boroughs, each of which had growing numbers of potential customers for their railway. The New Haven's directors were most interested in the Bronx, because of its proximity to the New Haven line as well as prospects for growth in that borough.

"They were looking for a plushier trade than the nickel business of the subway," said one observer of the rail scene. And they set about building one of America's finest electric railways.

When it was opened in May 1912, the N.Y., W. & B. *was* the best railway of its kind in America. Trains sped on a four-track right-of-way, along comfortable, deeply ballasted roadbeds over rails that gave the effect of a smooth, endless carpet. The railroad incorporated the most modern devices at a time when tremendous strides were being made in train technology. The directors refused to be overly thrifty and opted for a four-track line when a two-track right-of-way would have been adequate. They planned on a sensible long-range basis rather than for short-term benefits. And, finally, their area of operations encompassed one of the wealthiest and fastest-growing urban-suburban corridors in North America.

Few projects that seemed so certain of success have failed as egregiously as the Westchester, and the roots of the problem go back to just past the middle of the nineteenth century. The railway boom was approaching its peak then, and investors began casting their eyes on the lucrative metropolitan New York market in hopes of building additional steel links between Manhattan and the outside world.

Among the more attractive possibilities were the Southern Westchester and the New York, Housatonic & Northern railroad companies. The Southern Westchester, when plans were fully realized, would operate from the edge of Manhattan—and the juncture of the Harlem and East rivers—to White Plains in Westchester. At that point it would meet the New York, Housatonic & Northern. Joined together, the two railroads would then allow New Yorkers to ride all the way to Danbury, Connecticut, and, linking with other lines along the way, eventually to Boston.

The two companies merged in 1872 and construction of a modest one-track right-of-way was launched in Westchester County. Two years later the merged railroads folded. However, the disaster of the Southern Westchester and the New York, Housatonic & Northern merely inspired others to work on developing a new line from Manhattan to Westchester.

In the mid-1870s another group incorporated the New York, Westchester & Boston Railroad. Their plan was to run a line from the Harlem River through the Bronx, which then still was a part of Westchester County, with assorted branch lines to Long Island Sound and Elmsford.

"Together with the lines then operating—the New York Central & Hudson River, the New York & Harlem, and the New York, New Haven & Hartford—the New York, Westchester & Boston would form part of a rail network which virtually would guarantee the development of Westchester County as a major suburban residential area," wrote railway historian Roger Arcara in a book about the line.

But again the timing was wrong. Those who hoped to capitalize on the growth of New York City, which had consolidated in 1898 into five boroughs, had to wait for better financial times after the turn of the twentieth century.

Even then another venture, the New York & Portchester Railroad Company, failed to reach its goal. The roadbed was actually graded in 1906 and a bridge constructed over a creek dividing the towns of Harrison and Mamaroneck in Westchester. The bridge still stands, and the line itself didn't really die but, rather, was incorporated into the suddenly rejuvenated New York, Westchester & Boston which reemerged in 1906, after quietly acquiring property for years before.

This time the N.Y., W. & B. was being guided by Charles S. Mellen, president of the New York, New Haven & Hartford Railroad. Mellen's cronies, among the richest men in the country at the time, included J. P. Morgan and William Rockefeller, brother of John D. Rockefeller, Sr. In fact Morgan and Rockefeller helped put the Westchester back on the tracks in 1906 when they headed a committee that bought controlling interest in the New York, Westchester & Boston stock for $11 million.

Following a bit of litigation in which the Westchester swallowed up the New York & Portchester, Mellen and pals were ready to really roll—with elaborate prime plans, alternates, and lots of money with which to implement them. They could have utilized the facilities of the Grand Central terminal then under construction at 42nd Street and Park Avenue in Manhattan as their terminus or they could develop a new one. Unwisely, although it didn't appear so at the time, they decided to build a new one.

Few could have challenged the logic in 1909. Even then the Grand

152

Central terminal was overtaxed with rail traffic. Commuters from other lines who used the Manhattan station were screaming over the high cost of riding the railroads into the city when 5-cent subway rides were available in many parts of the city.

Mellen and his colleagues were aware of these complaints and believed that they had the answer. Instead of running the New York, Westchester & Boston Railway all the way to Grand Central, they would terminate the line in the Bronx. Their rationale was that they could lure commuters by lower prices, since riders would be able to connect with the city's 5-cent subways in the Bronx and ride the rest of the way to midtown Manhattan on the new underground. Knowing that much of the line would operate in what then was virtually uninhabited land, they nevertheless agreed to build a high-capacity railroad with four tracks, hoping that business and development would soon come.

Although the line was being built during the golden age of steam, Mellen decided to make the Westchester the only standard railroad in the area designed exclusively for electric power. Speed, efficiency, and beauty were the passwords. The Westchester scored on two out of three. It never really got a chance to prove how efficient it was.

"Though it was conceded that no really heavy volume of traffic was expected at first," wrote Roger Arcara, "the New Haven Railroad management at that time commanded sufficient resources to be able to sustain such an expensive undertaking while awaiting development of the much greater patronage the foreseeable future might bring."

Now came the key question for Mellen: "Where do we start and where do we terminate?" Since Grand Central Station had already been ruled out, the planners decided on the Bronx. They wanted the Westchester's terminus to link directly with the Interborough Rapid Transit (IRT) for the cheap connection to the city's subway. They searched for a prime location and finally found one at East 132nd Street and Willis Avenue.

The site was chosen for several reasons, not merely for the link with the IRT. It was deep in the South Bronx adjacent to the New Haven's Harlem River freight yards and passenger station. This enabled the Westchester to share the trackage of the New Haven's Harlem River Branch until West Farms junction, where the Westchester turned off to its own route.

At the Willis Avenue-East 132nd Street terminal, the Westchester connected directly to the IRT's shuttle elevated trains that ran to 129th Street, Manhattan (the Third Avenue el). Given a choice between Grand Central and a higher fare or the Bronx terminal and a lower fare, passengers by the thousands were expected to switch to the Westchester.

From Willis Avenue-East 132nd Street, the Westchester snaked up the Bronx. The second stop would be Port Morris (East 135th Street), followed by Casanova (Leggett Avenue), Hunt's Point (Hunt's Point Avenue), Westchester Avenue, 180th Street, Morris Park, Pelham Parkway, Gun Hill Road, Baychester Avenue, and Dyre Avenue. From there the route drifted over the city line north into Westchester County.

So ambitious was the project that the Westchester didn't need a press agent; its blueprints spoke volumes. For example, newsmen did not have to be coaxed into believing that the line would load and unload a great volume of passengers. All they had to do was glance at plans for the huge waiting rooms and the fact that freight facilities were virtually ignored. As for the speed potential of the line, Mellen merely had to take an inquisitive journalist for a tour of the construction sites to show that speed was guaranteed because designers had eliminated all sharp curves, steep grades, and grade crossings. They had learned their lessons well from the past.

Not to be overlooked was the cosmetic touch. Stations would get the grand architectural treatment. They would be, as one observer put it, "monuments, constructed of concrete in renaissance, mission or classic style." Or, as Roger Arcara put it, "The Westchester would have mansions where other lines were satisfied with sheds."

Structures built within the New York City limits—and now a part of the IRT system—were of the modified Mission type. Wherever possible, trees, shrubs, and hedges were planted around the stations. Terrazo facing was used in all station interiors, including the ticket booths. The respected *Electric Railway Journal* commented in June 1912:

"The passenger stations and signal towers may be said to constitute the most attractive group of way structures possessed by any electric or steam railroad in the United States. The result was made possible by the progressive attitude of the company, which was ambitious to erect buildings which would add to rather than detract from the expected high-class suburban development of this territory. . . . Many of the stations have cafes, haberdasheries and other stores in addition to the usual magazine and candy stands. Some stations have a room for baggage handling. At certain places the station building is being utilized as a natural headquarters for the local real estate development."

Since Mellen's New Haven Railroad had just electrified its own line with 11,000-volt, 25-cycle current, it immediately had a surplus of power and sold it to the Westchester. All that was needed now was to make the line operational. The first drills were put in motion in 1909, and construction proceeded rapidly. Instead of circling obstacles such as boulders and hills, engineers on the Westchester chose to bore right through them. Every item, from signal towers to viaducts, seemed to be built a little stronger, a bit more beautiful, and somewhat bigger than the best seen until then.

On May 29, 1912 the elephantine—at the time nobody dared call it a white elephant—project made its official debut. It ran from East 180th Street and Morris Park Avenue, near West Farms Square in the Bronx, to North Avenue, New Rochelle, Westchester. Much station and track work still remained to be done, but nobody noticed that. What caught the eye were the majestic stations, the broad, smooth right-of-way, and the splendidly speedy trains. The Boston & Westchester had purchased thirty steel cars, seventy feet long, which were equipped to draw current through the overhead pantographs.

The big green rolling stock, each of which could seat seventy-eight passengers, was equipped with powerful Westinghouse motors that could move the trains at speeds of sixty mph. Everything else about the cars' appointments was first-rate, from the electric lamps to white enameled ceilings, shaded windows, and roomy seats. From every aspect, the Westchester's cars were a 1912 commuter's dream-come-true.

Why, then, did the Westchester dream turn out to be the New Haven's nightmare?

One mistake—the fatal placing of the terminus in the Bronx instead of at Grand Central—was enough to convert the most perfect railroad of its day into a money-sapping failure. "Passengers," wrote rail analyst Bernard Linder, "given a choice between Grand Central and a higher fare, or the Bronx terminal and a lower fare, chose the former. They hollered louder when fares went up, but that's all—

they paid rather than change in the Bronx. The building boom came to Westchester, all right; apartment buildings sprouted on pastures and in woods, but not many of them elected to locate along the swift, low-priced line which made a change in the Bronx necessary."

At first, the officials who converged daily at the company's magnificent office building (now used by the New York City Transit Authority for field offices and police district offices) adjacent to the huge East 180th Street station were sanguine about the receipts. In its first full year of operation (1913) the Westchester carried 2,874,484 passengers. By 1920 the figure had more than doubled, and in 1928 over 14 million paying customers rode the line. But while the numbers were impressive on paper they failed to reassure bankers, who had been led to believe 140 million rather than 14 million would be a reasonable passenger total for a year such as 1928. The bottom line, year in and year out, failed to produce what the Westchester's supporters needed most—a profit. Rush-hour traffic was brisk but not substantial enough to offset the virtually nonexistent business at other times of the day.

In placing the Westchester's terminal in the Bronx, miles from mid-Manhattan, Mellen and his colleagues were operating on the Commodore Vanderbilt theory of city growth anticipation. In the middle of the nineteenth century when Cornelius Vanderbilt, boss of the New York & Harlem (later the New York Central) Railroad, considered a site for a new Manhattan terminal for his line as well as the New York, New Haven & Hartford and the Hudson River Railroad, New York City's center was near the southern tip of Manhattan Island. At that time the area around 42nd Street (where Grand Central Terminal is located) was regarded by New Yorkers as far distant as the North Pole. Yet Commodore Vanderbilt insisted on building his main depot in the suburbs of 42nd Street on the theory that New York City inevitably must expand northward. "Some day in the not-too-distant-future," Commodore Vanderbilt predicted, "Grand Central Station will be in the center of the city."

Vanderbilt's "folly" soon turned into Vanderbilt's gold mine. By the turn of the twentieth century it had become apparent that the commodore was correct in his assessment of the city's growth pattern. Mellen took that theory one step further. If Grand Central Terminal was the center of the business district in 1920 and expansion continued in the direction of Westchester, it was reasonable to assume that by 1930 the business and commercial district would extend to the South Bronx.

Mellen's theory was doomed with the city's first zoning law, written into the books in 1916 at a time when the Westchester was still hoping to have the Harlem River freight yards someday surrounded by tall office buildings. The new law limited Manhattan's commercial area to the precincts *south* of Central Park's southerly (59th Street) boundary. "Westchester's planners," wrote Roger Arcara, "could not reasonably be expected to foresee this development; to them it seemed, and rightly so at the time, that New York's business district was destined to go on expanding northward on Manhattan Island until, perhaps by the middle of the 20th Century, it would cover most of the Island, with its northern portion somewhere around 125th Street, right across the river from the New York, Westchester & Boston Railway."

Once the zoning law was approved, the Westchester's directors realized that Mellen's plan was obsolete and new thinking was necessary. The natural solution was to extend the line from its Harlem River freight yard depot into Manhattan and south down to the midtown commercial district. All the Westchester needed to accomplish this was money. Therefore, the solution at once was no longer simple.

Ideally, the Manhattan extension could be built from the line's profits and thereby build still more profits. But no matter how the Westchester's accountants juggled the books, there simply was never a profit with which to work; therefore, no extension could or would be built. Thus the Westchester's depot remained in the Bronx, and the line continued to operate only by the grace of its parent, the New York, New Haven & Hartford.

Patience and money simultaneously ran out on the New Haven in 1935 when the line reorganized and began to liquidate its unprofitable holdings. New Haven officials claimed they spent $50 million on the Westchester in a futile effort to put it in the black. Hence the N.Y., W. & B. was the first to go.

In a last, desperate attempt to revive the line, the Westchester was put by court order under the trusteeship of Clinton L. Bardo, an efficient railroad man who had been general manager of the New Haven. Bardo had some sound ideas for saving the Westchester, but his reorganization plans required money. There was no cash available, and on April 15, 1937 the line was declared irrevocably insolvent. Less than four months later Bardo died. The railroad itself enjoyed its last clickety-clack at about midnight, December 31, 1937 when some fifty passengers, most of whom were railfans, rode the final run.

The big bust that was Mellen's idea turned out to be the biggest bargain in subway history, considering that the New Haven invested $50 million in the Westchester and New York City paid less than $2 million for a major portion of the line. However, the transfer of the N.Y., W. & B. to the Board of Transportation did not come easy. When the Westchester ceased to operate after nearly twenty-five years, the 26,000 passengers who had been riding the railroad each day protested vehemently.

"Bring back the Westchester!" the commuters pleaded but in vain. Several ideas for resuscitating the railroad failed to crystalize. Ironically, the plan that eventually was implemented originated with New York City legislators and was to sever Westchester County completely from use of the Westchester's tracks. In the late thirties residents of the Bronx demanded that the line's right-of-way be annexed by the New York City Board of Transportation and linked with the then burgeoning city subway system.

Unlike other moves to save the Westchester—one such pathetic campaign was launched by employees of the line who offered to work for nothing until an angel was found—the plan to buy it for New York City gained momentum. Still more impetus was provided in June 1940 when New York City bought the Brooklyn-Manhattan Transit Company (BMT) and the Interborough Rapid Transit Company (IRT).

Having united the BMT, IND, and IRT, New York City now owned the greatest rapid transit system of any municipality in the world. Mayor Fiorello LaGuardia and his constituents were appropriately proud of their subways and looked to further expansion. One such possibility was an extension of the IND Bronx division past its 205th Street terminal farther eastward in the borough. This could be done for an estimated $2,500,000 and would probably have been done had it not been learned that the existing N.Y., W. & B. tracks within the Bronx from East 174th Street to the Mount Vernon (Westchester) border could be obtained for only $1,783,577. LaGuardia was persuaded that it would be more practical to buy the Westchester than plunge ahead with an extension of the IND.

The 205th Street extension was shelved, and New York City instead took over the Bronx portion of the N.Y., W. & B., installed a third rail, and assigned twenty Third Avenue elevated cars to the run. To make the adjustment, several mechanical alterations had to be applied to the Westchester's right-of-way. Unused BMT signals were hooked up on the Westchester route; clearances were adjusted for the wooden, open-platform elevated cars—a terrible comedown from the high-speed N.Y., W. & B. trains—and finally, the name of the line itself was changed to Dyre Avenue.

The new monicker was given because the city's latest rapid transit addition ran between East 180th Street and the Dyre Avenue station, the last stop in the Bronx. The first train rolled out of the terminal on May 15, 1941 and the shuttle remained in business with the antiquated rolling stock until 1954. Veterans of the Westchester had hoped that somehow the bankrupt line's passenger cars could be used, but the equipage was not meant for city subway service. Some fifty of the cars were returned to the New Haven and rebuilt for local service in Boston. Most of the remaining forty-five were sold to the United States government for wartime use, as emergency transport for workers in war-related industries.

Meanwhile, the Dyre Avenue line remained a curio to all but the few passengers who rode the shuttle during wartime and the immediate postwar years. "Even people who work for the city transit system are unfamiliar with it," was a comment in *Transit Magazine*, the journal of New York's subway workers. The Dyre Avenue shuttle was unique among all of the city's lines: it didn't always run. Every night it would close down at 1 A.M. and wake up again at 5:30 in the morning. What's more, its railway clerks worked only one shift, after which the conductors collected fares and made change right on the train in the finest Toonerville manner.

Slowly but surely, the Dyre Avenue line did what its predecessor could never do: it got better and better; healthier by the year, so that by 1955 *Transit Magazine* observed: "The white elephant's skin is darkening already. And, barring the unforeseen, the Dyre Avenue line will soon be more than paying its way." It would, too, especially after track connections were made in 1957 with the IRT's White Plains Road line north of the East 180th Street station. Now trains from the IRT Seventh Avenue (Broadway) line could run through, over the old Westchester route to Dyre Avenue.

In time the Transit Authority, successor to the old Board of Trans-

159

portation, switched the Dyre Avenue line to the Lexington Avenue IRT tracks on Manhattan's East Side. Now designated the "No. 5 Lexington Avenue express," it runs between Dyre Avenue in the Bronx and South Ferry, Atlantic Avenue, or Utica Avenue, Brooklyn. "The orphan has grown up," a Transit Authority official boasted, "and all New York City subway riders can be proud."

Westchester commuters were less fortunate. Their pleas for restoration of the N.Y., W. & B. continued until 1939 when the first pieces of equipment were removed. With each month, another chunk of what was once America's finest railway was hacked away by the voracious scrap workers until all that remained were a few vestiges of the line, most of them on the IRT's Dyre Avenue run. The 180th Street station, for one, stands handsomely, as it did in the early part of the century; likewise the enormous Morris Park station, built in 1912, which appears more suited to a European branch line than the No. 5 Lexington express.

To this day the Dyre Avenue line in its own way remains the most attractive and charming line on the city's transit network, although it is not likely that you will see the occasional rabbit scuttling away at the approach of a train, or the arboreal splendor that characterized the Westchester route when it wended its way through the last undeveloped area in the Bronx.

But as long as the Dyre Avenue line remains in business it will stand as a monument to the biggest bust—and bargain—in the annals of municipal transit.

The Freight Line,
the Farm Line,
and the Line That
Went to Sea

Only one branch of the New York City subway system has enjoyed the triple distinction of *(a)* being asked to carry a fully grown whale through its tunnels, *(b)* being the only railroad in the world where freight cars wore corsets, and *(c)* being the only New York rail line to turn a profit for more than fifty years. This remarkable line is known affectionately to Transit Authority officials as the SoB. And for good reason, because the SoB is the South Brooklyn Railway Company (officially listed as SBK, however, to avoid confusion with the South Buffalo Railroad), the TA's very own freight railroad, whose total rolling stock consists of two diesel-electric locomotives.

Nearly eighty years old, the SoB operates over six and one-half miles of Brooklyn track—including a short stretch of tunnel which it shares with the BMT Fourth Avenue subway. The SoB's run begins at portside along lower New York Bay. The waterfront yard at 39th Street and Second Avenue is adjacent to Bush Terminal, one of the large freight junctions in the country. From there the SoB heads west and then south, terminating at the TA's vast repair shop and yards in Coney Island.

The SoB's experience with the whale developed because of the line's proximity to the Coney Island amusement park. The whale had been killed in European waters, embalmed, and shipped to New York City for display at Coney Island. The SoB strapped the whale and its container atop a flatcar and directed the unique parcel toward the Fourth Avenue subway tunnel. It is an ancient tunnel built along extremely narrow lines—too narrow to accommodate the whale in its glass enclosure—and the SoB was unable to complete the trip.

The whale episode is symptomatic of the SoB's congenital problem: insufficient hauling space. That's how the TA's freight cars came to wear corsets. Unlike subway cars, freight cars have a tendency to develop middle-age bulge. Sometimes the bulge reached such obese proportions that the freight cars simply could not negotiate the tunnel. Instead of throwing in the towel George F. Preiss, who was freight manager of the line, and his brain trust found a solution. Wire was wrapped around the pudgy cars and then the corset was tightened until the men of the SoB were sure that the freight car could negotiate the tunnel. "It cost us four or five hundred a year for wire," said Preiss.

In its time the SoB has hauled some unusual pieces of freight. Once an Army plane crashed in Pennsylvania but the inquiry into the disaster was conducted at Floyd Bennett Field at the southern tip of Flatbush Avenue in Brooklyn. Since the airport was in the vicinity of the SoB's Coney Island terminal, the pieces of plane were shipped on the TA freight line.

Before Prohibition the SoB did a terrific business with breweries such as Trommer's and Piel's. The SoB also prospered during Prohibition, when it hauled a huge tonnage of wine grapes for Brooklynites who made their own. Those days the line also picked up mountains of ashes from factories, rubbish from all sorts of plants, and hauled these, for a fee, away from the premises. The ashes were carried to the Coney Island marshlands and dropped there, where they became valuable fill. Today thousands of homes in and around Coney Island rest securely upon these ashes and rubbish.

The SoB is credited with another freight first. In 1929 it instituted door-to-door delivery of carload freight lots by automobile trailer truck. "This," said Joe Harrington, "was some ten years before other railroads initiated such a service. The idea came because originally it operated freight trolleys, which, in the heyday of the trolley in Brooklyn, could snake through to almost any section of the city."

The flavor of a small railroad permeates the quarters of the SoB. "None of the flurry of a subway station exists in its offices," said Harrington. This has been the case "ever since the SoB emerged from its antecedent roads, including the Prospect Park and Coney Island Railroad, whose trackage ran along McDonald Avenue to Coney Island. Thus the SoB is the only freight line in the world that uses both former trolley tracks and subway tunnels," according to J. Porter Reilly, a member of the Transit Authority staff and author of *Doughty, Dazzling Diesels.*

Although the road owns no freight cars, it hauls boxcars from all parts of the United States and Canada, making virtual doorstep delivery to industrial customers whose facilities abut the right-of-way. Normally freight is lightered or floated to Brooklyn on barges from Hoboken by the New York Dock Railroad Company, where SoB locomotives pick them up and bring them to their destination. Speed along SoB tracks is kept down to five miles per hour.

Sometimes the line's freight cars are pulled the "wrong way" against vehicular traffic along McDonald Avenue. Equally strange to see is the SoB's procedure of switching the locomotive from front to back enroute from Bush Terminal to Coney Island. For the first half-mile of surface track before it reaches the subway tunnel, a diesel pulls the freight cars. Before entering the mile-long uphill tunnel, the diesel is detached, wrong-ended, and then pushes the boxcars over subway tracks.

"This is a safety measure," said Andrew DeLuca, freight traffic manager during the line's more recent operation. "On the open right-of-way, our engineer has visibility along his entire train; in the tunnel, he takes precautions against a break-away rolling downhill behind him. With the diesel pushing, the possibility of any break-away is averted."

The SoB's standard motive power for the first half-century was electric locomotives that resembled trolley cars with nothing more than a motorman's cab, a trolley pole in the middle, and a minicaboose in the back. Since the SoB is regulated by the Interstate Commerce Commission, the trolley locomotives were put through monthly inspections. By the mid-fifties it had become harder and harder to pass these inspections and, finally, diesel locomotives were introduced. In March 1955 one of the SoB's oldest locomotives (dating back to 1904) was scrapped. The line now has two diesels and no longer utilizes electric locomotives.

Although the SoB was a profit-maker for more years than most freight railroads, many of its profitable sources of revenue have vanished. It no longer can go in for scavenging the way it did when it was hauling fill for Coney Island. And the wine-grape tonnage has continually diminished as the art of wine-making died out in Brooklyn. But one customer not likely to take its business elsewhere is the TA itself. All the heavy equipment and supplies for the Coney Island yards are freighted in by the SoB.

Reilly noted that "when the TA obtains new cars they are floated in from Hoboken on barges to Bush Terminal at 50th Street and First Avenue. Here, the New York Dock Railway Company unloads them and moves the equipment to 38th Street and Second Avenue. At this point the SoB diesels take over to shuttle them to the BMT station at Ninth Avenue where they are electrified to make the last leg of their journey over regular TA tracks to the Coney Island yards for preservice preparation and testing.

Just how long the SoB can remain in business is a moot question. But in its own curious way the line Brooklynites call their freight version of the Toonerville Trolley is as popular as it ever was. On September 20, 1975 the Electric Railroaders Association ran a "fan" special over the route that drew a capacity crowd. As one rail buff observed: "You don't often get a chance to ride a freight line within the city; and one that once tried to carry a whole whale and boxcars that wore corsets!"

In its own way the Staten Island Rapid Transit line (SIRT) is the most offbeat passenger route in the five boroughs. Unlike the BMT, IRT, or IND lines, the SIRT never rolled outside of Staten Island. In contrast with the other lines, the SIRT always has suggested a farmland railroad, meandering from terminal to terminal at a slow pace.

From the very beginnings of New York City, Staten Island has been the stepchild borough across the bay. During the Revolutionary War, Staten Island remained loyal to King George. It has remained mostly rural while the rest of New York City is the epitome of urbanity. While much of Gotham traditionally votes Democrat, the good burghers of Staten Island go Republican.

In fact, Staten Islanders frequently even think of themselves more as New Jerseyites than New Yorkers. This, of course, can be explained by the fact that Staten Island sits right next to New Jersey while mainland New York looms far on the horizon. Were it not for an absurd boat race in 1687 Staten Island *would* be a part of New Jersey today. At the time both New York and New Jersey were vying for the island and it was decided that ownership would go to the colony that won a sailboat race from one end of the island to the other. New York's Captain Christopher Billop was the winner and New Jersey lost a very valuable piece of real estate. Ferry service began as early as 1713 but the first regular commuter service began in 1810 when Cornelius Vanderbilt, who was to gain fame as the boss of the

New York Central Railroad, launched a ferry service. The sixteen-year-old Vanderbilt, later to be known as "the Commodore," was on to a good thing. Staten Island (also known as Richmond, in honor of the Duke of Richmond) already had become a haven for transplanted New Yorkers, as well as others seeking a relaxed life within a relatively short ride of mad Manhattan. By the 1830s planners and investors realized that what the island needed to link its growing but far-flung communities was a railroad.

The first serious attempt at building one was organized in 1836 when Minthorne Tompkins, Harmon B. Cropsey, John Westervelt, John Thompson, and Richard Littell were granted a charter for the Staten Island Railroad. There was one catch; work had to begin on the new line within two years or the charter would be revoked. Work never did begin and the charter *was* revoked.

The second attempt at building a line, connecting Tottenville on the south of the island and Stapleton on the north, was developed in 1851. This time the project was promoted by both Staten Islanders and prominent citizens of nearby Perth Amboy, New Jersey. Like its predecessor, the second proposed Staten Island railway was almost immediately derailed by financial difficulties.

Searching for an "angel," the promoters approached Cornelius Vanderbilt, who had made a lot of money in the ferry business. In fact, at the time he was sought out by the Staten Island Railroad planners Vanderbilt had control of all the east shore ferries but he had never taken the plunge into railroading.

Vanderbilt came through with the money and in 1860 the line that eventually would become a part of the New York City transit system opened for business. It connected the towns of Vanderbilt's Landing (now Clifton) and Eltingville, seven and one-half miles south.

The railroad was a source of conversation even before its official opening. Its unique iron locomotive, the Albert Journea, named for the president of the railroad, caused quite a stir, as reported in the March 21, 1860 edition of the *Staten Island Gazette:*

"The locomotive has been indulging itself, since its arrival, by making pleasant little trips on the railroad as far as New Dorp, and has been quite useful in conveying materials . . . where required for use. Each day it is the subject of renewed comment and admiration by those who reside along the line transversed. . . . One old man among the number had never seen a locomotive. He said he lived between 'Iron Spring' and 'Skunk's Misery,' and has walked five miles to take a look. As 'She' advanced with a shriek, he jumped about a foot, and exclaimed 'I swear,' but as he was dumb thereafter, we cannot say what he thought of it."

A second locomotive was added in May 1860 and service extended to Annadale. A month later the line extended to Tottenville and the dream of a quarter century was realized. Staten Island had its railroad. But it wasn't a very pleasant dream right from the start. Revenue was slower in coming than the line's locomotives and, less than a year after it had opened, the railroad was threatened with foreclosure by the New Jersey Locomotive Works for failure to pay the bills for the two steam engines. An SOS was sent out to Commodore Vanderbilt, who responded by dispatching his son to Staten Island as the line's receiver and making some adjustments with ferry operators to synchronize their arrivals and departures with the railroad.

But good fortune never would smile on the Staten Island line and one of a long list of tragedies occurred on July 30, 1871 when the ferryboat *Westfield,* co-operated by the railroad, blew up at the Whitehall Street pier in lower Manhattan, killing sixty-six passengers. It also killed the railroad for a number of years.

The line made a comeback in 1883 when Robert Garrett, president of the Baltimore & Ohio Railroad was approached as a backer of a revived Staten Island Railway. Garrett realized that the Baltimore & Ohio needed a railhead in New York City and immediately supported the plan. The new company was called the Staten Island Rapid Transit Railroad Company, becoming the first to apply the words "rapid transit" to a railroad. Thus the country's oldest railroad to become a rapid transit operation merged with the Baltimore & Ohio, America's oldest railroad.

On July 31, 1884, thirteen years and a day after the old line had ceased to operate, the SIRT began service between Clifton and Tompkinsville. New lines were added, and by the early 1890s it appeared that boom years were just ahead. But they never materialized. Trolley cars were introduced to the island before the turn of the century and they began cutting into the SIRT patronage. By 1899 the railroad was in big trouble again. It went bankrupt and, this time, was bought outright by the Baltimore & Ohio for the "upset price" of $2 million at an auction.

Although ridership was less than encouraging in the early years of the twentieth century, the Baltimore & Ohio bosses saw some hope in the possibility of a connection with Brooklyn across the bay. Engineers for the Brooklyn Rapid Transit Company (later the BMT) suggested that as part of the Fourth Avenue (Brooklyn) subway project a connecting subway tunnel be bored under the Narrows (lower New York Bay) to St. George in Staten Island.

The idea was well received and likely would have been pushed to fruition were it not for a freakish turn of fate involving the BRT. In November 1918 a crash on the BRT's Brighton Line at Malbone Street in Brooklyn killed ninety-seven passengers and bankrupted the line. For the moment, at least, tunneling to Staten Island was out of the question.

Meanwhile revenues took an upward turn for the SIRT in the early twenties as the island's population grew. In 1921 more than 13 million people rode the Baltimore & Ohio's rapid transit route compared to only 2,460,000 in 1907. Tunnel talk was stirring again, and this time it appeared to be so much a certainty that realtors began speaking of a Staten Island land boom to follow the new subway tunnel. In 1925 headings for the tunnel were begun and an elaborate track connection in which the SIRT would link with the BMT Sea Beach line in the Fourth Avenue tunnel had been worked out. Unfortunately the planners never cleared it with the politicians.

New York's Mayor John Hylan had been an enemy of the BRT since 1907, when he had been working as a motorman on the line and his alleged carelessness had almost killed a towerman. He was fired and bore a grudge against the line, and its successor the BMT, ever afterward. New York State's Governor Al Smith was, in 1925, owner of considerable Pennsylvania Railroad stock. A link between the Baltimore & Ohio's Staten Island line and the BMT could, conceivably, have hurt the Pennsylvania Railroad.

Cynical New York City political pundits believe that neither Hylan nor Smith wanted a Staten Island-Brooklyn rail tunnel to be realized. Work on the tunnel, which had begun in both boroughs, stopped abruptly soon after it had begun. Nobody is certain why it happened, but the project was never again resumed. Meanwhile, in anticipation of a coupling with the BMT, the SIRT had electrified the system and purchased a fleet of BMT-type cars for use on its own lines.

Despite the tunnel setback, the SIRT continued to move forward.

Grade crossings were eliminated wherever possible, and by the early forties the line was as healthy as it ever would be. But soon after World War II had ended the city began consolidating transit facilities and, in 1948, the Board of Transportation annexed the Staten Island bus routes. It immediately reduced fares and, in so doing, sliced SIRT revenues by 60 percent.

The SIRT saw the handwriting on the wall and tried to unload the entire system on the city, but the answer for the moment was negative.

Once again there was hope of a rail link to Brooklyn—this time by bridge. The Triborough Bridge and Tunnel Authority was given approval to erect a huge bridge across the Narrows and in 1964 the span was completed. Unfortunately, its most vocal supporter was Robert Moses, who had vast political clout at the time. Moses, who consistently vetoed rapid transit in favor of the private automobile, insisted that the SIRT and the BMT be kept off the bridge and, as usual, Moses triumphed.

Still the SIRT limped along, serving those Staten Islanders who appreciated a pleasant train ride to the New York ferries. When the Metropolitan Transportation Authority (MTA) annexed the Transit Authority in 1968 new life was pumped into the SIRT. A fleet of shiny silver commuter trains was installed, replacing the old BMT-type cars that had been in use since 1925.

Cosmetically the SIRT was never in better shape but its financial state was less attractive. The failure of the line to link directly by rail with Brooklyn was its most significant drawback and ridership remained dishearteningly low in the mid-seventies.

Still another blow was delivered to the SIRT late in 1975 when trainmen, angered over the MTA's refusal to grant them equal pay with their New York City subway counterparts went on strike for four months. Charges rang back and forth, among them that the MTA was deliberately sabotaging the SIRT so that it could close the line and simply operate buses on Staten Island. The strike was settled in April 1976 and service resumed.

By far the strangest rapid transit line of any of the IRT, BMT, and IND divisions of the New York City Transit Authority is the Rockaway line, which extends from the mainland of Queens at Howard Beach to the long spit of land on the Atlantic Ocean known as Rockaway and Far Rockaway. To extend its IND line to the seaside area, the TA first had to build islands in Jamaica Bay, create bird sanctuaries, dig ship channels, and develop a few lakes here and there. The result was the longest single extension of the rapid transit lines since the subway was built in 1904, adding 11.62 miles.

The Rockaway line extension was completed in June 1956, but the rail route itself dated back to 1892. It was then that the Long Island Rail Road (LIRR) drove 50,000 piles deep into the mud and sand of Jamaica Bay and built a new line across the slightly more than four miles of shallow water. The LIRR then began running trains across the short route to the Rockaways, and simultaneously began wishing that it had never got involved with the idea of bridging Jamaica Bay.

Fire became the most common hazard. The trestle, only a few feet above water most of the way, was particularly vulnerable: The hot sun dried out ties; cigarettes popped out of open windows to land on dry, creosoted wood where they smoldered for five or six hours and then burst into flame, fanned by drafts through the open lattice of the ties.

But the Rockaways had many pleasures to offer the city dweller, and throngs continued to crowd the beaches despite the LIRR and its problems. The demand was so great in 1898 that the Brooklyn Elevated Railroad Company (BERC) made a deal with the LIRR to rent the track and run summer excursion trains over the trestle to the Rockaways. To do so the BERC had to build a special ramp at Chestnut Street and Atlantic Avenue in the East New York section of Brooklyn so that its trains could switch directly onto the LIRR tracks heading for the shore. As more and more Brooklynites took the trains to Rockaway, city planners began eyeing the Rockaway tracks for possible inclusion in the city transit system at some future time. But a succession of mayors managed to find a myriad of excuses for delaying the project.

It wasn't until 1950 that the project finally moved forward after someone flicked a burning cigarette out the window of an LIRR coach, causing a fire that burned out 1,800 feet of trestle. The LIRR, financially shaky at the time, threw up its hands over the Rockaway line and decided not to spend another fortune rebuilding its firetrap.

When the LIRR finally conceded defeat by petitioning for abandonment of Rockaway service, New York City moved in and acquired the line for $8,500,000, a bargain price. Of course the city had to spend an additional $47,500,000 to modernize the line and get it operative again but that, too, was considered a steal. It cost somewhat less than $5 million per route mile, the savings due primarily to large sections of road that were either salvageable or ready for use merely by modernizing the signals. Much of the money was invested in building a fireproof bridge across Jamaica Bay.

This was accomplished by creating two man-made islands, spanning most of the four-mile stretch across water. The ties were buried in ballast and sand, flush to their tops, so that no drafts could seep from underneath to fan into a destructive blaze started by a dying cigarette resting on a tie made flammable with creosote oil.

Among the more intense battles during reconstruction was a daily clash between transit men and squadrons of dive-bombing gulls that arrived from the nearby bird sanctuary which the TA also built as part of the new project. The gulls overflowed the sanctuary and began homesteading on the new railroad bed. When TA men approached the nests, the gulls attacked. "The damn things dive-bombed us," one of the field crew complained. "They knocked off hats and glasses in a wink."

The birds enjoyed the side benefits of the Rockaway trestle work. During the months that thousands of tons of sand were being pumped up to create the new islands, clams and fish also were pumped up, creating a cornucopia of gull goodies.

By construction standards, the Rockaway line was a topsy-turvy job. "It always had been a considerable problem *disposing* of fill," said Francis V. Hayes, division engineer of the project. "But in the Rockaway job we needed two million cubic yards *to fill!*"

To get it the contractors dug to the bottom of Jamaica Bay. Because the United States Defense Department wanted a ship channel, nearly one million yards of sand were pumped up and this formed what is now known as Sand Island. The birds almost immediately took possession of this island. The longer of the TA-created islands is known as the Embankment and runs for more than two miles across the bay.

To ensure that the new islands would not erode into the sea, the TA planted grass on a tremendous scale. At least 100 acres of the new land were planted practically foot by foot with beach grass, about the only vegetation that could thrive in the salty sand, to anchor the islands.

Before the new Rockaway line was completed it had scored several "firsts" for rapid transit. One was the dispatching of a field engineer,

Victor Lefkowitz, to the scene for the sole purpose of formulating a battle plan against mussels, creatures that destroy trestles as easily as lit cigarette butts do.

Camping in a pile crack, the mussels increase the size of the opening, permitting other marine life to get inside with them where they gorge themselves on tasty pile innards not protected by creosote. Piles used on the old LIRR trestle were found completely hollow inside the creosoted shell. Some 500 had to be replaced and these, together with the old ones, form the skeletons of the two man-made islands over which the line hops Jamaica Bay.

To outdo the destructive mussels, the TA engineers produced a concrete foundation. Another "first" was a floating concrete factory that was towed along the line. The factory precast thirty-ton slabs of concrete, which were lifted by a fifty-ton crane. It then dropped them on the concrete trestle foundations, forming a virtually finished roadbed. "Shovels and wheelbarrows were practically unknown," said a TA engineer.

Building the new extension was a remarkable accomplishment in itself, but completing it *on time*—considering the major roadblocks involved—was easily the most outstanding feat of the construction.

Studies of the old trestle and the surrounding terrain had been conducted by TA engineers as far back as 1950. When the actual heavy work began in 1955 the target date for completion of the mammoth project was set at June 28, 1956. The reasoning was that the new Rockaway line should open for business in time for the heavy July 4th crowds.

Construction moved along smoothly until the Westinghouse Electric Corporation went on strike on October 16, 1955. Westinghouse had the contract to provide the power equipment for the line, and as the strike dragged on, the deadline for completion seemed unlikely to be met.

The strike lasted for 156 days and when it was finally ended Westinghouse informed the TA that the equipment would not be ready until at least the second week of October, nearly four months after the deadline.

But the TA's bull-headed chairman, Charlie Patterson, would have none of that. He called a meeting on January 26, 1956 and asserted that the June 28 deadline would be met, come hell or high water.

Authority members were impressed with the chairman's determination but the workers at Jamaica Bay laughed when they heard what Patterson had said. "With this strike," one said, "how the hell does he expect us to open on time? What are we going to do for power equipment if Westinghouse can't deliver until the fall?"

Charlie Patterson had an answer to that one. He ordered his men to borrow some equipment from the IRT's Dyre Avenue line and the Aqueduct substation was skeletonized. Arrangements were made to buy other power. By spring a few optimists at TA headquarters began thinking they just might pull off the impossible. During a meeting with trestle builders at Jay Street headquarters in Brooklyn, one contractor told Patterson: "You know, I wouldn't be surprised if we are ready to run on June 28."

"Ready?" queried Patterson. We *will* be running then!"

In spite of strikes, dive-bombing gulls, and a horde of skeptics, the Transit Authority's trains rolled to Rockaway on June 28 just as Charlie Patterson had promised.

ANATOMY OF
THE UNDERGROUND

Signaling and
the Subway

One of the most perplexing problems confronting IRT subway planners early in the century was a very basic one: how to avoid crashes.
One major underground collision could put the new subway line out
of business. (That, by the way, *did* happen to the Brooklyn Rapid
Transit in 1918.) So August Belmont, founder the IRT subway, insisted that his engineers find an advanced, practical method of
signaling.

A primary function of this signaling system would be to allow
trains to operate regularly at headways of two and three minutes.

This would not be a simple accomplishment, since the IRT had no source of experience to turn to for practical advice. The London, Paris, Glasgow, Boston, and Budapest subways had not yet developed any sophisticated train regulatory equipment.

As so often was the case, New York City's first subway, the 1904 IRT, led the way in rapid transit innovation. When it came to signaling, the upstart IRT was the first completely electrically signaled railroad to operate in the United States. The IRT capped a series of signaling developments dating back to the early part of the nineteenth century when horses were being replaced by steam engines.

According to *Transit* magazine the locomotives brought tremendous speed—as much as fifteen miles an hour—but they also brought danger. Progressive-minded railroads maintained gangs of roustabouts at stations, who seized a train as it approached and dragged it to a stop by sheer strength at the station, or at least within walking distance of it. These monsters did not heed a cry of "Whoa!" And after the power was shut off, they rolled great distances. The human brakes and no signaling were all right until some prosperous railroads acquired two, even three, locomotives and operated several trains simultaneously on the single-track systems. The roustabouts weren't available between stations to stop the trains and accidents began to happen. Train schedules should have made it possible for trains to meet at predetermined points, where a second track was available for passing, but the schedules didn't mean much. Aside from the common breakdown, the farmers in many localities had the right, which they strongly defended, to use the railways to haul their produce to town in wagons fitted with flanged wheels. Thus many an engineer, whose schedule called for a twelve-mile speed, crept slowly behind a wagonload of turnips drawn at two or three miles an hour by a pair of weary farm plugs.

The first signaling in America was on the New Castle and Frenchtown Railroad, which ran seventeen miles through Delaware and Maryland from Chesapeake Bay to the Delaware River, an important rail link for steamship routes. Wooden masts, thirty feet high, were built three miles apart and from each was suspended an inverted peach basket. The baskets were covered with white or black cloth. When the train left the terminal, the white-covered peach basket was hoisted to the top of the mast. Three miles away, at the next tower, a man saw the signal through a marine spyglass, hoisted the white signal to the top of his mast, and so on. Thus, in a manner of minutes, the other terminal was apprised that a train was coming through. The white basket, at half-mast at a station, told the engineer to stop for passengers or freight. The basket was raised to the top of the mast at each station as the train went through; after it passed the basket was lowered immediately to the bottom of the mast, in which position it meant "Stop!" If a train was disabled and could not proceed, a black basket was hoisted to the top of the mast to spread the word. In some form or another the ball-and-mast system of signaling, as it became known, still exists in various parts of the country.

It was the beginning of railroad signaling, but a slow beginning. Other railroads were in no hurry to develop signal techniques. Indeed, twenty-five years later, the Tallahassee, Pensacola & Georgia was dealing with the problems of trains confronting each other between stations by making a rule that, in such case, "the dispute as to which shall retire shall be settled by the Conductors, without interference on the part of the engineers." The locomotive engineers were hotheaded prima donnas in those days, not to be trusted with diplomatic negotiations. Even so, the issue of which train was to back up to the nearest siding was not always settled by peaceable debate.

In America the saving of manpower by the use of signaling seldom entered the picture at all. In England, which was greatly ahead of America in signaling—the railroads were shorter, the traffic heavier—advocates pointed out that signaling could reduce the use of hired men. But here safety was the only issue. Railroads which could buy a gang of slaves to serve as brakes weren't at all concerned about conserving manpower. They were worried about passengers being injured in wrecks. Long lists of casualties discouraged people from riding new locomotive-hauled trains. Keeping people on the payroll simply to hoist a ball, or a flag, or show a colored light, or a disc—the semaphore had assumed many forms by now—was accepted casually. In retrospect this seems incredible, for the TA today has more than a million electric contacts doing the work of semaphoring, and 1,200 men who do nothing but serve the mechanical wants of these relays.

In 1863 the block system evolved in America. England already had a similar system, but in those days there was no free dissemination of information. Indeed, it is remarkable that railroad thinking in America developed so closely along British lines with virtually no interchange of thought.

In 1863 Ashbel Welch, chief engineer of the United New Jersey

Canal and Railroad Companies, divided the track between Trenton, New Jersey, and Philadelphia into sections, or blocks, about six miles apart. At each section border a building housed a crew and a simple telegraph apparatus. As a train passed, the telegrapher wired ahead that it was on its way, and an illuminated signal closed the track to all trains behind that one, until the telegrapher ahead flashed back word that the train had passed his point, at which time the track would be opened for another train. The system eliminated the danger that two trains could be on the same section of track at the same time, and even rear-end collisions could be avoided. The signal was manually operated, but "otherwise fool-proof."

To get around the problem of human failings, the signal man was replaced by an automated system. A train entering a block touched against an obstruction that immediately turned the signal behind it to "Danger!" It moved on and at the next block touched another obstruction—a rod or lever or arm—that did the same, and, in addition, turned the signal at the previous block to "Proceed." The automated semaphores worked fine in the south. They worked fine in the north, in summer. But in winter, sleet drove into the works and the all-clear locked in ice.

Lighted semaphores were even worse. In 1841 an international committee of railway men met in Birmingham, England, and decided to settle the light question once and for all. They declared that a white light meant "Full speed ahead," red meant "Stop!" and green meant "Proceed cautiously." All over the world railroads changed to this design. All over the world trains crashed and a lot of people were killed.

The theory was sound. A white light had many times the carrying capacity of red or green or blue. But the crashes promptly pinpointed two things: if the red glass disc was smashed by any means, the "danger" bulb showed white and beckoned to disaster; if the signal wasn't working at all, the engineer would glimpse any white light—a farmer's lantern, a street light—and charge ahead to a crash.

Dr. William Robinson, horrified by a couple of accidents he had witnessed, set out to devise a system that would end railroad crashes once and for all. In 1869 he constructed, and showed in New York a year later, an open-circuit system of block control with signals that were not dependent on human control, but actuated by every pair of wheels entering a block, or section. This was accomplished by having electric current pass up from one rail, through the wheels on that side, through the car axle, through the other wheels, and, by that flow of current, actuate the signal behind the train to red. A polished and refined version of this passing of current from rail to wheel to axle to wheel to rail, or the breaking of that current, is what activates the signals of today.

But that was 1869 and the railroads didn't like Robinson's system at all. It was newfangled, complicated, too tricky, expensive, and experimental. Here and there it was tried out on small sections of track. It was tried on the IRT thirty-five years later!

The electropneumatic interlocking signals of the IRT were considered the "marvel of the times" in 1904. At that time safety on the IRT was the primary issue. When the train passed a signal into a new block, the signal behind it turned red. As it did, the trip, a little metal arm beside the track, rose upright, to remain there as long as the signal remained red. A train that tried to pass before the signal changed struck this projection with its "trip cock," a lever which released compressed air from the braking system, causing the brakes to engage. Normally, the motorman would have to "key by"—that is, come a full stop, and turn a key to release the trip lever. In the overlap system, there are always two red signals behind each train, which means that the motorman would have to come to a full stop at least twice, turn the key, and proceed beyond two red lights before reaching the point where his own train could menace the train ahead. It was—and still is—possible for a motorman to crash into the car ahead, but it takes a lot of work to do it. In time the actual turning of a key was outmoded. Now the train simply comes to a stop at a signal, activating the trip arm by moving the train forward just enough to get its front wheels on the track circuit ahead. The time element device is also used to retard trains going into stations and curves and such. This isn't what standard railroads call speed control, although for all practical purposes it serves as such.

After 1904 the thought arose that signaling, used chiefly to stop or slow up trains, could also serve to increase track capacity and reduce delays. As subways filled to overflowing, and construction costs for new lines soared skyward, the need for squeezing every ounce of carrying capacity from the old tunnels became a primary consideration.

Under the old system a train waited to enter a station at a complete stop if a train was already in that station. Until the first train got under way and cleared the end of the platform, the second train had to remain motionless. Now, of course, a "station time signal" along the station platform lets the second train get under way, slowly, while the train ahead is beginning to leave the station.

"Theoretically, the track space, between trains," said one signalman, "is wasted space. The less of it there is, the better, from an economic viewpoint. The ultimate in efficiency would be one continuous train running around and around on a conveyor belt principle. That idea isn't here yet. But the closer we can come to it the higher goes the efficiency in moving cargo. All right, we've got to stop at platforms for passengers, we've got to stop and go.

"But we can, and are, cutting down on the need for such wide spaces between trains. More signals means it is possible to run more trains safely over the same track. In a sense, it is like braking a train going forty miles an hour, as compared to braking it at twenty. At twenty you need only a quarter of the distance to stop. We don't have to slow up the whole railroad; it's just a matter of slipping extra trains in between."

Movie-making on the Line

Ever since Hollywood began making talking pictures, the New York City subway has been a favorite locale for MGM, 20th-Century Fox, and United Artists. One of the first—and best—was *Subway Express,* by Martha Madison and Eva Flint and directed by Chester Erskin.

Mystery film buffs still talk about the *dénouement* in which a dying victim's last words to the police were "See Beach Express!" At first detectives mistakenly believe the victim was referring to the BMT's Sea Beach express and search in vain for the villain along the Brooklyn subway line. Only later is it learned that the victim was alluding to the Beach pneumatic subway tunnel which was adjacent to the BMT Broadway (Manhattan) line. It developed that the murderer was living in the old, abandoned Beach tunnel. Hence "See Beach Express!"

Just a few years later, the Third Avenue el (then part of the IRT) figured prominently in one of the most widely known films ever made, the original version of *King Kong*. In the movie's climax, the great ape lumbers down Third Avenue, smashing the landscape and, of course, the venerable el. The camera zeroes in on the interior of a train as unsuspecting straphangers read their newspapers and talk to one another. Unknown to them, Kong has ripped up the very tracks on which their local is rolling. Suddenly the motorman spies Kong up ahead and jams on the brakes. Passengers hurtle together. Kong's bloodshot eyes appear at the window of the car. Women shriek. Kong picks up the el car, flips it into the street, and ties knots in it.

Eventually Alfred Hitchcock, that indefatigable seeker of authenticity for movie sets, got into the act. He hired an IND train for *The Wrong Man*, a 1956 melodrama starring Henry Fonda. The master of suspense produced a scene with Fonda sitting in an R-1 car, reading a newspaper, as the train supposedly rattled through the tunnel. Actually, it was standing quite still in the IND's Fifth Avenue station.

As the demand for more subway filmmaking sites increased, the TA obliged by renting movie producers use of the Court Street shuttle line. Originally a tributary of the IND-Fulton Street line in Brooklyn, the Court Street shuttle (HH local) operated between the Hoyt-Schermerhorn Street station, where it connected with the A express and GG local, and Court Street near Atlantic Avenue at the fringe of Brooklyn Heights. This was one of the system's bigger blunders and in June 1946 the line was permanently closed. "It turned out to be a blessing for movie-making purposes," said Dennis Wendling, a TA public affairs man. "The old Court Street line has many of the features film directors look for in a subway—a curve, curtain wall, and switches."

Wendling, the TA's liaison with filmmakers, television producers, and anyone else who wants to use the subway for commercial purposes, has been called upon as the system's official safety adviser when actual filming takes place. One of the most unusual problems occurred during the shooting of the TV movie *A Short Walk to Daylight*, in which the script called for a subway derailment. To accommodate the producers, the TA jacked up a train off the tracks during the filming and then returned it to the rails once the movie was completed.

One of the busiest periods of subway filmmaking occurred from 1970 through 1975 when no less than thirty-six movies were made utilizing subway property in one form or another. In that period the most publicized film was United Artists' adaptation of John Godey's book *The Taking of Pelham One Two Three.*

The TA was not at all anxious to rent a subway to United Artists for the film because the story concerned the hijacking of an IRT local. "It had," said a TA official, "the potential to spark irresponsible and dangerous behavior."

United Artists' associate producer Steve Kesten was adamant about shooting the movie on the IRT system. "There was no way to do it without a real subway," said Kesten. "There was some talk about using the Boston, Philadelphia, or Montreal system, but who're you going to fool? The Transit Authority got cold feet. They didn't want to be responsible for somebody stealing a subway. It took [Mayor John] Lindsay going to the wall to get it done. We wound up paying a terrific whopping insurance premium to take care of any such risk."

The TA was so fearful that a subway train would be hijacked as a result of *The Taking of Pelham One Two Three* that it compelled United Artists to pay $275,000 for the train and $75,000 for the anti-hijacking insurance. The film was eventually done in part on the IRT and on the IND at the Court Street station. Starring Walter Matthau, Robert Shaw, Martin Balsam, and Hector Elizondo, the film received generally good notices.

The subway has done well on Tin Pan Alley. As far back as the nineteenth century the New York el inspired A. H. Rosewig to compose the "Rapid Transit Galop." By far the most popular tune of all was dedicated to the IND's speedy A express. Billy Strayhorn wrote the words and music for "Take the A Train" in 1941 and the immortal jazzman Duke Ellington recorded the tune, which has remained a pop classic to this day.

On Broadway, the New York underground made its greatest impact in David Merrick's production of *Subways Are for Sleeping,* which opened December 27, 1961 and ran for 205 performances.

The closest the New York transit system came to making an imprint on comic strips was Fontaine Fox's legendary Toonerville Trolley. The creation, interestingly, was modeled after a system within the greater New York area. Fox said he was inspired to draw the Toonerville Trolley by a friendly old bearded motorman who ran a rundown trolley in Pelham, New York.

"Fox had traveled on this line to visit cartoonist Charlie Voight's home," said Herb Galewitz, who compiled a collection of Toonerville cartoons. "By the time Fox returned to his own home, he had recalled another rundown trolley line in Louisville, the Brook Street run. He merged the two lines into *The Toonerville Trolley That Meets All Trains* and its conductor-motorman, the Skipper. It was an immediate success."

The Toonerville Folks reached the end of the line when Fontaine Fox retired in 1955.

The Most Dangerous Job on the Subway

Steel-nerved workers who constantly examine the subway's energy source are a special breed reared only in the murky tunnels of New York's underground. Some 250 PD (power distribution) men drill, bolt, and weld the third rail while it is alive with enough current to kill a man in one blinding flash. Theirs is rated the most dangerous transit job. Outside maintenance men—topflight ones, too—can't take it. The IND division discovered that when it developed its special welding process. Outsiders accustomed to the sunlight on elevated tracks were lost in the subway darkness! A world that was alternately dazzling in the glare of welding arcs, or uncomfortably black in the presence of the deadly rail terrified them, while PD men leaned right on the rail with precisely three-sixteenths of an inch of rubber between themselves and the current. One or two days of this and outsiders quit, their nerves frazzled.

The IND has since recruited its men from among the track-walkers and other subway people who, over the years, developed a respectful familiarity with live third rails. They are goodnaturedly contemptuous of standard electric railroaders. Subway PDs view as sissified the custom of turning off the juice wherever possible, as practiced on some roads. Subway men always work with "hot" equipment, race

181

tight headways that would stagger outside power crews, make no bones about considering themselves a sort of rail aristocracy.

A chief supervisor once told about the time his two brothers urged him to take a railroad job with their line—a busy one. "Those fellows work in daylight a lot of the time, they can see what they're doing, and damned if they don't think they're working fast when trains are on a fifteen-minute headway. Hell—that's not even interesting."

One job they all dread is rescuing dogs and cats—and once a goat—that continually stray into subway tunnels, become terrified, and crouch under the third rail. Invariably the dogs snap at the PDs, the cats maul them, and the goat butted them. All in a day's work, caring for and repairing the subway's power supply.

The Rails They Ride On and How They're Replaced

To an uneducated eye the endless miles of rails lacing New York's subway system are permanently locked into place and will remain usable as long as the system is operating. Actually, the reverse is closer to the truth. There isn't a network of rails anywhere in the world subject to the incessant pounding and abuse absorbed by the New York system.

As a result subway maintenance men must constantly replenish the old rail with new steel, and do it without disturbing the normal flow of train traffic. Usually this happens at about midnight.

The lights are going off throughout the city. Out of the 207th Street yards rumbles the work train of the IND. For the twenty-four men who make up its crew, this is the dawn of a new workday. While the city sleeps, while trains interrupt at only twenty-minute intervals— that is the time when worn-out rails are replaced by new. The rusty new rails (in this particular field, it is the old, worn-out rails that glitter brightly) are laid out in rows on the flatcar.

On tangents—straight lines—rails live a long time. "Indefinitely" is the word. But on curves, the grind of steel wheels wears them out fast. Seventeen or eighteen months is a fairly long life for a curved rail; on sharper bends they may last as little as twelve or thirteen months. And most of the rails on the flat car are for bends. Unlike standard railroads, where rails are fitted at the point of repair, every inch of new IND rail is fitted in advance for the particular few feet where it is to be placed—sawed to size, bent to fit the curve, drilled to take the plate.

As described in *Transit*, the work train rumbles into the dark tunnel, just behind a southbound passenger train. In the passenger car the crewmen and the spare motorman drowse during the long trip down to the forties. This, like many work trains, is a double-ender. When the time comes to unload and load rails there will be a motorman fore and aft, for each full section of this rail weighs 1,100 pounds, and the movement of the train itself is used to load and unload.

They're up and alert, though, when the train comes to a halt in the forties. Now begins the operation that calls for footwork, as one observer put it, "as neat and dainty as the Rockettes—except that they don't have pretty legs."

Twelve men, six on each side, each pair sharing a set of tongs, hoists the rails up to a chute, falling away as its tip finds the chuteway. The train twitches forward a little, and the rail goes down to the roadbed with a thundering clang. For perhaps seventeen minutes this work continues. Then the flagman whistles that a downtown local is coming. The work crew scrambles down, and the work train pulls away on its runaround.

This runaround is a fantastic jaunt. The train may go down to 34th Street (Pennsylvania) station where it can be switched over to the northbound track. Now it may have to travel to 125th Street before it can be switched over to the southbound track on which the men are working. Before being switched over, it waits for a downtown train, so it can trail it. This is the only means by which the trackmen can be sure of having seventeen or eighteen minutes to unload, or, as the night progresses, to load the worn-out track. The runaround continues hour after hour until, just as the first sleepy work-bound passengers are appearing on the platform, it picks up its last used rails and heads back toward the 207th Street yards.

When rails originally were put into place, the men who exerted the elbow grease required became known as gandy dancers. Railroads were built and rebuilt at the price of their sweat and aching backs.

They swung six-pound spiking hammers for eight hours. Or plucked the great spikes out with clay bars. Or tamped ballast. Now *there* was a test of whether a man would ever make a TA trackman. You stuck a tamper in his hands and set him to pounding away. If he lasted the first day through—a great many didn't—he had possibilities. If he showed up for work the next day and could still move his arms and legs, he was a likely prospect.

In 1956, Leo Casey, the TA's public relations boss, assigned one of his researchers to find the roots of the term "gandy dancer." He went to three authorities.

"Gandy dancer," the first authority said, "derives from gander. Originally it was gander dancer. You'll find gander in the dictionary meaning 'simpleton' or 'fool.' Well, long ago railroads used to recruit their track crews from the flophouses of the Bowery and skid rows elsewhere. They were pretty low specimens—weak minds and strong backs. Hence the term gander dancers, changed later to gandy dancers."

Double-checking, the researcher went to another top authority.

"It's an old term," the second etymologist said. "Once upon a time there was a slave-driving track foreman who worked his men so hard that they practically had to dance. The foreman's name was Gandy. Hence the term gandy dancer."

Triple-checking, the researcher tried a third authority.

"Sure, I know the origin," said he confidently. "Whereas now it is applied to all trackmen, originally it referred only to those tamping ballast. Ever notice the way a male goose will turn slowly and stamp when upset—well it's remarkably like the old walk of the man tamping ballast by hand."

So much for the origins of the term.

The gandy dancer is disappearing fast from the TA scene, and probably in time from the American railroad scene. Tireless little gasoline engines and compressed air are replacing the bulging biceps and mighty back.

Perhaps the surest sign of the times came in 1956 when the TA rebuilt the track and roadbed for approximately 1,000 feet between 25th Street and 36th Street, Brooklyn, on the northbound express of the Fourth Avenue line.

By the standards of years ago, or even months before, this was a nine-week job, to be done in the late shift, and to produce, in addition to a new roadbed, the usual crop of sprained ankles, cuts, bruises, a hernia or two, countless backaches, and gallons of sweat. But this time it was different.

Into the tunnel, after rush hour Friday night, came new pieces of equipment, some never seen before in a subway. By rush hour Monday the job was finished—no cuts, bruises, hernias.

Not only were nine weeks of work compressed into a single weekend, but it was done more easily, at less cost, with fewer men. Toting up figures later, the engineers discovered they came to just 50 percent of the cost of doing it by the sweat-and-muscle method.

First the rails had to be taken up. The first of the new tools—a mechanical spike puller—yanked 425 spikes in an hour and a half. It would have taken five times as long using manpowered claw bars.

The freed rails were pried out of their seats with crowbars and lifted to the toe bench—biceps and backs were still used here, and in the next operation, as the old ties were removed by hand.

Payloaders and bulldozers—new to subway rebuilding—scooped up the old ballast. The roadbed was cleaned down to the concrete base. The flatcars hauled away fifteen carloads of the old ballast. In the old days this stuff had to be cleared by laborious hand shovel.

Now came the rebuilding process.

Tie plates had been laid on track ties in the yard at 38th Street and Tenth Avenue. These were brought to the work area, set on the concrete base, and the rails lifted back in place.

The power spike driver, the second new piece of equipment, drove spikes into holes previously drilled in the yards. Not a spike maul or muscle was called into play for all the spikes driven.

In came fifteen hopper carloads of stone ballast (broken trap-rock) which was distributed over the rails. Then, by track jacks, the track was raised and ballast tamped under it.

Again, not a muscle was raised for this—ordinarily the most tedious and back-breaking of the jobs. Instead, the third new piece of equipment came rolling through—a $45,000 mechanical ballast tamper, or mechanized gandy dancer. This machine was built by the Pullman Standard Manufacturing Company to TA specifications. It rolls, like the spike puller and spike driver, on wheels on the track. It has sixteen spade-shaped tamping heads of special steel, which bite into the ballast and jam it under the ties to a firmness not possible with the strongest human muscles. Tamping with this machine costs one-sixth the price of hand-tamping.

Revolutionary as the Fourth Avenue operations were, they were just the beginning of a great new line of equipment that has written doomsday for the gandy dancer.

A Guide to Knowing and Enjoying the New York Subways

New York City's subway system opened on October 27, 1904, and from that day until the present, New Yorkers have complained about it. While critics of the subway have valid arguments, it is high time someone came along and touted its virtues.

The IRT, BMT, and IND divisions together have 708.55 track miles, making the New York subway system the largest in the world. During rush hours it operates 635 trains throughout the system.

For cleanliness, Toronto's underground is tops. Montreal's rubber-tired Metro is quieter and Moscow's subway is unquestionably more ornate and beautiful. But when the mechanisms are right, no subway is faster (top speed, fifty-five mph), more exciting, more complex, more diverse, and more colorful than New York's. And it's still the best bargain in transit. What better proof than the fact that a rider can travel from 241st Street and White Plains Road in the Bronx to Coney Island—a total of 29.31 miles—for a lower price than a five-block cab ride?

The Smith-9th Street station in Brooklyn, at eighty-seven and one-half feet the highest in the city, offers a breathtaking panorama of lower New York harbor and Staten Island. At the other extreme is the 191st Street (Broadway) station in Manhattan, which burrows 180 feet below street level.

Curiosities abound on the subways for those willing to seek them out. For example, after midnight, the Transit Authority operates a rail-grinding machine, designed to smooth the ride by leveling the tracks. When in action, the rail-grinder creates a bizarre visual and audible scene as it shoots sparks and screeches from its Rube Goldberg-like grinding cars.

186

The rail-grinder's first cousin, the vacuum-cleaner train, tours the system each night inhaling steel dust and other debris. If the results aren't obvious at your station it's because there is only one such contraption on the system.

To the train buff, the most exciting aspect of any subway system is the ride itself. Tastes vary, to be sure. Speed fanciers prefer the breathtaking run on the new Sixth Avenue tunnel from 34th Street to West 4th Street; or the IRT's Broadway express dash from 72nd Street to Times Square. Those who prefer scenery combined with long and fast runs lean toward the Rockaway line, especially the route between Howard Beach and Broad Channel stations—3.7 miles—the longest distance between stops on the system, past the Jamaica Bay Wildlife Refuge.

In general, a good subway or elevated trip must include at least some of the following ingredients: a speedy run, interesting scenery, rhythmical track music, and something to see and do at the end of the line. For example, any one of the six lines (B, D, F, M, N, QB) converging on Stillwell Avenue-Coney Island gets points because both the original Nathan's Famous and the Aquarium are only blocks away.

For children, the outdoor sprint of the Brighton express (D) from Prospect Park to Sheepshead Bay, is one of the fastest and most exciting rambles on the system.

Now that the old Myrtle Avenue el has been demolished, Brooklyn's best elevated rides include the Broadway (Brooklyn)-Jamaica BMT (J) express and the IND (F) route. The J operates on the center of a three-track right-of-way as a city-bound express in the morning and a Jamaica-bound express in the late afternoon. It develops excellent speed and rhythms between Eastern Parkway and Essex Street stations. Highlight of the F run is its long slow climb out of the tunnel at Carroll Street and then its high curve overlooking the Gowanus Canal and lower New York Bay.

Similarly, Queens has a splendid elevated express on the Main Street IRT Flushing line that can match BMT's Jamaica run for speed and scenery. But unique is the IRT Dyre Avenue line in the Bronx. This route once was a section of the old New York, Westchester & Boston Railway, and the original handsome stations remain alongside the dirt embankment.

From the same era is the IND Rockaway line, which travels a right-of-way that once belonged to the Long Island Rail Road. This delight has the special attraction of crossing Jamaica Bay at two points before swinging south to the Rockaway Park terminus or north to Far Rockaway.

For the information of historians, the city's original subway station, which was built in 1904 and is no longer in use, was located at City Hall. This first line ran along Lafayette and Fourth Avenue to Grand Central Station and then crossed to the West Side on the right-of-way now used by the 42nd Street shuttle.

In the following summary, subway ratings (based on scenery, speed, uniqueness, historical qualities, and rhythm) are denoted thus:

****Highest rating
***Among the best
**Good, but not great
*Hardly worth the carfare

IRT

**Broadway-Seventh Avenue local (1), Van Cortlandt Park to South Ferry. Running time, fifty minutes. Slow, generally dull except for interesting climb from subway to el at 125th Street and Broadway, and good view from el at 225th Street. Excellent park at the north terminus and Staten Island ferry at the south.

****Seventh Avenue-White Plains Road express (2), 241st Street, the Bronx, to New Lots Avenue, Brooklyn. Running time, one and one-half hours. One of the best. Combines a good el run with great speed under Broadway, especially between 96th Street and 72nd Street, and between 72nd Street and Times Square. A winner for kids, who will be entranced by the old-fashioned, angled tunnel struts in the subways.

*Seventh Avenue-Lenox Avenue express (3), 148th Street, Lenox terminal, Manhattan, to Flatbush Avenue, Brooklyn. Running time, one hour. An inferior cousin to No. 2. Lacks scenery, and run into Flatbush remains underground throughout.

**Lexington Avenue-Woodlawn express (4), Woodlawn, the Bronx, to Flatbush Avenue, Brooklyn. Running time, one hour and ten minutes. The northern segment—in the Bronx—is the best for scenery and speed. The sprint from 86th Street to 59th is especially exciting, but the enjoyment tails off in Brooklyn with a dull ride to Flatbush.

188

***Lexington Avenue-East 180th Street-Dyre Avenue express (5), Dyre Avenue, the Bronx, to Utica Avenue, Brooklyn. Running time, one hour and twenty minutes. Real good start in the Bronx features a ride along the former New York, Westchester & Boston trackage above ground, then to some speedy tunnel work under Lexington Avenue before the ride turns boring in Brooklyn. Not much at the end of the line but Chinese restaurants and delicatessens.

**Lexington Avenue, through express (5), 241st Street, the Bronx, to Utica Avenue, Brooklyn. Running time, one hour and twenty minutes. Very similar to its sister line above except for a different opener. Some good scenes and very good speed.

**Pelham express (Lexington Avenue local) (6), Pelham Bay Park, the Bronx, to Brooklyn Bridge-Worth Street. Running time, fifty minutes. Doesn't compare with other IRT runs except for a pleasant above-ground stint in the Bronx.

**Lexington Avenue-Pelham local (6), Pelham Bay Park to South Ferry. Running time, one hour. A slower, slightly longer version of the Pelham express, above, and not really worth the effort. Wins an extra star, though, for being the only line to have a movie made about it (*The Taking of Pelham One Two Three*).

***Times Square-Flushing express (7), Main Street, Flushing, to Times Square. Running time, twenty-five minutes. A delightful elevated *tour de force* past the old World's Fair Grounds, Shea Stadium, and through Jackson Heights and Woodside; then to the Queens Plaza maze overlooking the Penn Central rail yards below. Stunning speed throughout Queens right up to and including the tunnel to Manhattan. Highly recommended but too short a ride to earn the highest rating.

**Times Square-Flushing local (7), Main Street to Times Square. Running time, thirty minutes. Same as the preceding but slower.

IND

****Eighth Avenue Express (A), 207th Street, Manhattan, to either Lefferts Boulevard or Far Rockaway. Running time from 207th Street to Far Rockaway, one hour and forty minutes. When Duke Ellington recorded "Take the A Train" the run wasn't quite as long as it is now. Addition of the Rockaway segment makes this a highly recommended attraction. It begins slowly in Washington Heights and then picks up fine speed buzzing downtown Manhattan underground; slows up a bit in Brooklyn but then elevates in East New York and heads over the tracks past Aqueduct and, finally, to the shore. It's a delight for kids.

*Eighth Avenue local (AA), 168th Street, Manhattan, to Chambers Street, Manhattan. Running time, thirty-five minutes. One of the most drab, listless offerings on the system. Forget it.

**½ Avenue of the Americas (Sixth Avenue)-West End line (B), 168th Street, Manhattan, to Coney Island, Stillwell Avenue. Running time, one hour and twenty minutes. Recommended only for the Brooklyn segment, which is a pleasant elevated run through Borough Park and Bensonhurst on out to Coney Island. In addition to Nathan's Famous, there are a few dandy Italian restaurants near the terminus.

*Eighth Avenue-Bronx local (CC), Bedford Park Boulevard, the Bronx, to Hudson Terminal, Chambers Street, Manhattan. Running time, fifty minutes. Blah!

****Avenue of the Americas (Sixth Avenue)-Brighton express (D), 205th Street, the Bronx, to Stillwell Avenue, Coney Island. Running time, one hour and twenty-five minutes. Highest rating because of variety: subway, el, embankment, open-cut run, East River bridge crossing, and dazzling speed. The dash from Newkirk Avenue to Kings Highway is a scenic delight, and the track-wheel music as the express rounds the Beverley Road curve is right out of Benny Goodman's "China Boy." Another gem is the direct run from the Brighton el tracks onto the dirt embankment at Sheepshead Bay, not to mention the neat hill from Avenue H down to Newkirk Avenue. A stop-off at Sheepshead Bay is suggested for the clams at F. W. I. L. Lundy Bros. on Emmons Avenue, or simply for a walk along the quay where the fishing boats dock.

**Prospect Park-Franklin Avenue shuttle (SS), Franklin Avenue to Prospect Park, Brooklyn. Actually a part of the BMT line, this ten-minute offshoot of the Brighton line is worth taking for historical purposes (site of the Malbone Street disaster) and for a lilting run from grade to an elevated terminus at Franklin Avenue in Bedford-Stuyvesant.

***Eighth Avenue-Queens express (E), 179th Street, Jamaica, to either Euclid Avenue or Rockaway Park. Really good speed along the Queens Boulevard express segment is a highlight, as well as the outdoor spin to the Rockaways. The long local haul through Manhattan is a drag, and a similar run through Brooklyn is not much fun either. But the start and the finish represent good railroading.

****Avenue of the Americas (Sixth Avenue)-Queens-Brooklyn line (F), 179th Street, Jamaica, to Stillwell Avenue, Coney Island. Running time, one hour and twenty-five minutes. Combines the good rhythm of the Queens Boulevard express with the pleasant climb out of the Carroll Street tunnel up over the Gowanus Canal. Wonderful panorama of New York Bay, followed by an elevated lope over Bensonhurst on out to Coney Island. It lacks the overall speed of the Brighton run but has enough variety to rate top billing.

**Brooklyn-Queens local (GG), 71st Street-Continental Avenue, Forest Hills, to Church Avenue, Brooklyn. Running time, fifty-five minutes. A slow meandering trail that ends with the pleasing climb over the Gowanus Canal.

BMT

**14th Street-Canarsie line (LL), Eighth Avenue, Manhattan, to Rockaway Parkway, Brooklyn. Running time, thirty-five minutes. Pretty much of a drag until the subway lifts out of the tunnel at Broadway Junction and heads for Canarsie. Everybody should go to Canarsie at least once in a lifetime.

***½ Myrtle Avenue-Brighton line (M), Metropolitan Avenue, Queens, to Stillwell Avenue, Coney Island. Running time, one hour and ten minutes. This is the only section of the Myrtle el still extant. The initial run from Metropolitan Avenue is bouncy and fun. A fascinating crossover curve just past the Broadway-Myrtle junction brings the train through brownstone backyards and up over Myrtle Avenue. After the Williamsburg Bridge rumble—and the tunnel crossing back to Brooklyn after Broad Street—the train finally surfaces at Prospect Park for its dance to Coney Island.

***Broadway-Sea Beach express (N), 57th Street, Manhattan, to Stillwell Avenue, Coney Island. Running time, fifty minutes. Lots of that good BMT rail rhythm and speed, especially when it bypasses DeKalb Avenue during rush hours. Fascinating right-of-way in Brooklyn as the train heads for Borough Park and Bensonhurst, ultimately landing in Coney Island.

**Broadway express-Brighton local (QB), 57th Street, Manhattan, to Stillwell Avenue, Coney Island. Running time, fifty minutes. The express under Broadway is a delight when it gets going and the climb over the Manhattan Bridge offers good vistas of downtown Brooklyn and the lower East Side. The creep along Brighton local trackage is one of the more scenic slow runs and not to be put down, unless you're in a hurry. Don't be!

**½ Jamaica line (J), 168th Street, Jamaica, to Broad Street, Manhattan. Running time, forty-five minutes. An abbreviated version of the old QJ train (to Stillwell Avenue, Coney Island), most of which was taken over by the M. Still features the old Broadway el and a pleasant East River crossing.

*½ Broadway-Fourth Avenue local (RR), from Ditmars Boulevard, Astoria, to 95th Street, Brooklyn. Running time, one hour and ten minutes. The subway section in the middle is a bore, but the Queens segment offers pleasant (albeit slow) elevated views.

Dubbed "art" by a small minority of avant garde critics, subway graffiti is regarded as an unsightly disgrace to the system by most riders. *Sprague Library, Electric Railroaders Association, Inc.*

One of the seldom-seen pieces of subway rolling stock is the garbage collection train which operates in the wee small hours of the morning. *Bob Leon*

One of the Transit Authority's specialty cars is the ballast-tamping machine. *New York City Transit Authority Photo File*

Another specialty item is the steam bath machine, employed by the Transit Authority to make its stations spic-and-span, if such a feat is possible. *New York City Transit Authority Photo File*

When he was Transit Authority chairman, Charlie Patterson boasted that his subway owned the world's largest vacuum cleaner, to inhale steel dust that accumulated in the tunnels. *New York City Transit Authority Photo File*

Like automobiles, subway cars sometimes visit the car wash. This one is at the Coney Island yards. *New York City Transit Authority Photo File*

Repairing a "live" third-rail is regarded as one of the most dangerous jobs on the subway system. *Bob Leon*

The city's subway system, incredibly, has its own freight line, which has operated since the nineteenth century, linking Bush Terminal on New York Bay with the Coney Island yards. For years, the chief means of propulsion was an electrified locomotive which pulled everything from freight cars to the BMT's own subway rolling stock. *Sprague Library, Electric Railroaders Association, Inc.*

The subway car's main power switch. *Sprague Library, Electric Railroaders Association, Inc.*

The BMT added this work train to its fleet in 1927. The car now serves as a signal equipment dolly. *Sprague Library, Electric Railroaders Association, Inc.*

Old 998 was the BMT's first steel car for elevated train service. The car sat in the Coney Island yard, where it was used for storage after being retired from passenger service. It has since been scrapped. *Sprague Library, Electric Railroaders Association, Inc.*

An IRT "Low V" takes the curve near the old Yankee Stadium in the Bronx. *Sprague Library, Electric Railroaders Association, Inc.*

The line that nobody knows—except residents of the borough of Richmond—is the MTA's Staten Island Rapid Transit railway, here enroute to Tottenville from the ferry terminal at St. George. *Sprague Library, Electric Railroaders Association, Inc.*

In the early twenties, when a subway tunnel was planned to link Brooklyn's BMT with the Staten Island transit system, Staten Island purchased a fleet of BMT-type cars. The tunnel never was built but the cars ran for years. *Sprague Library, Electric Railroaders Association, Inc.*

Rather than scrap an old, but useful, "Low V" IRT car, ingenious Transit Authority mechanics simply converted it for winter work as a snowplow. *Sprague Library, Electric Railroaders Association, Inc.*

A workman puts some of
the finishing touches on
a new R-46 car in the
Pullman Company plant.
*Sprague Library, Electric
Railroaders Association,
Inc.*

The Transit Authority started taking delivery of shiny new R-46 cars starting in the early seventies. Here one is being unloaded at Hoboken, New Jersey, on its way to New York City. *Sprague Library, Electric Railroaders Association, Inc.*

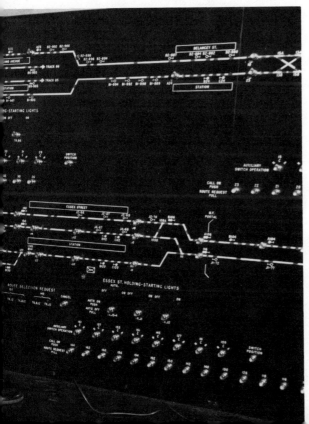

The contemporary subway signalman employs the most sophisticated electronic equipment available. *New York City Transit Authority Photo File*

Whenever a Hollywood filmmaker requires a subway station for a back-drop, the Transit Authority rents out its abandoned Court Street station, which also serves as a transit museum. *Dennis Wendling*

Hollywood went underground to film *The Taking of Pelham One Two Three*, a story about the hijacking of an IRT local. *United Artists Corporation*

The art of subway construction has progressed immeasurably since the first IRT line was built in lower Manhattan. However, costs have risen so steeply that many projects such as the Second Avenue line have been abandoned because of lack of funds. *New York City Transit Authority Photo File*

One of the Transit Authority's most ambitious projects in the late fifties was the Chrystie Street connection in lower Manhattan. The "cut-and-cover" method of subway building was used here. *New York City Transit Authority Photo File*

An electrical fire on April 21, 1964, brought about destruction of the IRT's SAM, the automated subway train that operated between Times Square and Grand Central station. *Sprague Library, Electric Railroaders Association, Inc.*

Track repair on the Williamsburgh Bridge can be difficult and nerve-wracking with the waters of the East River glistening through the ties. *New York City Transit Authority Photo File*

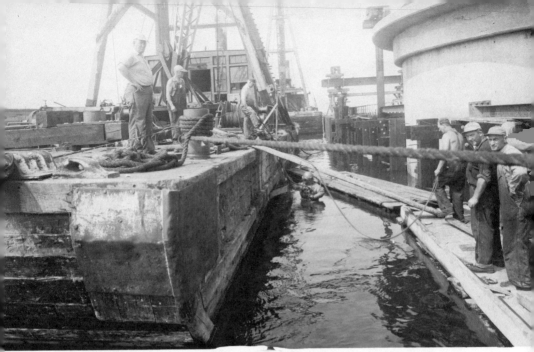

Once operated by the Long Island Rail Road, the Rockaway line was annexed by the Transit Authority (following a major trestle fire) and repaired so that New York had another "subway that went to the sea." *New York City Transit Authority Photo File*

While a seagull glides in the background, the Transit Authority's Rockaway line rolls over Jamaica Bay enroute to the Atlantic Ocean beach. *Sprague Library, Electric Railroaders Association, Inc.*

It's hard to believe that a New York subway operates in such a bucolic setting, but the IRT's Dyre Avenue line (once part of the New York, Westchester and Boston Railway Company) is the exception, here meandering through the upper reaches of the Bronx. *Sprague Library, Electric Railroaders Association, Inc.*

The term *subway crush* was coined in 1904 after the IRT made its debut. More than seven decades later, the crush continues. *Bob Leon*

THE SUBWAY SUPERSTARS

Man's—and woman's—love for railroading is at once limitless and amazing. In New York City alone there are ten different transit-fan organizations devoted to the care and adoration of subway and elevated cars. The folks who belong to these groups represent only a small fraction of train buffs in the city and throughout the country. (Who says you have to be a card-carrying member of the Electric Railroaders Association to be a transit nut?) Some of them, such as Ed Silberfarb of the Transit Authority's public relations department, are fortunate enough to be paid for working at their hobby.

Then there are people such as Karl Stricker, a Vietnam veteran, who operates a computer for a living but knows more about subways than most employees who run them. "My husband," said Audrey Stricker, "is always wrapped up in things like the BMT." Karl Stricker represents the intense rail buff; he will not miss a chance to stop, look, and listen to trains wherever he may be.

Twice Audrey managed to get Karl to agree that they take their vacations in Hawaii. Both times he called on Honolulu's mass-transit

207

director. When the director complained about the massive jams on his freeways, Karl promptly suggested he run a few express buses at a 25-cent fare from the outlying areas to downtown Honolulu. He did, and the jams eased.

The subway or train addict is a special species, some outstanding representatives of which can best be described as subway superstars. Some, like George Horn, Harold Wright, and the Reverend Francis J. Cosgrove, have been mentioned earlier. Five more subway superstars are included here.

The subway superstars who follow were selected from a cast of thousands. The qualifications were *(a)* display love of the line; *(b)* uniqueness; *(c)* have made a contribution to railroading in some form; and *(d)* have an interesting story to tell.

Don Harold, who works for the Transit Authority, knows as much about subways and streetcars as anyone alive. He is revered by his transit peers and is the man most sought out when anyone from a film producer to a subway buff wants information from the TA's public relations office. Harold was still in diapers when he became a rail fan—he can recall the precise moment when he first saw a trolley car—and now is regarded as one of the foremost rail experts in the world.

By contrast, Rebecca Morris came by her love of subways in adulthood. A native of Youngstown, Ohio, Rebecca holds degrees in library science and English literature from Columbia University. Her claim to superstardom began with her nonstop riding performance in 1973 when she rode every line on the TA system.

Bob Leon was chosen a superstar on the strength of his subway photography, which is without peer. A former photographer for the TA, Leon has combed every transit nook and cranny both underground and above, to compile the most definitive collection of single station (Times Square) photos (of trains and people) in the world.

Perhaps *the* unique superstars are Howard and Suzanne Samelson, a married couple from Manhattan who own the only antique store devoted exclusively to transit matériel. The shop, Broadway Limited, is located directly over New York's first subway line, the IRT Broadway West Side local, which regularly causes tremors among the antique china and other memorabilia in the store at Broadway near 106th Street.

Each of the superstars has in his or her own way made a distinctive contribution to the world of subway fandom. Here, in their own words, the subway superstars tell about themselves and their love of the New York underground, as well as of trains in general.

Rebecca Morris, Ms. Subways

In the fall of 1973 Rebecca Morris did what nobody else has ever done for the New York subway system. She rode every inch of track, from Brooklyn to the Bronx, and then published in the New York *Daily News* Sunday magazine a definitive chronicle of her odyssey.

Rebecca, who lives in a venerable high-rise apartment overlooking Riverside Drive (and the Hudson River) at 114th Street in Manhattan, owns one of the most exhaustive personal indices of the New York subways and enjoys sharing her rail buffery with others. Here is her account of her corner-to-corner ride on the system.

The Lefferts Blvd. Station at four in the morning could be the loneliest place in New York. Or maybe just the coldest. Wind blows across the elevated tracks. I look out of the train—suspended here—waiting for the return run to Manhattan. Outside the night is dark except for some metal lamps on the deserted platform. Bare light bulbs form little circles of heat in the cold air. I am absolutely alone. Reflected in the train windows are its baby-blue walls splashed magenta and orange with graffiti. Beyond them I can see the black tops of trees, the low buildings of Queens stretching west toward Brooklyn. Far off, a yellow glow indicates Manhattan. Shivering, I cross to the open door and step out onto the platform. It is very still. A quarter moon hangs over Ozone Park where all sensible people are asleep.

It might be warmer below near the token booth. Perhaps there is even a candy machine. But if the train should suddenly pull away. . . ? No, I decide. Even if there is a machine, it won't be working. There are some 6,600 vending machines in the New York Subway System. I know of four that work. The Interborough News Co. owes me eighty-five cents. Dear Sirs . . . I begin composing a letter in my head—then stop. If I give the locations of all the stations where I lost coins yesterday, they'll think I'm mad. Some of those stations are 50 miles apart!

It seems to me that I have been here an eternity. I look at my watch: 20 minutes. This wait could ruin my chance at the world record. It stands at 21 hours and 8 minutes.

The first subway riding record—traveling the entire system of routes for a single fare—was set October 27, 1904: IRT Opening Day. . . . Scheduled time for an express was 26 minutes; the local took 46. Although those early riders were conscious of making history, it is doubtful that they had any thoughts of setting track records. It was just too simple.

In 1940 the three lines (BMT, IRT, IND) were unified under city control in June. Two days before that unification, Herman Rinke, a curious and indefatigable electric railroad enthusiast, decided to tour the existing system for a single five-cent fare. He had no thought of setting a record. With unification, the IRT-operated 9th Ave. el was scheduled for demolition. His trip was a 25-hour sentimental gesture. It turned out to be the first recorded try. Since that day, more than 66 people have ridden the entire system in 24 recorded trips. These records are kept in an unofficial file at the [TA's] Public Relations Dept. No one knows how many have done it just for fun. The 1961 subway map cited the example of a Flushing youth who had ridden all the routes in 25 hours and 36 minutes for a single token. The TA's aim may have been to point out the scope or convenience of the subway, but that record—set Jan. 25, 1957 by Jerome Moses, 16— instead seemed to invite competition. During the 1960s, subway derbies became a fad with urban students; 11 of them were completed during the peak years of 1966 and 1967. On April Fools' Day of 1966, the M.I.T. Rapid Transit Club began a highly publicized ride. They had used a computer to route their attempt and informed the newspapers. On April 2, they were feeling foolish by 1 hour and 1 minute. And Geoffrey Arnold, who had held the 24 hour, 56 minute record since 1963 when he was 17, remarked "Pacific Street was a ridiculous place to start." That June, nine boy scouts from Troop 290 in Queens further shamed the computer by logging 23 hours and 18 minutes. And on Aug. 3, 1967, 16-year-old James Law, with six buddies, rode from 168th St., Jamaica, to Pelham Bay Park in 22 hours 11½ minutes; a time cited in the current *Guinness Book of World Records.*

When the Bronx Third Ave. el was closed in August 1973 subway route mileage was diminished 5.5 miles. On Oct. 8, Mayer Wiesen, 35, and Charles Emerson set a "modern record," riding over 230.8 route miles, changing trains many times, and passing through the 462 operating stations, in 21 hours and 8 minutes. A record which looks as if it will stand unless I get out of the Lefferts Blvd. Station.

At 8 yesterday morning, I am just starting out, entering the 168th St. terminus of the Jamaica spur, an old elevated line taken over and extended by the BMT. The 1893 span between Alabama Ave. and Cypress Hills may be the oldest el track still in continuous use. The train I board is one of the oldest also: rolling stock built in the mid 1930s. Sixty-watt bulbs light the cars. Hanging down from the ceiling are fans with black blades. I make my way to the front car, intending to ride looking out the window next to the motorman's cab, but a handsome black kid, about 13, has got there first. He stands hands in his pockets, nose to the glass, alert, ready to "drive the train." At 8:03 we head toward Manhattan—looking down long streets, old houses, over expressways clogged with morning traffic, rattling past Cypress Hills Cemetery where miles of tombstones cast small neat shadows in the early light. At Broadway Myrtle, I change to the M train, yoyo-ing up and back to cover the Myrtle Line—past houses whose third-story windows, with pulled blinds are often no more than six feet from the train.

9:15. Manhattan comes into view from the Williamsburg Bridge. Below the East River is gray. It is a postcard approach. The train "zooms-in" like a 1940s movie—so familiar that I almost expect to see titles flash across. No matter. The Manhattan skyline still makes me gasp.

10:00. I am changing trains in Brooklyn when I see the kid from Jamaica el again. We grin in recognition. "Hey," I shout, "Are you doing the system, too?" As the train doors shut I see him nod. He swings off to Coney Island while I race up in search of the Astoria train. On the DeKalb overpass I spot a snack bar and buy Coke for breakfast. Aside from some coins in my jeans, a notebook and map, I have decided not to carry anything. I want to see if I can live off the subway—sort of an urban Camp Fire Girl.

11:12. Enroute to Flushing on a blue World's Fair train. To my left

Shea Stadium passes; while off to the right lies Flushing Meadow. The ribbed Unisphere and skeletal towers of the '64 Fair rear up out of the flat landscape—fossilized like dinosaurs.

12:05. Returning to Manhattan, I change at Jackson Heights for the newer IND. On the underpass is a Nedicks—coffee and a hot dog—breakfast is shaping up. I am wiping mustard off my fingers when I reach the underground Roosevelt Ave. platform. On May 20, 1970, this was the site of the first passenger fatality due to collision or derailment in 42 years; two GG trains collided during morning rush hour killing two passengers and injuring 71.

1:55. The F train to Coney Island is one of the new, longer R-44 models: pristine and elegant, with seats of muted orange and yellow. Panels of fake wood are set into its walls and fluorescent lights line the ceiling. Just before the doors close, a chime sounds. . . . The advertising cards, color transparencies lit from behind, glow.

I am about to succumb to the quiet style of these long, air-conditioned cars, when I notice that the doors between them are kept locked. These new, 75-foot units do not mesh properly on curves; the space between cars becomes dangerous. Motormen, conductors, and presumably transit police, have keys, but New Yorkers are naturally leery. Many feel that being trapped in one car could become a risky situation.

The IND Coney Island line becomes elevated for a brief span entering Brooklyn; the highest point in the system, 87.5 feet above street level, is at the Smith and Ninth St. Station. Here the view is open in all directions: back toward postcard Manhattan, out into the harbor. Little automobiles crawl over the arched expressway ahead; below the Gowanus Canal and the Red Hook neighborhood. Too soon, we are underground.

At Church Ave. the line ramps upward again, joining the 1919 BMT el track at Ditmas Ave., where it emerges and begins the long approach to the ocean. Coney Island, cold and closed, decorates our passage. Orange and green spokes of the Wonder Wheel circle blue sky; flags and bits of banner blow. A deserted but honky tonk air prevails. We pass the roller coaster, webbed and delicate in the afternoon light. The air is bracing.

2:54. The Brighton Line heads back to Manhattan, for a while paralleling the sea. Short views down streets end in ocean. The pastel acres of Brighton Beach Baths stretch, patterned, toward the sand.

We stop at Sheepshead Bay before heading northwest along an embankment and cut through the tree-hung backyards of Victorian mansions facing Buckingham Road.

3:15. At the Prospect Park Station hundreds of high school kids mill, going home. Cops range the platform and one accompanies us onto the Franklin Shuttle. The kids are wonderfully natty; boys and girls stride aboard wearing platform shoes that defy balance, pants with big bells, hats, lots of jewelry, elaborate hair-dos. While I am aware that teenagers in groups are responsible for a fair amount of subway crime, I cannot imagine this stylish group doing anything to muss their clothes. Subway history is full of accounts of rampage and vandalism. Two days after the 1904 opening; eight youths armed with buckshot blowers boarded the new subway at 145th St. and proceeded to shoot out the electric lights while doing gymnastic stunts on the straps. Two were arrested at 96th St., the rest escaped. But this was not the first subway crime. *That* occurred opening night. During the crowded ride north from Brooklyn Bridge Station, someone lifted the $500 diamond stickpin that had been holding down the tie of Harry Barret of W. 46th St. When he reached Grand Central, his necktie was flapping.

3:50. The return shuttle is almost empty. As it approaches Prospect Park again, we pass near Empire Blvd. In November of 1918 it was still called Malbone St. The name was changed after the Brighton train, jammed with evening rush hour passengers, failed to make a curve at the tunnel there, causing the worst subway disaster ever.

5:02. I am picking up a few stray miles under Rockefeller Center when evening rush hour begins. While I know the total 3.8 million daily subway riders cannot all be taking the D train tonight, it *feels* as if they are. Jammed shoulder to shoulder, passengers have no-where to look but up. Above our heads, "Miss Subways" stares out of her poster, giving us a strained smile, "hoping to do some modeling." Since 1941, when the contest began, over 200 New York working girls have become "Miss Subways." Currently, two winners, out of six finalists, are chosen every eight months by passenger vote. Miss Subways receives a $40.00 charm bracelet dangling silver tokens, and her picture decorates the 6,700 subway cars for a three-month period. I ride standing all the way to 205th St., the Bronx. Sheer endurance does not win a girl the title.

6:35. At 168th St. and Broadway, I change trains again, and descend into the IRT on a hot automated elevator to ride the Broadway local to Van Cortlandt Park. The ride is through the deepest section of track in the whole system: 180 feet below street level at the 191st St. and St. Nicholas Ave. station.

7:00. Moving under Harlem on the No. 3, a rather splashy train with big graffiti—mustard yellow and pink predominate. Despite $10 million spent to remove graffiti and 1,562 arrests in 1972, the TA is losing the "spray can war." I read off the names: Supreme King 219, Snake II, Lopez 138, and amuse myself trying to think up my own subway logo—in case graffiti should become legal. Outside the stations pass, dingy, written all over. Two Black Muslims move in and out of the straphangers selling *Mohammed Speaks*. On this line, I am a "token white"—the pun lifts my spirits.

8:02. TA police range the E. 180th St., Bronx platform where the No. 2 pauses. One boards, walkie-talkie mumbling at his waist. He will be riding until 4 A.M. Since May of 1965, a uniformed transit patrolman has been assigned to every train during these hours.

10:30. I stand in the first car, face pressed against the glass, speeding through a dark underground world, the lighted coach behind me forgotten, as the black tunnel comes on. Tracks in perspective lines rush, disappearing under my feet, crossing, converging ahead. Signal lights change: yellow—"proceed with reduced speed," green over yellow—"on diverging track." Express lines mount, as local tracks sink in the dark. In the distance, tiny orange lights flicker above the tracks, then disappear where track-men carrying lanterns dive into the sidings. Now the square, metal-pillared cut rounds into a tube; we approach the old, 1908, Joralemon Street tunnel. Green lights signal us through. I make myself useful peering intently at the dark curved walls, checking for leaks.

1:12. The Wilson Ave. station on the Canarsie line is a narrow, double-decked curiosity: one track occupies each level—the eastbound track emerges, briefly elevated, traveling above the underground westbound span. We pass the deserted platform in half light. It faces—a single track away—the Cemetery of the Evergreens. No one in his right mind would get off at Wilson Ave. at 1:12 in the morning. No one did.

2:30. The A train heads out over the waters of Jamaica Bay leaving the huge glow of JFK that arc-lights the eastern sky. I have made the Rockaway Round Robin on schedule and can relax. Only between

214

the hours of midnight and 6 A.M. is it possible to cover the entire Rockaway peninsula on a single train.

The train moves further out across the vast, dark bay. Only feet below on either side, water laps the narrow trestle. Far out, a crescent of lights veers gently inward on the long railroad stem. Beyond that brilliant curve, the ocean pounds. For miles around the night is black and cold, the water deep. A strange place for a New York subway train.

4:00. And farewell to Lefferts Blvd.

5:30. Waits are long now. The work trains move slowly underground through nearly empty stations, picking up trash and cleaning out tunnels. The New York bars have closed, and some standees on the Hoyt St. platform bear witness to this fact. A heavy, black woman joins me; she walks as if her feet hurt, and I suspect she has just got off work. The trains always take a while at this hour, she tells me. We stand together on the platform, unacknowledged sisters, re-enforcing each other. In 1907, the Hudson Tubes were still running Women Only Cars with guards aboard to insure privacy. I guess we *have* come a long way.

At 6:26 the sun rises over Greenwood Cemetery where I am passing, for the second time, over an elderly bit of track known as the Culver Shuttle; 1.1 miles still bear tribute to Andrew Culver, who built a steam railroad to Coney Island that passed over this site in the 1880s.

7:00. Coney Island for the second time in two days! Crossing the Stillwell Terminal overpass, I go by the employees cafeteria and smell breakfast. On the Sea Beach Line, morning rush hour is just beginning. This is the third rush hour I have ridden through without leaving the subway. The poignancy of that situation might be enough to make one who has dined off Zagnut bars, peanuts, and Lucy Ellen orange slices for two days, get a cramp. I try not to think of hot coffee.

8:10. Changing trains at Union Square I am especially careful, warned by history. The first subway passenger accident occurred here Opening Day, 1904. A Miss Sadie Lawson, 26, of Jersey City, who had been riding north and south for several hours, fell getting off the southbound train and broke her hip. I grab a metal strap and hang on tightly all the way to 42nd Street.

8:25. Times Square. The 42nd Street shuttle contains 2,700 feet of original 1904 IRT Right of Way, now semi-isolated. In 1928, the second worst accident in New York subway history happened just south of here on the Seventh Avenue line, the infamous "Times Square Disaster."

9:30. The Lexington Avenue Express emerges into bright sunlight just before the old Yankee Stadium. On the golf course below Woodlawn terminus, lucky men tee off across the rolling fairways. It is a splendid day for riding elevated trains.

10:39. Pelham Bay Park. I have made the trip—on 67 different trains—in only 26 hours and 36 minutes. 26 hours and 36 minutes! The thought that I may be the first woman to complete the ride does not console me at all. But the sun is shining. And I have my logo: Ms. Subways 114.

Reprinted by permission of Rebecca Morris and the New York Sunday News.

Don Harold, Mr. Traction

To label Don Harold simply a rail fan is not enough. His involvement with transit is more serious than the word "fan" suggests. Harold's knowledge of the New York City transit system is encyclopedic.

As a child growing up in Brooklyn, Don was influenced by many employees of the old BMT system. By the time he was seven he had a complete understanding of all the subway, elevated, and trolley lines in Brooklyn. He has since translated that knowledge to his job as public affairs officer for the New York City Transit Authority.

From his Jay Street office in downtown Brooklyn, Harold strives to make the system work. At home in Flatbush, as a collector of transit memorabilia he spends endless hours preserving the history of the transit system.

To a rail fan, "traction" is the word used to describe a rail system. To rail fans Don Harold is unequivocally "Mr. Traction!" Here is the story of how rails have guided his life from its very beginning.

My mother once told me that when I was a baby, sitting in my carriage, and she wanted to do some fast shopping at the grocery store, all she had to do to keep me quiet was leave the carriage in a spot where I could see the trolleys go by.

Later, from Grandad, I learned about the community each trolley served and the transfer privileges for each line. He taught me about the various privately owned companies, the equipment, and who owned each piece. I can remember being on the Broadway (Brooklyn) trolley and hearing him explain how those cars had been rebuilt. He knew *everything* about trolleys and he constantly tried to pass this knowledge on to me. Many times we would pass a piece of equipment he had discussed earlier and he would ask me questions about it. If I didn't remember he would bawl the daylights out of me! I really had to remember, or else. . . .

One of my fonder memories dates back to when I was five years old and my whole family went to Manhattan to have dinner and see a movie. We were standing in the rain on Broadway (Manhattan) watching the old open-bench trolley cars go by and Grandad said, "Well, the boys aren't going to have a chance to ride one of these again—they are going to do away with these cars." So we got on these beautiful old cars with the running boards along the sides, and took a trip all the way down Broadway. I really cherish that memory, rain and all. I still remember the conductor swinging along the running board.

The only thing my grandfather didn't teach me was the bus routes; he had absolutely no use for them—like most train buffs. To satisfy him a vehicle had to ride on rails. I feel the same way.

My fascination for rail systems began with a great love for streetcars. After getting interested in trolleys I became fascinated with elevated trains and then subways, which are an outgrowth of the elevated system.

Once I learned all about the BMT system I found it necessary to learn the IRT system simply because that was the system serving the area in which I lived. Then I decided that as long as I knew the BMT and the IRT I ought to know the IND as well, so I set about the business of learning that system too.

In 1943 when I was twelve years old, my grandfather died. By then my involvement with rails was firmly implanted. I made a big step forward in 1946 when Sammy Shiffter, at the time a trolley motorman and now a conductor for the Transit Authority, sponsored me for membership in the Electric Railroaders Association. By 1947 I was accepted as a member and have been going to the fan trips, movie shows, and other activities ever since. The early fan trips were great because there was a tremendous variety of equipment to use at the time—more than now—and there were so many lines to ride. The things we did back in the forties before the system began to diminish were really something. I once took a fan trip all over New Haven on an open trolley when the lines were still open there. When I was fifteen I took a trip on the old Third Avenue elevated line in Manhattan. We rode in an open flatcar with a railing around it. I shared the car with a whole bunch of old-time rail fans.

George Horn, who is one of the greatest of all train buffs, rode on that trip with me. We became good friends and have remained so for over thirty years. George became a trolley motorman on the BMT. We always made sure to get George assigned as our motorman for the fan trips; he was that good.

One night when I was on the way home from a date I saw George at the depot at Ninth Avenue and he asked me to make his last run with him. Once we were out he asked me if I wanted to try my skill at operating the car. I had done it a number of times so I said, "Why not?" The McDonald Avenue trolley run was scheduled to last thirty-eight minutes but all you really needed was twenty-five. George told me that if I could get down to Coney Island and back to the depot in nineteen minutes I could catch the Vanderbilt Avenue car that would take me home. We must have been moving pretty fast because I had to wait for the Vanderbilt.

Since I had been infatuated with trains all my young life I really wanted to deal with transit as a career. My family wasn't too happy about this because of my grandfather's experience. He had been an inspector with the BMT until the worst part of the Great Depression, about 1937, when he was one of sixty inspectors demoted to the rank of trolley motorman because of the line's financial problems. When I talked about going into railroading my mother would say, "Look at how they treated your grandfather. After twenty-five years they demoted him. They don't treat anyone nicely, so why get into that kind of business?"

Obviously I listened, but didn't obey. My decision to pursue a career in transportation came one night when I was in my early twenties. I was at a Holy Name Society meeting at my parish church in Brooklyn and they had a wonderful speaker who was a priest. He mentioned that many of us there hated our jobs, and hated even to go to work. He encouraged the younger men to find out what they *liked* to do and make a career out of that. He made a lot of sense to me, so I decided there and then that somehow I'd get myself into the transportation business.

It took me quite a few years, because the Transit Authority is somewhat hamstrung by Civil Service regulations and there aren't always tests given for the positions I wanted. In those days there was no such thing as a management program like we have today. You came in as a Grade Two clerk, a conductor on the subway, bus operator, or some kind of maintenance position. These jobs were all on the operating level. The tests weren't given too frequently and then you had to wait a long time for your name to be called. I had to wait ten years to realize my goal of a career in transit.

While working at other jobs I kept in touch with a lot of people in official positions with Transit Authority, especially people in the personnel department. Many of these guys had come up through the ranks and I knew them when they were trolley-car motormen and inspectors.

Then I finally got my big break. During the mid-sixties the Authority was in the process of scrapping a lot of its vintage subway cars. Many of them had already been wiped out of existence and more were on the verge of disappearing completely. Len Ingalls, who was the boss of the public affairs office at the Authority, and I had been friends. One day we discussed the situation and Len asked me for suggestions about which cars to save. He said it would be tough to save all the cars. I said, "Look, Len, if I worked for you I'd get the job done!" I think Ingalls was impressed, and the wheels started to turn in my favor. The next thing I knew I was working for Ingalls.

One of the first projects I was assigned was saving the museum cars. I had to use a little subterfuge here and there in the beginning to get the job done, since not everyone thought it was such a good idea. But I found a peg—a ceremony to celebrate the "50th Anniversary of Subway Service to Queens." It gave us the opportunity to restore some vintage cars to the condition they were in fifty years ago. Today the Authority has set aside five trains of museum cars representing the type of car you would find for each period of transit history. Until recently they were available only to people who chartered them for fan trips and to moviemakers. Starting this summer, however, there will be an exhibit for the public at the Court Street (Brooklyn) station. Antique trains will take people there from midtown Manhattan. I've been in charge of the museum cars for eleven years now and haven't lost one yet.

My involvement with traction systems goes beyond my work with the Transit Authority. I'm a member of the Electric Railroaders Association. I also belong to the National Railway Historical Society and Branford (Connecticut) Electric Railway Association.

I have a collection of railroad transfers that I started in 1939. It covers the entire United States and many foreign countries. I also have been taking all kinds of transit photographs since 1944 and have collected thousands of pictures. The most prized part of my collection is a set of four albums of photos that are part of a series that the BMT took in 1930 showing complete views of every type of rapid transit and surface transit car, both passenger and service type, that they owned at the time. They have a broadside, a three-quarter, and an interior view of each car, mounted in books with a specification sheet over each set of prints. I was able to get hold of the whole set of books when they were going to dispose of them fifteen or twenty years ago.

More recently I've acquired movies of rapid transit and trolleys. I still try to make as many fan trips as I can and when I get to go on vacation I like to visit other cities and inspect their systems. I usually spend half my time taking a busman's holiday and half my time just being a tourist.

A large part of my collection consists of books and literature as well as many old transit files that were to be destroyed. These files help to document the history of the BMT system and the quality of the people who worked for them.

William S. Menden was president of the BMT and William G. Gove was the superintendent of equipment for the system back in the thirties. When you read some of their correspondence you realize that these were men who really knew how to run a railroad and they did a fantastic job. For example, there was a very bad snowstorm in 1935 that shut the Sea Beach line down for several days. Menden and Gove, as well as others, realized that they could never let this sort of thing happen again.

Throughout the next year Menden and Gove came up with various ideas for a special piece of equipment to keep the tracks and switches from getting covered with ice and snow. The most feasible was a special car that would spray alcohol on the third rail. They decided to test their idea by converting an old wooden elevated car for the purpose.

Gove wrote to Menden proposing that they convert No. 673 for this purpose. In replying Menden questioned the use of Car 673, since it still was in passenger service and in excellent condition. He suggested that they use No. 995, which was being used for a work car and was already in need of repair. That really showed me something about their knowledge of the system. There was the president of the company who knew the condition of every single car on the property. Menden made sure the right car was used and that no equipment was wasted. That's the kind of management I admire.

The new theory of management is that the man running the system doesn't really have to know the nuts and bolts behind the system. He has to know only the *procedures* and can have people working for him who know the nuts and bolts. Sometimes, though, when you place too much confidence in others, it can lead to trouble. *Big trouble.* I know some guys out on the road—motormen, conductors, and maintainers—young fellow in their twenties. They love their jobs and they are dedicated. They eat and sleep railroading and I think that this is the type of individual who should be encouraged and be given the chance to advance more. They could provide the good subway management we need in the future. We have assistant general superintendents on the property now who have come up through the ranks, and no one can dispute their expertise in operating the system.

If you want to see how to run a city railroad just go to Canada. The Toronto Transit Commission has a fantastic operation. That would be my second favorite system after New York City and I think there is a lesson to be learned from the Canadians.

First of all they run a well-balanced system. In Toronto they have rapid transit, trolley cars, trolley coaches, and buses. The equipment is impeccable and the operation is neat, tidy, and efficient. I've inspected it several times and I think it should be the model transit system for the entire country.

As for the future of the New York subways and surface transit, a lot can be done. For instance I'd like to see some consideration given to the restoration of trolley lines. These types of cars are most economical. We should have a more varied and balanced surface transit system. The rapid transit system is fine the way it is, and while I love all the old cars and I hate to see them scrapped, the practical point of view is that you don't win new riders by giving them forty-year-old cars to ride in. We have to make people come back and ride the subways, and I think that with the new R-46 and R-44 cars we're headed in that direction.

As I think back and try to understand what it is about traction systems that attracts people like me, I realize that there is a certain amount of order in a rail system. It's a planned, fixed system. To me it's very disturbing to see a train of mixed subway cars. There is a certain challenge in achieving the efficient operation of a traction system and this is one of the appeals of rail transit. For those who work in transit, the chance to contribute to this orderly enterprise can be a very rewarding experience.

Howard and Suzanne Samelson, the Broadway Limited Family

Howard and Suzanne Samelson are partners in life as well as in business. They are among the fortunate few who have been able to build a thriving business around their hobby, the love of trains.

The Samelsons, both in their twenties, own and operate the Broadway Limited Antique Store in New York City. It is the only one of its kind in North America. At their depot for railroad nostalgia as well as on the fan trips they take, they earn their living buying and selling old railroad antiques.

Howard is a third-generation rail buff. Suzanne married into the tradition and is now hooked for life.

Howie, Suzanne, and I met at their store on Broadway near 106th Street in Manhattan for the interview. A set of H.O. electric trains sat in the window surrounded by such railroad artifacts as station signs, lanterns, and a spring from the IND A train. The Samelsons were busy filling catalog orders when I arrived. The store was empty, since they close on Mondays. Settling down between stacks of timetables and Delaware & Hudson dining-car china, we began to explore precisely how railroading became the focal point in their lives.

Howard: I owe my interest in trains to my father. His started with a love of Brooklyn trolley cars and then spread to subways and finally railroads. My involvement started with the subway and spread to trains. I had no choice because by that time there were few trolleys left! My father and I used to spend many afternoons at the Jamaica station of the Long Island Rail Road and Penn Station watching the trains come and go.

Both my parents and my father's father were rail fans. They were historically interested as hobbyists, but there were no professional railroaders in our families. Suzanne and I are the closest thing to professional railroaders in the family.

Suzanne: When Howard told me of his interest in railroading I thought that was fine, everyone has a hobby. I had no interest in it at all when we first met. Then, one time at the end of December we decided to take a train to visit a friend of ours in Scranton.

It was the middle of the winter and the train went through the Delaware Water Gap. It was such a nice ride in the middle of the afternoon and then we had dinner in the dining car. It was a wonderful trip and I'm sure that was when I realized that I could be just as hooked on trains as Howie was.

Howard: Suzanne and I had decided that we would ultimately like to convert our hobby into a living. We thought that perhaps in thirty or forty years we could make it into our retirement business. But events began moving faster than we anticipated. I started to get fed up with my job at the ticket agency. We heard about an antique store that was for sale so we decided to try to buy it.

At first we were selling both transit and nontransportation antiques, but our goal was to sell only railroad-related material. One of the hobby publications recently did a survey indicating that there are at least one hundred thousand people in the United States that consider themselves rail buffs. That convinced us that there is a need for a store like ours. If there is going to be one it should be in New York City.

Suzanne: We mostly sell railroad memorabilia and nostalgia items, although we do have some steamship material. We have timetables, books, magazines, postcards, dining-car china, silverware, and station signs. We have some smaller metal items like builders' plates.

Timetables are by far the most popular item we have. They contain all sorts of information about what type of equipment was used, the kinds of schedules, the types of services offered, and what the advertising looked like. They really represent history.

Howard: Listening to the people come in and ask for the stuff is a riot. "Do you have a 1948 Pennsylvania Railroad timetable?" "Do you have the route sign from a subway?" In terms of the real world it's all unusual. In the collector's world there is nothing at all unusual about it.

Locating merchandise isn't always easy. The New York City Transit Authority doesn't own most of its equipment. The city gives it to them, and when it's time they sell it for scrap.

Railroads are not a prime source for collectors. The most likely place to find something is with another collector. We are always keeping an eye out for a new source of supply. We really are very aggressive in our attempts to find interesting pieces for the store.

I started collecting on my own before I met Suzanne. Now we collect very little. It was a real problem at first but we decided when we started the store that we would save only specific types of items for ourselves. All timetables are for sale. All brochures, no matter how fabulous they may be, are for sale. Right now all we collect is dining-car china.

For the most part the china is hard to find. They are, to a great extent, one-of-a-kind pieces. Many are out of production. By the way, the china in our collection doesn't sit on the shelf. We use it as our regular dinner service.

To a large extent Suzanne and I earn our living riding trains. We operate the souvenir car on the fan trips sponsored by the tour operators and charter groups. We are the concessionaires for the Delaware and Hudson Railroad. We make about two trips a month although we have made as many as eight trips in a three-week period. Most of the trips are scheduled for the summer. These excursions are round trips that originated at one time from New York City, but now start from such places as Binghamton, New York, or Wilkes-Barre, Pennsylvania. We also work with the Southern Railroad out of

Alexandria, Virginia. These trips are lots of fun and very colorful. Many of the fans dress up in costumes of the period.

At trips sponsored by the Electric Railroaders Association it's more of a free-for-all. Anyone can come and sell.

Suzanne: Howie and I have been working together for more than four years. It hasn't hurt our marriage, but there have been problems. When you're partners in business you're bound to have tensions, but when you are also partners in life there are twice the number of opportunities for trouble. The experience of working together has made us closer.

The last *real* vacation Howard and I had was our honeymoon. For the occasion we got on the first train headed west. We made it all the way to Los Angeles and back. It was on this trip that I realized I was just as much of a rail fan as Howard.

There is really something special and personal about leaving New York City in the late afternoon on the Broadway Limited, having dinner, going to your private room to sleep, and waking up the next morning in Chicago. To us there is a mystique about riding on trains.

Bob Leon, King of the Transit Photographers

Bob Leon and the New York City Transit Authority began their relationship in 1949 when Bob was hired as a staff photographer in the TA's legal department.

In the twenty-five years since then Leon photographed virtually every mile of the subway and surface transit systems in New York City. Some of his more exceptional work is on permanent display at the subway passageway underneath the New York Public Library. But Bob Leon is more than a photographer.

An accomplished painter, Bob is an innovator. His efforts to modernize the TA's photography department resulted in greatly increased productivity, and a fascinating career. This is the story as he related it to me.

I was working as a textile designer in New York in 1948 when my wife saw a notice in the newspaper saying that New York City needed a photographer for one of its departments. I applied for the job and took a test. Once the grades were in my name was placed fourth on the list. All I could do was sit and wait, but fortunately the wait wasn't too long. The Transit Authority called me in May 1949 to start a career with them as a photographer. The job was to last for twenty-five years, until I retired in 1974. I'm the third generation of Leons to earn a living with a camera.

To get the job was really satisfying. My grandfather was a photographer in Alexandria, Egypt, a hundred years ago. When he moved to Budapest, Hungary, in 1898, he opened a photo studio that remained until 1938 when my family moved to the United States. My father was a photographer until he retired in 1975. It was only natural that I carry on the family tradition. Before coming to the United States I worked as an art teacher in the high school in Budapest. I have always thought of myself as a photographer and an artist. To me the two are interchangeable. The only difference is the medium they use.

May 1949 was a turning point in my life. My family moved into a new house in Laurelton (Queens) in the beginning of the month. On May 19 I started my job with the Transit Authority, and my son Bobby was born May 28.

During my twenty-five years with the subway system my responsibilities went through four phases. When I started, I was assigned as a staff photographer attached to the legal department, when it was still located at the site of the old Paramount movie theater on Flatbush Avenue in Brooklyn. When a case came up and there was a need for a picture I would go to the scene and take it. That accounted for about 35 percent of my time. At the time we were divided into two units. My unit handled the BMT, while the Manhattan unit handled the IRT and the IND. When the Authority moved into its building on Jay Street (Brooklyn) in 1951, I got a real break.

The TA has a house organ that the public affairs department writes for the other employees. I was assigned to the public affairs department shortly after the move, and I did almost all the photographic work for the magazine. That, combined with the other pictures I took for the department, took up most of my time.

I am very interested in people's reactions to unusual things. That's why I always had so much fun in the subway.

Once I had to take some photos for an article on the hazards to track workers working on the Williamsburg Bridge. The bridge has no protection underneath so all you have to walk on are the ties and tracks. Believe me, it's a long way down if you fall. Well, to show the dangers involved I had to climb up on the bridge girders. The smallest slip and I would have fallen, and bye-bye Bob Leon! Someone should have taken my picture if they wanted to see dangerous working conditions.

Another time when I was working at the 86th Street station we were using a big camera and I was holding the people back while the other fellow took the picture. I had a flashlight in my hand and as a woman came down the stairs I held my arms out and said, "Hold it lady, hold it!" She grabbed the flashlight from my hand, looked at it, looked back at me, then demanded, "Why should I hold it?"

One of my most interesting assignments occurred when I photographed the crown princess of the Netherlands on her visit to the World's Fair in 1964. I had to photograph her in the subway car on the way out to and back from the site on the fair, in Flushing, Queens. Was it crowded in that subway car with all the press and photographers surrounding the princess! We were on the way back when I finished my last roll of film. Some high school girls got on the train and squeezed in next to the princess. I told the girls who she was and you should have seen those girls. They were so excited. The princess had a long talk with them and we all had a grand time. My only regret is that I was out of film and couldn't capture the excitement in the girls' faces.

Not all my subway assignments were fun, however. The first time a train passed me when I was standing along the wall in a tunnel I was scared stiff. When you stand at track level the train looks like a giant as it goes past you. You flatten yourself against the wall and just hope for the best. It happened to me so many times that I eventually got used to it, but you have to learn not to take any chances. One false move underground near the third rail or a speeding train and you're in big trouble.

When I wasn't on assignment, I became involved in a number of other transit-related projects. Each one of them was aimed at beautifying the subway. One was an art club I helped to start nearly twenty years ago. Many of us who worked for the TA got together to put on an exhibition of our paintings in the Transit Authority's Brooklyn building on Jay Street. Since then, we have had shows for two weeks every spring. Now these shows are on display at the 57th Street station of the Sixth Avenue line so everyone can see them. These exhibitions are the only time the Transit Authority gets undividedly good publicity. The shows were so successful, in fact, that after many years I prepared detailed plans to make one portion of that station into a permanent exhibition area. I would have extended invitations to various community groups and charities to exhibit art. I submitted it to Transit Authority Chairman William Ronan and he wrote back that he liked the idea and would study it. That was in 1972. All the departments that examined the facility agreed that it was a good idea and could be put into motion very cheaply.

Then Ronan resigned as chairman and David Yunich moved in. I sent my idea to him and explained what had already been done. Unfortunately the city hit a financial crisis with all kinds of budget cuts and the project was put aside. When I retired I offered to organize the project and arrange for the exhibits on my own time. I even offered to do this for no pay in the beginning. The answer was familiar: "We don't have the money!"

There is one project I worked on that has given me a great deal of satisfaction even though I didn't get much credit. Our art shows were so successful that it gave me the idea to have the TA get together with the Board of Education and arrange to have each school in New York City "adopt" a subway station. The school would be responsible for using it as an exhibiting area and keeping the station graffiti-free. This way the kids would learn that the subway is, in a way, their property and it's their responsibility to keep it beautiful. You might not see an immediate end to the graffiti, but I'm sure that if this were carried on year after year, eventually everyone would look at the subway from a different point of view. I thought the mayor should declare a "Let's Beautify Our Subways Week" and have all the stations open their exhibits at the same time. The impact would have been tremendous.

No one wanted to help at first. I met with the heads of the art departments in some of the schools, and they were against it because they didn't want to work the extra hours without pay. The TA didn't want to upset the Board of Education, so they let the project drop. Nothing happened for several years until the heads of the art departments in two schools came to the TA to ask if they could exhibit their students' artwork in the subway station near the school. One of the schools was on Twenty-fifth Avenue in Brooklyn and the other was a high school in Flushing. This was the type of support I had hoped for, so I started the wheels in motion again.

The situation was very difficult. We couldn't get any security for it and no one wanted to assume responsibility. I was told, "The subway is for moving people and if they stop to look, you have a problem." So we had to hang the exhibits in out-of-the-way places. There were innumerable problems to solve, but I was convinced this would be a major step in the beautification and cleaning of the subways. All other attempts to control graffiti had been largely unsuccessful. I'm glad to say that in any stations where art is now being displayed the area is graffiti-free and the pictures are never vandalized. I like to start training with the kids. By the time people are adults, it's too late to change their ways.

Not all the changes I made at the Authority were for the benefit of the riding public. When I started with the TA the photographers were using eight-by-ten cameras. You had to be a packhorse to carry all the equipment. If you wanted to take more than twelve pictures, two people had to go to carry the extra equipment. After a while we changed over to the smaller but still cumbersome four-by-five camera. We stayed with that until 1968 when I thought the time had come to switch to 35mm cameras. The cameras were smaller and just as good. I got permission from my department chief to use a test camera on assignments, so I went out and bought a camera to prove its worth. With the 35mm I could take two hundred pictures in the time it would take me to do twenty-four with the four-by-five. This time everyone agreed on the value of the project. Within six months everyone in the department had switched to 35mm. I had developed a tennis elbow packing all the old equipment around. The 35mm camera was the solution to my problem.

I got involved in a scheme about ten years ago that was supposed to be the first in a series of projects to make the subways visually beautiful. The architectural department thought it would be nice to display pictures in the stations that would show the passengers what they were going to see when they went out of the station. Mike Portilla, a coworker, was one of the originators of the project and came to me to discuss it. We worked very closely on the project. The passageway between the IND and the IRT that runs under 42nd Street from Fifth to Sixth avenues was chosen for the pilot project.

Now the area is decorated with a beautiful display of pictures that cover two eras in history.

We found pictures in the library that showed what the area looked like when the old Crystal Palace was still up. My photos show what is there today. I covered Bryant Park and the library from front to back. I must have taken two hundred or three hundred pictures of the area under every type of weather condition. It took a year to come up with the pictures we finally selected. The four that were eventually chosen were one inside the library, one outside, a picture of the fountain, and one of those beautiful statues at the base of the flagpoles in front of the library that no one ever sees. That's my favorite shot. I used a telephoto lens to compress the image so that I could get the statue in front and the great stone lion in the background.

We realized that these displays had to be made permanent and the process we settled on makes them look like graphic artwork rather than photos. It has a finish like that on a refrigerator or stove. The area is kept under twenty-four-hour surveillance to guard against vandalism. After the first pictures went up, the budget crunch forced people to decide what they consider necessary, so more displays like this have been delayed.

Meanwhile I kept trying to improve myself in school and in 1974 I received my master's degree in fine arts from Herbert H. Lehman College. As part of the program I took a course in photography that required each student to turn in a term project. For me the choice was easy. I picked the subject I had come to know better than any other. I did a photo essay on the Times Square subway station. I wanted to make people aware of certain underground forms of beauty they don't usually notice. For example there is a kind of beauty to the "high exit turnstile." The spokes form beautiful designs. Even a dirty old stairway can have something interesting about it. After I photographed the surroundings, I concentrated on my favorite subject: people.

I divided the people part of my project into sections. The people caught in the crush of rush hour represented a visual excitement that we have all felt when we got caught in it. I stood on a stairway on the north end of the station platform. When you stand there in the morning, all you see is backs of people. In the evening all you see are faces. This ebb and flow is very interesting to me.

I actually noticed that everyone had a different way of putting tokens in the turnstile. Some push, some drop. Then came the subway readers. People read under any and every condition in the subway. For many it's a way to avoid a waste of time, for others it's an easy way to block out the world around them.

I knew the Times Square subway station well because I had photographed it thousands of times, day and night, during every season. I saw and took pictures of things the average person never gets to see—everything from the TA's garbage train coming in at night to the scrubbing of the station walls by the maintenance department.

I was proud when I was asked to have a one-man show of my project at the Soho Gallery. I made the entire exhibit area look like a subway station. I had imitation bricks on the walls and mounted the pictures on billboards. It created a nice effect. After the show the public affairs department asked me if they could use the photos as a traveling exhibit to promote the TA and I agreed, but once again budget cuts prevented this from happening. It was just the wrong time. I thought about having the Times Square photo project published, but I never pursued the idea. By nature I'm not a businessman so, to me, just taking the pictures was reward enough.

Unlike many people who work for the Authority, I was not a rail fan when I started. Every form of transportation has its buffs. There are automobile freaks and there are subway freaks. I always thought the motion of the trains has a great deal to do with it; the motion creates an excitement. The basic tom-tom rhythm of the wheels adds to the effect.

When I ride the subway I try to make my time productive. I do crossword puzzles and sleep. I don't like the noise. It doesn't allow conversation, although the new R-44 and R-46 cars are beautiful and very quiet.

During my twenty-five years with the Transit Authority I learned that a Civil Service organization is not the type to grab at innovation quickly. The TA would need a different set of priorities and economic structure to make many of the projects I started possible. A Civil Service organization doesn't make a big thing out of the efforts of the individual. They didn't even give me credit in most of the photos I took, although somewhere I'm sure they mention me as photographer. I didn't fight for it and they didn't want to do it. It is gratifying, however, after a year and one-half of retirement, to find that what I did on the subways does mean something to someone.

APPENDIXES

Opening Dates of
New York Subway Lines

Explanatory Notes

Name of Line: The name by which the line may be most easily followed on the map (not necessarily the official name).

Section of Line: For quick location on the map, each new section is listed by the names of the nearest stations (not necessarily the exact section placed in public operation). (U) next to the station name indicates that the actual station is underground although the section of line is aboveground. (A) indicates that the station is aboveground on an underground section of line. (G) indicates that the station is on an elevated structure although the section of line listed is on the surface.

Type of Line: C=Open cut; E=Raised full or embankment; L=Elevated structure (virtually all are over public streets); R=Private surface right-of-way. S=Subway.

Tracks: The number shows how many tracks are constructed into the main body of the section indicated. It does *not* include sidings, storage tracks, etc., but *does* include express or middle tracks if in existence, whether or not in use by regular trains.

Opening Date: This is the date *regular* service began for the public. It is not the date of *(a)* the first test train or *(b)* "official" opening by the mayor, etc. Both events were sometimes held several days before the public opening. With less than a dozen exceptions, the dates came from two sources: The Rapid Transit Commission reports and the daily newspapers, which were checked against each other.

IRT DIVISION

Section of Line

Name of Line	From	To
Original Route Opened	City Hall Loop	Brooklyn Bridge
	Brooklyn Bridge	Broadway & 96th St.
	Broadway & 96th St.	Broadway & 145th St.
Broadway-Van Cortlandt Pk.	145th St.	157th St.
	157th St.	Dyckman St. (A)
	Dyckman St.	215th St.
	215th St.	225th St.
	225th St.	242nd Street
Lenox Ave.-White Plains Rd.	Lenox Ave. & 145th St.	148th St.
	Broadway & 96th St.	Lenox Ave. & 145th St.
	Lenox Ave. & 135th St.	Jackson Ave. (A)
	149th St. & 3rd Ave.	180th St.-Bronx Park
	(el station)	
	177th St.	219th St.
	219th St.	238th St.
	238th St.	241st St.
Brooklyn	Brooklyn Bridge (Manhattan)	Fulton St. (Manhattan)
	Fulton St.	Wall St.
	Wall St.	South Ferry
	Bowling Green	Borough Hall (Brooklyn)
	Borough Hall	Atlantic Ave.
	Atlantic Ave.	Utica Ave.
	Utica Ave. (U)	Junius St.
	Junius St.	Pennsylvania Ave.
	Pennsylvania Ave.	New Lots Ave.
Nostrand Ave.	Franklin Ave.	Flatbush Ave.
7th Ave.	Times Square	Pennsylvania Station
	Pennsylvania Station	Chambers St.
	Chambers St.	South Ferry
	Chambers St.	Wall & William Sts.
	Wall & William Sts.	Borough Hall
Lexington-Jerome Aves.	Grand Central	125th St.
	125th St.	138th St.-Grand Concourse
	138th St.-Grand Concourse	149th St.-Grand Concourse
	149th St.-Grand Concourse (U)	Kingsbridge Rd.
	Kingsbridge Rd.	Woodlawn
Pelham Bay Park	125th St.-Lenox Ave.	138th St.-3rd Ave.
	138th St.-3rd Ave.	Hunts Point Rd.
	Hunts Point Rd. (U)	177th St.
	177th St.	Westchester Square
	Westchester Square	Pelham Bay Park
Queensborough	Times Square	5th Ave.-42nd St.
	5th Ave.	Grand Central
	Grand Central	Vernon-Jackson Aves.
	Vernon-Jackson Aves.	Hunters Point Ave.
	Hunters Point Ave. (U)	Queens Plaza
	Queens Plaza	103rd St.
	103rd St.	111th St.
	111th St.	Willetts Point Blvd.
	Willetts Point Blvd.	Main St., Flushing (U)
Dyre Ave.	180th St.	Dyre Ave.

Type of Line	Length in Miles	Tracks	Opening Date	Note Reference
S	.1	1	Oct. 27, 1904	1
S	6.5	4	Oct. 27, 1904	
S	2.5	3	Oct. 27, 1904	2
S	.6	2	Nov. 12, 1904	
S	2.1	2	Mar. 12, 1906	
L	.8	3	Mar. 12, 1906	
L	.4	3	Jan. 14, 1907	
L	1.2	3	Aug. 1, 1908	
S	.3	2	May 13, 1968	
S	3.0	2	Nov. 23, 1904	
S	1.1	2	July 10, 1905	3
L	3.2	3	Nov. 26, 1904	3
L	3.4	3	Mar. 3, 1917	
L	1.1	3	Mar. 31, 1917	
L	.4	3	Dec. 13, 1920	
S	.3	2	Jan. 16, 1905	
S	.2	2	June 12, 1905	
S	.5	2	July 10, 1905	4
S	1.6	2	Jan. 9, 1908	
S	.9	4	May 1, 1908	
S	2.8	4	Aug. 23, 1920	
L	1.9	2	Nov. 22, 1920	
L	.4	2	Dec. 24, 1920	
L	.6	2	Oct. 16, 1922	
S	3.0	2	Aug. 23, 1920	
S	.4	4	June 3, 1917	
S	2.6	4	July 1, 1918	
S	1.0	2	July 1, 1918	5
S	.8	2	July 1, 1918	
S	1.5	2	Apr. 15, 1919	
S	4.2	4	July 17, 1918	
S	.7	2	July 17, 1918	
S	.4	3	July 17, 1918	
L	3.8	3	June 2, 1917	6
L	1.7	3	Apr. 15, 1918	
S	.9	2	Aug. 1, 1918	
S	2.5	3	Jan. 8, 1919	
L	2.0	3	May 30, 1920	
L	1.1	3	Oct. 24, 1920	
L	1.3	3	Dec. 20, 1920	
S	.4	2	Mar. 14, 1927	
S	.4	2	Mar. 22, 1926	
S	1.3	2	June 22, 1915	
S	.3	2	Feb. 15, 1916	
L	.9	2	Nov. 5, 1916	
L	4.3	3	Apr. 21, 1917	
L	.4	3	Oct. 13, 1925	
L	.6	3	May 14, 1927	
L	.9	3	Jan. 21, 1928	
	4.0	2	May 15, 1941	7

IRT Division Notes

1. From Brooklyn Bridge station to City Hall and back is a single track loop, and the City Hall station is the most ornate in New York. However, it is no longer open to the public, although Lexington Avenue locals operate around the loop without stopping in order to reverse their direction.

2. Due to a deep valley at that point, the 125th Street station on Broadway is on an elevated structure. The line emerges from underground at 122nd Street and returns underground at 135th Street.

3. Before subway train operation was extended under the Harlem River to the Bronx from 135th Street and Lenox Avenue, that portion of the new line between 149th Street and Third Avenue, and 180th Street, Bronx Park, was serviced by Third Avenue el trains reaching the new line via a connecting structure from the 149th Street el station. When through subway operation began, the trains emerged from underground beyond the subway's 149th Street and Third Avenue station, and climbed up to the previously used structure near the Jackson Avenue station. The stub end of the line at 180th Street was shut down after August 4, 1952 and the 0.2-mile structure demolished.

4. The South Ferry loop is double track and is accessible to both Lexington Avenue and Seventh Avenue trains. The original station is on the outer loop, and the inner loop was at first used for midday storage. The present station on the inner loop was added in 1918.

5. The South Ferry station on this section is the same one described in 4, above.

6. This section operated by shuttle service in advance of through Lexington Avenue train operation from Grand Central.

7. The Dyre Avenue line operates along the former right-of-way of the defunct New York, Westchester & Boston Railroad, an electrified suburban line which extended to points beyond the city via two routes. The City of New York purchased that portion existing within the city limits for rapid transit use. Connecting tracks for through operation off the White Plains Road branch at 180th Street are completed but not yet in use. Although it was originally four-track, only two exist today. The character of the line varies, with short adjacent portions of open cut, raised embankment, and tunnel. The Pelham Parkway station is underground.

An IRT "Low V" executes the screeching turn around the curve at South
Ferry, at the southern tip of Manhattan Island. *Sprague Library, Electric
Railroaders Association, Inc.*

BMT DIVISION

Name of Line	From	To
Centre & Nassau Sts. Loop (Manhattan)	Essex St. (Delancey)	Canal St.
	Canal St.	Chambers St.
	Chambers St.	Connection to Tunnel from Whitehall St. to Court St.
Manhattan Bridge-So. Side	Chambers St. (U)	Myrtle Ave. (Brooklyn) (U)
-No. Side	Prince St. (U)	Myrtle Ave. (Brooklyn) (U)
4th Ave. (Brooklyn)	Myrtle Ave.	59th St.
	59th St.	86th St.
	86th St.	95th St.
Sea Beach	59th St. & 4th Ave. (U)	86th St.
	86th St.	Stillwell Ave. (G)
West End	36th St. & 4th Ave. (U)	*9th Ave.
	9th Ave.	*18th Ave.
	18th Ave.	*25th Ave.
	25th Ave.	*Bay 50th St.
	Bay 50th St. (G)	Stillwell Ave. (G)
Brighton Beach	DeKalb Ave.	Prospect Park (A)
	Prospect Park	*Church Ave.
	Church Ave.	Newkirk Ave.
	Newkirk Ave.	Sheepshead Bay
	Sheepshead Bay	*Ocean Parkway
	Ocean Parkway	*West 8th St.
	West 8th St.	*Stillwell Ave.
Culver Line	9th Ave. (U)	*Ditmas Ave.
Myrtle Ave.	Broadway (Brooklyn)	Central Ave.
	Central Ave.	*Wyckoff Ave.
	Wyckoff Ave.	*Fresh Pond Rd.
Jamaica	Essex St. (Manhattan)	Marcy Ave.-Broadway (Brooklyn)
	Marcy Ave.	*Myrtle Ave.
	Myrtle Ave.	*Alabama Ave.
	Alabama Ave.	Cypress Hills
	Cypress Hills	111th St.
	111th St.	168th St.
Brooklyn to Manhattan via Tunnel & Broadway	DeKalb Ave. (Brooklyn)	Whitehall St. (Manhattan)
	Whitehall St.	Prince St.
	Prince St.	14th St.-Union Square
	14th St.-Union Square	Times Square
	Times Square	57th St. & 7th Ave.
	57th St. & 7th Ave.	Lexington Ave.-60th St.
	Lexington Ave.-60th St.	Queens Plaza (A)
Astoria	Queens Plaza	Ditmars Blvd.
14th St.-Canarsie	8th Ave. & 14th St.	6th Ave. & 14th St.
	6th Ave. & 14th St.	Montrose Ave.
	Montrose Ave.	Broadway Junction (A)
	Broadway Junction	*Sutter Ave.

* Dates for these portions refer to new construction replacing older route either on surface or older structure.

Type of Line	Length in Miles	Tracks	Opening Date	Note Reference
S	.8	4	Aug. 4, 1913	1
S	.4	2	Aug. 4, 1913	
S	1.0	2	May 30, 1931	2
B	2.3	2	June 22, 1915	3
B	2.4	2	Sept. 4, 1917	3
S	4.4	4	June 22, 1915	4
S	1.4	2	Jan. 15, 1916	
S	.4	2	Oct. 31, 1925	
C	4.4	4	June 22, 1915	
R	1.1	2	June 22, 1915	5
	.9		June 24, 1916	6
L	2.7	3	June 24, 1916	
L	1.1	3	July 29, 1916	
L	.7	3	July 21, 1917	
R	.8	2	July 21, 1917	
S	2.3	2	Aug. 1, 1920	
C	.8	4	Sept. 26, 1919	
C	1.0	4	1907	7
E	3.4	4	1907	7
L	1.1	4	Apr. 22, 1917	
L	.4	4	May 30, 1917	8
L	.4	2	May 29, 1919	9
L	1.1	3	Mar. 16, 1919	10
L	.6	2	July 29, 1914	
L	.7	2	July 1, 1918	
L	1.0	2	Feb. 22, 1915	11
B	1.7	2	Sept. 16, 1908	12
L	1.4	3	Jan. 17, 1916	
L	2.5	3	Dec. 21, 1916	
L	1.9	2		13
L	2.0	2	May 28, 1917	
L	2.4	2	July 3, 1918	
S	2.0	2	Aug. 1, 1920	
S	1.8	2	Jan. 5, 1918	
S	.8	4	Sept. 4, 1917	14
S	1.4	4	Jan. 5, 1918	
S	.8	4	July 10, 1919	
S	1.7	2	Aug. 1, 1920	
L	2.5	3	Feb. 1, 1917	15
S	.3	2	May 30, 1931	
S	3.9	2	June 30, 1924	
S	3.6	2	July 14, 1928	16
L	.6			17

BMT Division Notes

1. There are three tracks through Essex Street station.

2. Last portion of the Dual Contracts completed.

3. Manhattan Bridge, spanning the East River, has two separated pairs of tracks, one on each side of the bridge. The pair used by trains between Brooklyn and Times Square is on the north side; the pair on the south side is used by trains between Brooklyn and the Centre-Nassau streets loop.

4. This section includes a six-track portion through the DeKalb Avenue station due to the two Brighton Beach line tracks merging with the Fourth Avenue line at that point.

5. Before the completion of the eight-track Stillwell Avenue terminus, trains used a temporary Surf Avenue terminal.

6. This section has both a short two-track tunnel and a six-track open-cut approach to the double-decked Ninth Avenue station with three tracks on each level.

7. The section Church Avenue to Sheepshead Bay was converted from two to four tracks in 1907 by the Brooklyn Rapid Transit Company for Fulton Street-Brighton Beach el train operation. The open cut ends south of Newkirk Avenue.

8. West 8th Street station has two 2-track levels.

9. This portion is a double-deck structure with two tracks on each level. The data on this line refer only to the upper deck.

10. This is part of an original through route to Stillwell Avenue. On October 30, 1954, the IND division assumed Culver operation to Coney Island, and thereafter the BMT terminated at Ditmas Avenue.

11. The line from Fresh Pond Road to Metropolitan Avenue is an original unimproved el train surface right-of-way.

12. Original el train route.

13. Original unimproved el structure.

14. This portion opened in connection with the north-side tracks of the Manhattan Bridge.

15. Opening date refers to original IRT operation. Although originally built for and part of the IRT's Queensboro lines, this section transferred to complete BMT operation on October 17, 1949.

16. The Wilson Avenue station on this section is double-decked with one track on each level. The upper, or outbound, track is on a raised embankment; the lower, or inbound track is underground.

17. This section (Broadway Junction-Eastern Parkway to Atlantic Avenue) is a very complex network of intertwined tracks providing connections from the Broadway line to the Jamaica, Fulton Street, and Canarsie lines, and from the 14th Street line to the Fulton Street and Canarsie lines. It is an improved former el. Atlantic Avenue station has six tracks. Various connections were placed in service between October 17 and December 18, 1918.

The Park Row terminal housed the BMT Myrtle Avenue line. *Sprague Library, Electric Railroaders Association, Inc.*

IND DIVISION

Name of Line	From	To
Washington Heights to East New York	207th St.	168th St.
	168th St.	Chambers St.
	Chambers St.	Jay St. (Brooklyn)
	Hoyt-Schermerhorn Sts.	Court St.
	Jay St.	Rockaway Ave.
	Rockaway Ave.	Broadway-East New York
	Broadway-East New York	Euclid Ave.
	Euclid Ave.	Lefferts Blvd.
Rockaway	Rockaway Blvd.	Rockaway Park
	Rockaway Blvd.	Wavecrest
	Wavecrest	Mott Ave.
Bronx-Grand Concourse	205th St.	200th St.
	200th St.	145th St.
Coney Island	Jay St.	Bergen St.
	Bergen St.	Carroll St.
	Carroll St. (U)	4th Ave.
	4th Ave. (A)	Church Ave.
	Church Ave. (U)	Ditmas Ave. (A)
	Ditmas Ave.	Kings Highway
	Kings Highway	Ave. X
	Ave. X	Stillwell Ave.
Queens-Manhattan	50th St. & 8th Ave.	Queens Plaza
	Queens Plaza	Roosevelt Ave.
	Roosevelt Ave.	Union Turnpike
	Union Turnpike	169th St.
	169th St.	179th St.
World's Fair	71st & Continental Aves.	World's Fair
Queens-Brooklyn Crosstown	Queens Plaza	Nassau Ave.
	Nassau Ave.	Bergen St.
Sixth Ave.-Houston St.	59th St. & 8th Ave.	50th St. & 6th Ave.
	50th St. & 6th Ave.	34th St.
	34th St.	West 4th St.
	West 4th St.	2nd Ave. & Houston St.
	2nd Ave. & Houston St.	Jay St. (Brooklyn)
	50th St. & 6th Ave.	57th St. & 6th Ave.
	34th St.	West 4th St.

244

Type of Line	Length in Miles	Tracks	Opening Date	Note Reference
S	2.4	2	Sept. 10, 1932	
S	9.8	4	Sept. 10, 1932	
S	2.2	2	Feb. 1, 1933	
S	.4	2	Apr. 9, 1936	1
S	4.3	4	Apr. 9, 1936	2
S	.4	4	Dec. 30, 1946	
S	2.0	4	Nov. 28, 1948	
L	2.0	2	Apr. 29, 1956	
L	5.6	4	June 28, 1956	
L	3.9	2	June 28, 1956	
L	.5	2	Jan. 16, 1958	
S	.6	2	July 1, 1933	
S	5.1	3	July 1, 1933	3
S	.5	2	Mar. 20, 1933	
S	.5	4	Oct. 7, 1933	
L	1.4	4	Oct. 7, 1933	
S	2.4	4	Oct. 7, 1933	4
	.3	4	Oct. 30, 1954	5
L	2.3	3	Mar. 16, 1919	6
L	1.0	3	May 10, 1919	6
L	1.3	2	May 1, 1920	6, 7
S	3.0	2	Aug. 19, 1933	8
S	2.6	4	Aug. 19, 1933	9
S	4.0	4	Dec. 31, 1936	
S	2.4	4	Apr. 24, 1937	
S	.5	4	Dec. 10, 1950	
R	2.0	2	Apr. 30, 1939	10
S	2.3	2	Aug. 19, 1933	
S	4.8	2	July 1, 1937	
S	.9	2	Dec. 15, 1940	8
S	1.0	4	Dec. 15, 1940	
S	1.3	2	Dec. 15, 1940	
S	1.0	4	Jan. 1, 1936	
S	2.3	2	Apr. 9, 1936	
S	.4	2	July 1, 1968	
S	1.3	2	July 1, 1968	11

IND Division Notes

1. Hoyt-Court streets stub not in service.

2. There are six tracks through the Hoyt-Schermerhorn streets station.

3. 145th Street station has two levels—the four Washington Heights tracks above and the three Bronx tracks below.

4. Between Seventh Avenue and Fort Hamilton Parkway, the express tracks use a more direct route than the local tracks.

5. This section is a ramp between the IND underground line and the former BMT el structure (see also note 6, below).

6. The section Ditmas Avenue to Stillwell Avenue is part of the former BMT Culver line el structure that replaced an original el train route on the surface. The opening date shown is the date when the structure replaced the surface route. The transfer of this portion from the BMT to IND and the extension of the IND operations from Church Avenue to Stillwell Avenue took place on October 30, 1954, at which time the Culver line ended at Ditmas Avenue.

7. That section of the line between West 8th Street and Stillwell Avenue is double-decked and this item refers only to the two tracks on the lower deck. BMT division 9 refers to the upper deck.

8. The Seventh Avenue station on this portion is double-decked. The Queens-Manhattan line shown opening on August 19, 1933, uses the north track on each level. The Sixth Avenue-Houston Street line, shown opening on December 15, 1940, runs on the south side track on each level.

9. Between 36th Street and Northern Boulevard the express tracks use a more direct route than the local tracks.

10. Temporary line built only to run during the two seasons of the World's Fair in 1939 and 1940. It has since been torn up.

11. Express service began on this date between 34th Street and West 4th Street on the D line.

Reprinted by permission of the Electric Railroaders Association

A classic (and classy) IND "A" train. *New York City Transit Authority Photo File*

Pioneering Subways
of the World

This table includes only passenger subway systems. It omits underground sections of railways which are mostly surface lines, such as in Oslo; Athens; Newark, New Jersey; and Rochester, New York.

Year First Link of System Was Opened to Traffic	City
1863	London
1886	Glasgow
1896	Budapest
1897	Boston
1900	Paris
1902	Berlin
1904	New York
1908	Philadelphia
1919	Madrid
1920	Barcelona
1927	Tokyo
1928	Buenos Aires
1932	Sydney
1933	Osaka
1935	Moscow

The Electric Railroaders Association

The Electric Railroaders Association, Inc., is "a non-profit educational organization, founded in 1934 and devoted to the history and development of all types of electric railways," including main-line electrified railroads, rapid transit lines, interurban electric railroads, and streetcars. The association publishes a magazine, *Headlights*, for distribution to members and subscribers, and this magazine presents news, historical articles, and technical articles. The association also operates special fan trips over electric railway lines, conducts tours of shops and yards, and holds a yearly convention with activities of interest to anyone interested in electric railroads. Current membership is approximately 2,200. The ERA's address is 145 Greenwich Street, New York, New York 10006.

CHRONOLOGY OF
THE ELEVATEDS

August 26, 1878: The Third Avenue el line opened. This line was built by the New York Elevated Railroad Company under permission from the Rapid Transit Commissioners. Since the company now operated the Ninth Avenue line to South Ferry, they were permitted to construct a line up the East Side, which was begun at South Ferry and Chatham Square in November 1877. The route was via State Street, Front Street, Coenties Slip, Pearl Street, with stations at South Ferry, Hanover Square, Fulton Street, and Franklin Square; New Bowery, the Bowery with stations at Chatham Square, Canal Street, Grand Street, and Houston Street; while on Third Avenue the stops were at 9th, 14th, 23rd, 28th, 34th, and 42nd streets. Here the line went west to the new Grand Central depot of the Hudson River Railroad. The line was extended north from 42nd Street and Third Avenue, with service opening up stations at 47th, 53rd, 59th, and 67th streets on September 16, 1878, and extended further on December 9, 1878, to stops at 76th, 84th, and 89th streets. A new yard with offices was opened at 99th Street, between Third and Fourth avenues, when stations were opened at 99th, 106th, 116th, 125th, and 129th streets on December 30, 1878. By this time, the New York Elevated Railroad was carrying over 84,000 passengers daily on its two lines.

February 25, 1879: The Sixth Avenue Line began through service to 53rd Street and Eighth Avenue replacing a temporary shuttle that operated from 50th Street from the previous January 9. This connection with the Ninth Avenue line was begun on July 8, 1878.

March 17, 1879: The Third Avenue line extended operation south to a new station at City Hall from Chatham Square. This spur line construction was begun in June 1878, and traversed the thoroughfare known as Park Row. It

251

was closed down again on March 27, ten days after it opened. The remainder of the line from South Ferry to 129th Street inaugurated all-night service on April 15.

June 9, 1879: Both Sixth and Ninth Avenue lines extended their operations to 81st Street and Columbus (Ninth) Avenue, opening stations at 59th, 66th, 72nd, and 81st streets. Since it was a double-track structure, it was built jointly by the New York Elevated Railroad on the western side of the street and the Metropolitan Elevated Railroad on the opposite side. Service was further extended and stations were opened at 86th, 93rd, 99th, and 104th streets on June 21.

September 1, 1879: The Manhattan Railway Company assumed control of both the New York Elevated Railroad and the Metropolitan Elevated Railroad under an agreement signed the previous May 20. The Manhattan Railway Company was organized on November 10, 1875, at the suggestion of the Board of Rapid Transit Commissioners appointed by Mayor Wickham. This company had a capital stock of $2 million and was headed by Edwin Jay Gould with offices at 10 Dey Street. It also undertook to complete all remaining structural contracts of the previous companies under their franchises and to unify operations under one management. When the previous firms had passed from existence, they had built 81.44 miles of structure, the Metropolitan having contributed 44.25 miles and the New York Elevated contributing 37.19 miles.

September 17, 1879: The Sixth and Ninth Avenue lines further extended their lines north on Columbus Avenue to 110th Street, then east one block to Eighth Avenue, and then north again to 125th Street, opening a station at 116th Street. This structure was the highest of its kind ever built and was called Suicide Curve because of the large number of people who leaped to their death from this point. The 130th and 135th Street stations were opened on September 27 while 145th and 155th Street stations opened on December 1.

March 1, 1880: The Second Avenue Elevated Line opened. This route was constructed to 65th Street by the Metropolitan Elevated Railway Company and north of that point to the Harlem River by the Manhattan Railway Company, with work beginning at Allen and Division streets on February 24, 1879. From Chatham Square, the route followed Division Street, thence north on Allen Street and First Avenue, with stations at Canal, Grand, Rivington, 1st, 8th, 14th, and 19th streets. At 23rd Street the line turned west one block to Second Avenue and then north for the remainder of its route. Stations were opened at 23rd, 34th, 42nd, 50th, 57th, and 65th streets. A storage yard for the line's equipment was opened at 66th and 67th streets, between Second and Third avenues. This yard was abandoned on March 17, 1905. Coincident with this opening, Third Avenue line trains resumed service to City Hall.

May 2, 1880: Work was completed and trains began operating over a completely rebuilt structure on the west side of the Ninth Avenue line. The original track on the easterly side of Greenwich Street and the westerly side of Ninth Avenue, as well as sections reinforced in 1874, 1875, and 1876, were torn down section by section and replaced. During this reconstruction, service was maintained by using the sidings and turnouts, and afterward the sidings were used as a center express track, so that it became a three-track line from 14th Street to 59th Street, the only such line then in existence. The work had begun in October 1879.

July 1, 1880: The 34th Street branch opened. This spur, running from the Third Avenue line, connected with the East River ferries of the Long Island Rail Road, serviced by a shuttle service, with an intermediate station at Second Avenue.

August 16, 1880: Service was extended on the Second Avenue line from South Ferry to 127th Street, opening stations at 86th, 99th, 111th, 117th, 121st, and 127th streets. With the Second Avenue line going to South Ferry, service there of the Third Avenue line was discontinued and all Third Avenue trains terminated at City Hall.

November 1, 1881: The Sixth Avenue line operated to South Ferry, and all-night service was inaugurated on the line. The night trains operated until January 1, 1883, when the management discontinued them for economy reasons. So many complaints were received, however, that passengers were permitted to ride the employee trains until January 31, 1883, when half-hourly night service was reinstated and made permanent.

June 18,1882: The Second Avenue line terminated at Chatham Square, while the Third Avenue line alternated service between City Hall and South Ferry. An interlocking switch machine was installed at Chatham Square for the routings. The Second Avenue line used a platform just south of the junction, while the Third Avenue line used the original platform north of the junction. A shuttle was run in nonrush hours to City Hall from the Chatham Square (Third Avenue) station, and on September 25 an overhead pedestrian bridge was opened connecting the two platforms. The resultant congestion at this point was so acute that on January 11, 1885, the shuttle was extended to Canal Street station, for the South Ferry-City Hall interchange. Finally on April 12, 1885 track adjustments were made and both lines went to South Ferry.

August 27, 1885: The first electrically powered train ran on the Ninth Avenue line. The locomotive Benjamin Franklin made a number of experimental trips on the center tracks from 14th Street to 50th Street under the sponsorship of Leo Daft, pioneer electrical engineer. This locomotive weighed nine tons and used a bronze wheel of fourteen-inch diameter to pick up the current from a center third rail. It ran at a speed of twenty-five miles per hour and pulled four cars.

May 17, 1886: The Suburban Rapid Transit Company began operations. This new company was organized on March 6, 1880 for the purpose of constructing several elevated routes through the Annexed District, as the lower section of the Bronx was then known. Its original plans were to construct routes over a private right-of-way, but as the plans progressed it was found to be a prohibitively expensive program. In March and April 1886 it acquired through merger and lease the routes and franchises of the New York, Fordham & Bronx Railway Company which were almost parallel with the Suburban Company's routes. This second company had not built anything, but possessed many property consents and easements. The Suburban Rapid Transit Company built a center-bearing drawbridge across the Harlem River, an S-route over the yard and terminals of the New York, New Haven & Hartford Railroad, as well as the Harlem River & Portchester Railroad. The bridgework was begun on October 24, 1883. Service began operating from a newly opened station on the Second Avenue line at 129th Street to 133rd Street in the Bronx. The fare was 5 cents. Service was extended to 143rd Street on May 23. The old Second Avenue station at 127th Street was closed.

June 1, 1886: The fare on the Second and Ninth Avenue lines was reduced to 5 cents at all hours. It previously had been 5 cents only from 5:30 to 8:30 A.M. from 4:30 to 7:30 P.M. and was 10 cents to the remainder of the time.

The lower fare went into effect permanently on the Third Avenue line on October 1, 1886 and on the Sixth Avenue line on November 1, 1886. By this time, additional stations on the Second Avenue line were in use at 80th and 92nd streets.

October 26, 1886: Two elevated cars that were electrified by Frank J. Sprague (including heating, lighting, starting, and stopping) were tested on the 34th Street branch. It marked the first time a station platform was electrically lighted as well as the first application of dynamic braking. The car picked up 600-volt power from a center third rail. The power plant for this operation was located in a storage warehouse at East 24th Street and the East River. Mr. Sprague was Electric Railroaders' Association No. 1 member and is known as the "Father of Electric Traction."

November 25, 1886: The Harlem River branch of the Suburban line opened. A single-track structure that went down an incline to Willis Avenue and 132nd Street, where the Willis Avenue station of the New Haven Railroad was located. The cost of a transfer over this line was based on the New Haven fare schedules.

January 1, 1887: The 138th Street station opened on the Suburban line. During 1887 service was extended to 149th Street and Third Avenue on June 16; to 156th Street on July 1; to 161st Street on August 7; to 166th Street on December 25; and in 1888 to 169th Street on September 2; to 170th Street on September 29th.

September 1887: Another test of an electric motor (pulling an electrified passenger car) was conducted o the 34th Street branch of the Third Avenue line by Stephen D. Field. This motor was built at Yonkers, brought over the Hudson River Railroad to High Bridge, thence over the New York & Northern Railroad to 155th Street. It then was hauled over the Sixth Avenue line to South Ferry and then up the Third Avenue line.

November 26, 1888: Another test of an electric engine by Leo Daft (see August 27, 1885) on the Ninth Avenue line. This was a rebuilt Benjamin Franklin from the tests of 1881. The tests were begun in October and were completed on February 12, 1889. Power was supplied from a dynamo in an old factory on 15th Street. As many as eight cars were pulled at fifteen miles per hour.

June 4, 1891: The Manhattan Railway Company assumed operating control of the Suburban properties, as a result of a lease dated April 1. From the beginning of Suburban operations, their trains used a joint station with the Second Avenue line at 127th Street and then a station built on 129th Street between Second and Third avenues. The passenger load of all lines under Manhattan Railroad Company operation had reached 547,000 passengers daily.

July 20, 1891: The Suburban line was extended north on Third Avenue in the Bronx to 177th Street, with a station also at 174th Street. Stations at 180th Street, 183rd Street, and Pelham Avenue (Fordham Road) were opened on July 1, 1901. A new yard at 179th Street was put into use at this time, which supplemented one in use at 133rd Street near Willis Avenue. The Bronx Park spur and station were opened on May 21, 1902. An unusual operation of this spur was the hydraulic passenger-car elevator which lowered cars for storage from the structure to a small yard beneath, beside the New York Central Railroad tracks.

August 1, 1891: Service on the Harlem River branch was operated by the New Haven Railroad. The branch was closed down from December 18, 1887 until July 19, 1891 when service was resumed by the Manhattan Railway Company. It appears that some sort of New Haven through service to 129th Street lasted until May 11, 1905.

June 2, 1892: Third-tracking of the Ninth Avenue line was completed from 59th Street to 116th Street. The Sixth Avenue line also had new stations added by this date at 18th and 28th streets. Turnstiles were first installed on the Second Avenue line at 1st Street (downtown side) on August 10, 1896.

September 25, 1896: Through service (rush hours only) was instituted on the Third Avenue line from South Ferry to Bronx Park and from City Hall to Tremont Avenue (177th Street). On August 15, 1898 platform changes were made at 129th Street and this through service was extended to all hours.

October 5, 1896: Experimental operations with cars pulled by an electric motor were instituted on the 34th Street branch. This was the first application of an outside third rail and the use of batteries. This engine weighed ten tons, was eighteen feet long, and eight feet high in the center, and had a steeple cab. It carried a storage battery of 256 cells for use in case of a power failure. The two passenger cars that it pulled were lighted by fifteen lamps of sixteen-candle power. These experimental trips were under the guidance of Mr. J. B. Entz of the Electric Storage Battery Company. The powerhouse for this testing was in a building at First Avenue and 34th Street.

March 27, 1897: A new era in car lighting was introduced on the Sixth Avenue line with the placing in service of 400 cars equipped with Pinstch gas fixtures. There were four lamps in each car, nine feet apart, and each lamp had four jets at forty-candle power. The gas was manufactured at the 155th Street yards, and placed in seven-foot-long tanks under each car.

April 11, 1897: The famous "Bicycle Train" service was inaugurated. This service was operated each Sunday over the Ninth Avenue line from 155th Street to Rector Street, since platforms at South Ferry were too congested. Stations and trains involved in the service had "Bicycle Trains" (station) signs. Seats were removed on one side of cars and bicycle racks installed for twenty-four-inch bikes. The fare was 15 cents per passenger and bike, or 25 cents for two with a tandem. Thirty-five 2-car trains were run until autumn when the service was permanently discontinued.

August 19, 1897: The second test of an air-pressure locomotive began on the Sixth Avenue line. This was No. 400, built under the patents of Robert Hardie by the American Air Power Company. It was operated by compressed air from a plant at 100 Greenwich Street that put it into the engine tanks at 2400 pounds per square inch. On October 23, 1881 the Second Avenue line had one of its trains pulled by "Pneumatic Tramway Engine No. 1" under the same principle. Neither attempt met with great enthusiasm.

November 21, 1900: The first public test of a multiple-unit electric on the Second Avenue line took place between 65th and 92nd streets. This train, using the Sprague system of multiple-unit operations, had one motor car at each end with four trailer cars. The results of this test train convinced the management to spend $5 million to electrify the whole system, and on May 1, 1901 contracts were let to General Electric to electrify the rolling stock and structures, while Westinghouse built the powerhouse and generating facilities at 74th Street and the East River. This was the largest electrification project of its time and its final cost was about $18 million. It was the end of the steam era.

December 20, 1901: The first regularly scheduled electric train went into service on the Second Avenue line. Full service was inaugurated on March 11, 1902, with the exception of rush-hour "extras." On September 2, 1902 the last steam engine ran on this line.

March 24, 1902: Electric service commenced on the Third Avenue line and was completed on August 15, when the last steam engine was operated. On May 31, 1902 two new open-sided cars were placed in service on the Third Avenue line.

October 1, 1902: Electric operation began on the Sixth Avenue line from Rector Street to 58th Street. It was extended to 155th Street on November 2, and the last locomotive ran via Sixth Avenue on April 4, 1903.

February 18, 1903: Electrified operation began on the Ninth Avenue line from South Ferry to 155th Street. The last locomotive to run in passenger service on the el lines was a 66th Street local-express pulled by Engine No. 135. They were used in work-train service for a number of years afterward, however. A new station was also opened on this line at 110th Street on June 3. Situated at the so-called Suicide Curve, it boasted four elevators to whisk passengers up from the street level.

April 1, 1903: The Manhattan Railway Company was leased to the Interborough Rapid Transit Company for 999 years in order that the new subway system being built could be coordinated with the el lines. The first instance of this new arrangement came on November 26, 1904, when the Westchester Avenue elevated extension of the Lenox Avenue IRT subway was opened to

Bronx Park. Because the Harlem River tunnel was still unfinished, the subway was unable to make use of the new extension. Temporary service was provided by the Second Avenue el line to Bronx Park via a new connection opened at 149th Street and Third Avenue. This service was discontinued on July 9, 1905 and the connection was seldom used. Beginning on July 10, 1905 paper transfers were issued at 149th Street between the el and subway stations. On or about October 1, 1907 the Second Avenue line was extended to Freeman Street during the morning and evening rush hour. The last new station of the Second Avenue line was opened at 105th Street on April 1, 1911, while the last new station of the Sixth Avenue line opened at 38th Street on January 31, 1914.

September 15, 1904: The U.S. Express Company began freight service over Third and Ninth Avenue lines. The distribution point for this unique enterprise was on Morris Street, just behind 7 Broadway, where the first shops were located for engine repairs. Livestock and less-than-carload freight were carried in the el baggage cars, which made five round trips daily to uptown points. Mail was also carried on regular passenger trains on the front platform of the first car, accompanied by a U.S. Post Office messenger, with a limit of seven bags per man. Both services were discontinued shortly after World War I. No railroad freight cars or special mail trains were ever operated. The mail service began in 1872.

March 19, 1913: With the combined subway and el lines carrying over 1,500,000 passengers daily, it was deemed of the utmost urgency to expand the el lines so that the expected additional traffic could be handled. On this date the Public Service Commission granted approval for the Manhattan Elevated improvement work to begin. When it was completed, fifteen miles of new single track, nine miles of old track, and forty stations had been built or rebuilt. This tremendous engineering feat required 50,000 tons of steel girder, 65,000 tons of new rail, 12 million feet of track ties, and 70,000 gallons of paint at a cost of $44 million. It provided seventeen double-deck express stations—and the whole job was accomplished without delaying one train!

January 17, 1916: Center tracks opened for operation on the Second, Third, and Ninth Avenue lines. The Second Avenue express trains went to Bronx Park or Freeman Street via 149th Street, while the Ninth Avenue line inaugurated an express service north to 125th Street that previously had terminated at 116th Street. The Sixth Avenue line began faster service also, using the Ninth Avenue center track north of 53rd Street.

July 1, 1917: The Bergen Avenue-West Farms connection opened to eliminate delays at the Manhattan connection at 149th Street and Third Avenue. Following the original franchised route of the Suburban line, it provided a direct connection from 143rd Street on the Third Avenue line with the Westchester Avenue subway line structure. Second Avenue trains used it in rush hours only. The els were at their peak of use, carrying 1,014,883 passengers daily. On July 9 the Third Avenue line inaugurated through-express service from City Hall to 177th Street.

July 23, 1917: Elevated service to Ditmars Avenue, Astoria, was begun via the Second Avenue line over the Queensboro Bridge, replacing the IRT subway service which had opened the line from Queensboro Plaza the previous February 1. This arrangement lasted until January 17, 1918, when the el service was alternately operated to Astoria and Alburtis (104th Street) Avenue on the Flushing line, with IRT subway service from Grand Central via the Steinway tunnel. A new station on the Ninth Avenue line opened at 151st Street on November 15.

July 1, 1918: The Sixth and Ninth Avenue lines extended their operations to 167th Street and Jerome Avenue on the IRT Woodlawn line, opening a station at Jerome-Anderson Avenue. The Sedgewick Avenue station had been opened on January 6, when the New York Central (successor to the New York & Northern Railroad) terminated their operations over their bridge to 155th Street station of the el. The bridge, last of the steam-powered swing-type Harlem River drawbridges, was leased for 999 years to the IRT, which instituted a shuttle service on a single track until March 1, when both tracks were placed in use. Express-track operations were also extended on the Ninth Avenue line from 125th to 155th streets on July 1. Jerome Avenue el service was further extended on July 17 to Kingsbridge Road, and the Sixth Avenue rush-hour express ran to Woodlawn on January 2, 1919.

October 4, 1920: The last of el expansions took place on this day in the Bronx, when the Webster Avenue extension opened with stations at 200th, 204th and 210th (Williamsbridge) streets and a lower-level platform at the Gun Hill Road station of the IRT White Plains Road line. Third Avenue rush-hour express service was provided to 238th Street, while a shuttle train ran at other times between Fordham Road and 219th Street, until December 13, when rush-hour service was run through to 241st Street.

April 24, 1923: Faced with rising costs and being refused applications for a fare rise above 5 cents, the Manhattan Railway Company sought means of effecting economies and attracting riders. On this date it introduced the "Goldenrod" paint scheme for its cars and stations. The first train operated on Sixth Avenue, and the 38th Street station was the first to be painted bright orange with a black roof and the words OPEN AIR LINE on the sides. The preceding January, at the 106th Street station of the Third Avenue line, the first turnstiles replaced ticket collectors; while the first multiple-unit door-controlled train went into service on Second Avenue on November 8, whereby one man operated all the doors on a train from a central position. December 6 saw the closing of the 42nd Street spur of the Third Avenue line.

June 16, 1924: The last train operated on the 58th Street branch of the Sixth Avenue line. This spur had through service to downtown in rush hours and a one-car shuttle the remainder of the time. Demolition began on August 11. The Willis Avenue branch also discontinued shuttle service that year, on April 15, although the spur remained in occasional use for car deliveries and special trips until 1954.

June 1, 1927: A passageway was opened between the el and the IRT subway station at 149th Street and Third Avenue, discontinuing paper transfer issuance and eliminating the heavy crowds crossing that busy intersection.

258

On January 21 of the following year the Second Avenue line extended its service in Queens to the Willets Point Boulevard station. It also began using the new Corona Yard of the IRT.

July 14, 1930: The 34th Street branch closed. Traffic began to decline on this spur when the Long Island Rail Road terminated its operations at Pennsylvania Station and discontinued the 34th Street ferry. Razing began on July 15, 1931, and was completed on September 5.

December 4, 1938: The Sixth Avenue line discontinued operations from Morris Street to 53rd Street and Ninth Avenue. It was replaced on December 15, 1940 by the new IND subway built beneath, real estate and political groups having fought for its removal.

June 11, 1940: The Second Avenue line discontinued operations between 60th and 129th streets. The service to Freeman Street was assumed by the Third Avenue line. On this same date, the Ninth Avenue line discontinued operations between South Ferry and 155th Street. The remainder of the line was serviced by the IRT subway division using "composite" cars in a shuttle to Burnside Avenue. On June 12 the remaining properties of the Manhattan Railway Company came under the ownership and management of the New York City Transit System operated by the Board of Transportation. A paper transfer issuance was established between the el and subway stations of the IND-Concourse line at 155th Street. Board of Transportation offices were located at 250 Hudson Street.

June 13, 1942: The Second Avenue line discontinued operations from South Ferry to Queensboro Plaza. For patrons formerly served by the trains to Queens, a paper transfer issuance was established between the Third Avenue line and the IRT Queensboro line at 42nd Street.

November 5, 1946: With World War II over, agitation was renewed to rid Manhattan of its last remaining elevated route. On this date service to Freeman Street via the Bergen Avenue cut-off was discontinued. On July 1, 1948 the fares of the New York City Transit System were raised to 10 cents, and a 2-cent transfer between surface line trolleys and buses and the el was established in the Bronx. This arrangement was discontinued on June 30, 1952.

December 22, 1950: Third Avenue el service was discontinued from Chatham Square to South Ferry and from Gun Hill Road to 241st Street. A paper transfer issuance was begun between the city-owned bus line and the el at Chatham Square and between the el and the IRT-BMT subway stations beneath City Hall station. The Bronx Park (Botanical Gardens) station and spur were closed to service on Friday, November 14, 1951, while weekend and night service after 7 P.M. were discontinued on the Third Avenue line below 149th Street after March 14, 1952.

June 15, 1953: The operations of the New York City Transit System were leased for ten years by the newly created New York City Transit Authority and taken over on this date. Fares were raised to 15 cents and the use of the tokens was instituted, effective July 25. The City Hall branch of the el was closed on December 31. The express track through 149th Street station was closed on September 24, 1954, forcing express trains to use the ramp between upper and lower levels from 138th Street to 143rd Street.

May 12, 1955: The Third Avenue el discontinued service south of 149th Street. The last train left Chatham Square at 6:04 P.M., ending elevated service on Manhattan Island. Demolition began August 3 at 115th Street and was completed on February 16, 1956 at 42nd Street.

So ended the elevated era in Manhattan; subways had superseded the railroads-in-the-air, seemingly forever.

INDEX